The coffin of Zemathor and other rectangular coffins of the late Middle Kingdom and Second Intermediate Period

Wolfram Grajetzki

GHP Egyptology 15

London 2010

This title is published by
Golden House Publications

Front cover image:
reconstruction of Zemathor's coffin, using Garstang's notebook drawings

Back cover image:
Text panel from the coffin of Senebhenaf, Oxford, Ashmolean Museum, E 1953; photo: Grajetzki (top)
detail from a coffin found at Thebes, compare p. 55 (photo: Gianluca Miniaci), Cairo, Egyptian Museum (middle left)
falsedoor on the coffin of Senebni, Cairo CG 28029; (photo: Grajetzki, middle, right)

Printed in the United Kingdom
by

CPI
Antony Rowe
Bumper's Farm
Chippenham
Wiltshire SN14 6LH

London 2010

ISBN 978-1-906137-22-9

Contents

Acknowledgments

For photographs and help in museum collections and archives I would to like thank Steven Snape, Patricia Winker (University of Liverpool), Ashley Cooke (World Museum, Liverpool), Christina Riggs (Manchester Museum), Janine Bourriau (Cambridge), Patricia Spencer (EES). Furthermore I would like to thank Günther Lapp for the latest version of Visualglyph, which is especially useful for this book because it includes 'incomplete hieroglyphs', Masahiro Baba and Lutz Franke for providing me with literature, Stephen Quirke for reading my English and several discussions. Special thanks goes to Paul Whelan for making several drawings, reconstructions and reading and editing my English. All remaining mistakes are my responsibility. I am grateful to Gianluca Miniaci for providing several pictures and information on coffins.

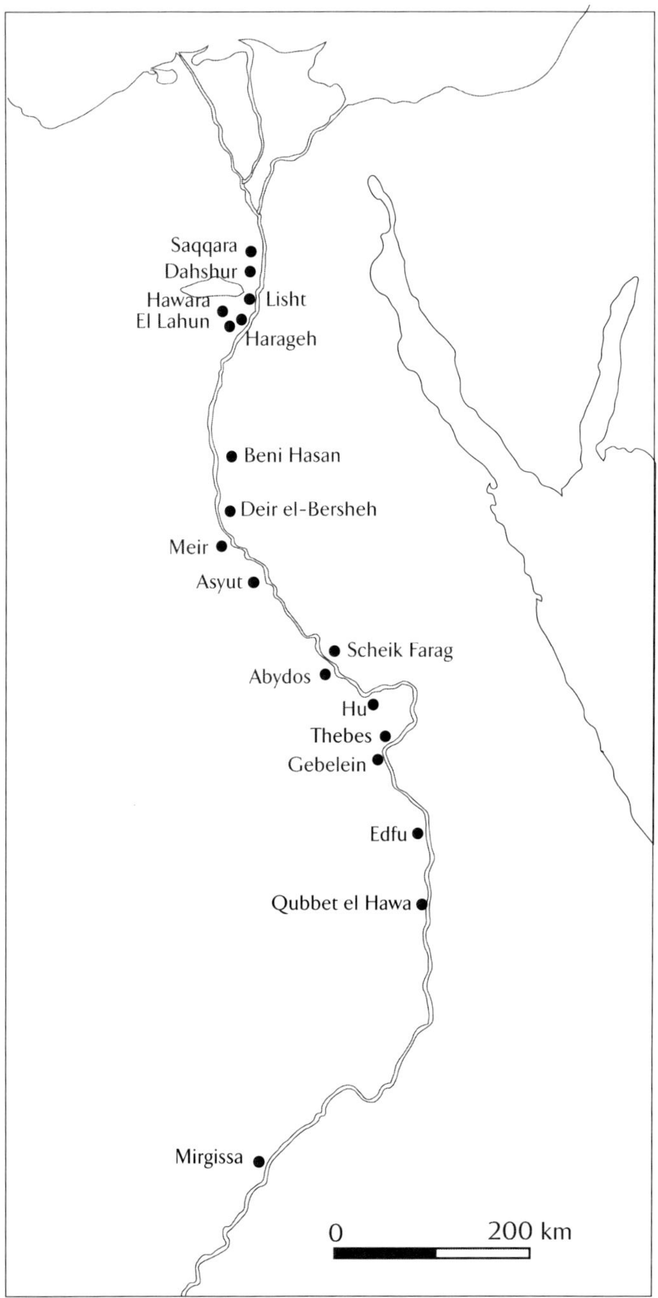

Map of Egypt and Lower Nubia

Introduction

The first chapter is the starting point of this publication with the coffin fragments of Zemathor, found at Abydos and only preserved in rough copies by John Garstang made at his excavations in 1906. In addition, in the second chapter some badly published coffin and canopic box fragments of the Second Intermediate Period will be presented. Many of them I found in archives with old excavation records. The coffins all were discovered at the end of the Nineteenth or beginning of the Twentieth Century. The present location of most of these fragments is not known to me, but in most cases it can be assumed that they were left on the sites and are most likely perished by now. The third and fourth chapters present a catalogue of already published coffins of the late Middle Kingdom and Second Intermediate Period. For the late Middle Kingdom, the time after Senusret II, I am presenting just a selection of coffins which show already features also appearing on Second Intermediate Period coffins. For the Second Intermediate Period I am listing all published coffins known to me. Model coffins are only presented in a selection. There are certainly many more unpublished coffins, especially from Lisht and Thebes. I did not take these into account, because, these coffins cannot be controlled by any reader, before any scientific publication appears. Chapter five provides a brief discussion of the main texts found on the coffins, chapter six the conclusions.

Coffins and tomb groups of the classical Middle Kingdom, that is, the late Eleventh and Twelfth Dynasty, are relatively well researched and well datable. Coffins of officials and court members of the Eleventh Dynasty provide a perfect guide for dating. Many of these officials are also known from inscriptions dated to a reign or even to a regnal year. For the Twelfth Dynasty there are the tombs of the local officials, several of whom are mentioned in the tombs of the local governors. These governors are often again well datable. This once more provides a good chronological sequence of burials and coffins, reign by reign. Under Senusret III the rich provincial cemeteries were no longer used to the same extent as before. Certainly, there were still many people buried in the provinces and their burial equipments was still often quite wealthy. However, decorated coffins seem to become less common in the provinces and more importantly, it is often almost impossible to relate burials to a certain reign of a king. The problem becomes worse for the Second Intermediate Period, which is here broadly speaking the Thirteenth to Seventeenth Dynasty. While there are some coffins and burials of the late Twelfth and early Thirteenth Dynasty, belonging to members of the royal family and therefore again well datable, there is nothing like that for the time after king Hor, whose tomb is the last that can be placed in a chronological frame. For the next 150 years there are no secure datable tomb groups and coffins. Certainly, there are still some coffins and tombs related to king's names, such as the coffin of the 'royal sealer' and 'overseer of marshland dwellers' Senebni (datable by an inscribed staff under king Sewahenre) and the coffin of queen Mentuhotep. Although these burials can be placed under a certain king, there is the problem that none of these kings is securely datable within the Second Intermediate Period. All attempts to provide a sequence need to be seen with great caution. We are only again on firmer ground at the very end of the Second Intermediate Period with the rishi coffins of several kings. These kings are often not exactly datable either, but there is little doubt that they belong in general rather to the end of the Second Intermediate Period.

Notes on the chronology

The late Middle Kingdom is here defined as the period after Senusret II up to the end of the Twelfth Dynasty. For the development of the Second Intermediate Period, from the Thirteenth to Seventeenth Dynasty, I follow in general, the outline presented by Kim Ryholt.[1] The capital and burial ground for the national ruling class was in the Twelfth and Thirteenth Dynasties in the Memphite region. Several Thirteenth Dynasty coffins of these high ranking people were found at Dahshur. Whether Lower Egypt was lost to foreign rulers, at the very end of the Twelfth Dynasty (as proposed by Ryholt) is not of relevance for this study.[2] At some point in the Second Intermediate Period, the royal court moved its power centre to Thebes. Indeed, there are some burials and coffins in late Middle Kingdom tradition (rectangular and inscribed with texts, known from the late Middle Kingdom) found at Thebes, belonging to the circle of the

[1] Ryholt, *Political Situation*, 293-310; with the exception of one article I was not able to consult M. Marée (editor), *The Second Intermediate Period (Thirteenth-Seventeenth Dynasties), Current Research, Future Prospects*, Leuven, Paris, Walpole, MA, 2010 in time for the book.

[2] It seems indeed likely that most kings of the Thirteenth Dynasty still ruled over the whole of Egypt, see Ben-Tor, *BASOR* 315 (1999), 58-59.

highest court officials. There is even one coffin in late Middle Kingdom tradition from Thebes, belonging to queen Mentuhotep. That the royal burial place was located at Thebes seems to attest that the city became a major centre for Egypt and most likely the capital; perhaps of an Upper Egyptian state. This phase is labelled here Sixteenth Dynasty. Whether the beginning of the Sixteenth Dynasty was contemporary with the last phase of the Thirteenth Dynasty is unknown. So far there is no secure evidence for that. The Seventeenth Dynasty are those kings belonging to the latest Second Intermediate Period, buried at Dra abu el-Naga and known from their rishi coffins and small pyramids. In terms of burial culture they belong already to a different phase, closer to the early Eighteenth Dynasty.

Coffin sigla

The sigla used in this study follow Willems, *Chests of Life*, 19-40. New coffins, not included in Willems' list have been assigned additional numbers (in *italics*). Only coffins with texts receive a siglum. Also following Willems, uninscribed coffins are not included in this list. The relevant uninscribed (or little inscribed) coffins already belong to the second half of the Second Intermediate Period and early New Kingdom. They are considered in this study but are not the main focus of this book.

Aswan
A1X Neferhesut (Willems, in J. van Dijk (editor), *Essays on Ancient Egypt in Honour of Herman te Velde*, 356-57, note 47)
A2X Nebetneheh (Edel, *Die Felsgräbernekropole der Qubbet el-Hawa bei Assuan, I. Abbteilung Band 1*, 436)

Abydos
Aby1 Nakht (Garstang, *El Arabah: A Cemetery of the Middle Kingdom*, pl. VI-VII)
Aby2 Sobekhotep (Peet, *Cemeteries of Abydos II*, 61, pl. XIII, 4, pl. XXXVI)
Aby3 Amenemhat (Peet, *Cemeteries of Abydos II*, 62, 122, fig. 88, 123, fig. 89)
Aby4 Dedmut (Peet, *Cemeteries of Abydos II*, 60, fig. 28, pl. XIII, XIV; p. 12, pl. V, XIa, below)
Aby5 Zemathor (pp. 6-8, plate I, VIII below)
Aby6 Nemtyemweskhet (Bourriau, *Pharaohs and Mortals*, 93-94, no. 74; pp. 13-14, pl. IVbelow)
Aby7 Senebhenaef (Grajetzki, *SÄK* 34 (2006), 205-216;)
Aby8 Sehetepibankh (p. 11 below)

Deir el-Bersheh
B9C Amenemhat (CG 28091)
B10C Amenemhat (CG 28092)

Dahshur
Da1C Zathathomeryt (Cairo CG 28101)
Da2C Nubhetepti-khered (Cairo CG 28104; de Morgan, *Fouilles à Dahchour I*, 110, fig. 263)
Da3C Zatsobek (Cairo CG 28105)
Da4C King Awibre Hor (Cairo CG 28106; de Morgan, *Fouilles à Dahchour I*, 101, fig. 241, 241 *bis*.)
Da1X Zatip (de Morgan, *Fouilles à Dahchour I*, 36, fig. 73; Willems op. cit. p. 23 provides no name of the coffin owner)
Da2X Ita (de Morgan, *Fouilles à Dahchour II*, 46-48, fig. 105, 109)
Da3X Khnumet (de Morgan, *Fouilles à Dahchour II*, 57-58)
Da4X Itaweret (de Morgan, *Fouilles à Dahchour II*, 73-74)
Da5X Keminub (de Morgan, *Fouilles à Dahchour II*, 70, fig. 116, 117)
Da6X Amenhotep (de Morgan, *Fouilles à Dahchour II*, 70, fig. 113-115)
Da1 Senu (Yoshimurra, *Excavating in Egypt*, 192-193, 228, no. 248; Yoshimura, *Excavating in Egypt for 40 years* (2008), 30, no. 47)

Gebelein
G1 Unknown owner (Cairo CG 28031)
G2 Unknown owner (Cairo CG 28032)

Harageh
Ha1 Senusretankh (Engelbach, *Harageh*, 23-24, pl. LXX)
Ha3 Zatimpy (Engelbach, *Harageh*, 24, pl. LXV, 2)
Ha8 Harageh tomb 219 (Grajetzki, *Harageh*, 46; pp. 38-39 below)
Ha9 Harageh tomb 128 (Engelbach, *Harageh*, 16)

Hawara
Haw1 Zatrenenutet (see p. 21-22 below)
Haw2 Neferuptah (Grajetzki, *GM*, 205 (2005), 55-66)
Maz1 Bebut (found at Hawara; Flinders Petrie, Wainwright, Mackay, *The Labyrinth, Gerzeh and Mazghuneh*, 35, pl. XXXVII, compare pp. 32-33 below)

Hu (Diopolis Parva)

Hu1 Tomb Hu Y 196 (p. 15 below)
Hu2 Tomb Hu Y 219 (pp. 16-17 below)
Hu3 Ib, tomb Hu 15 (pp. 17-18 below)
Hu4 Tomb Hu Y 467 (p. 18 below)
Hu5 Tomb Hu Y 480 (p. 19 below)
Hu6 Tomb Hu Y 511 (pp. 20 below)
Hu7 Tomb Hu Y 217 (pp. 21 below)

Lahun

La1 Zathathoriunet (tomb no. 8) (Brunton, *Lahun I*, 14, 18)
La2 Tomb no. 7 (Brunton, *Lahun I*, 16)
La3 Tomb no. 10 (Brunton, *Lahun I*, 14)

Lisht

L1Li Sesenebnef (Gautier/Jéquier, *Mémoire sur les Fouilles de Licht*, 76, pl. XVI-XX)
L2Li Sesenebnef (Gautier/Jéquier, *Mémoire sur les Fouilles de Licht*, 77, figs. 95-96, pl. XXI-XXVI)
L4 Senebtisi (outer coffin; Mace, Winlock, *The Tomb of Senebtisi at Lisht*, 23-26)
L5 Senebtisi (middle coffin; Mace, Winlock, *The Tomb of Senebtisi at Lisht*, 26-32)
L6 Bener (Arnold and Dorman, in Arnold, *The Pyramid of Senwosret I, The South Cemeteries at Lisht I*, 34-36, 147-49)
L7 Wahneferhotep – Lisht (Arnold and Dorman, in Arnold, *The Pyramid of Senwosret I, The South Cemeteries at Lisht I*, 37-39, 147-49, pl. 14)
L9 Zay (Allen, in *World of the Coffin Texts*, 6)
L10 Unknown (Allen, in *World of the Coffin Texts*, 6)
L11 Debehni (Allen, *The Egyptian Coffin Texts, Volume 8, Middle Kingdom Copies of Pyramid Texts*, 389; Bourriauin P. Der Manuelian (editor), *Studies in Honor of William Kelly Simpson, Vol.I*, 110-111)

Meir

M2NY Hapyankhtifi (Kamal, *ASAE* 14 (1914), 82-86)
M20 Khakheperresenb Iy (Kamal, *ASAE* 14 (1914), 75-77)
M56 Hapyankhtifi (middle coffin of M2NY, unpublished, compare: Forman, Quirke, *Hieroglyphs and the Afterlife in Ancient Egypt*, fig. on p. 93)

Mirgissa

Mi1 Tomb 117 (Vercoutter, *Mirgissa II*, fig. 61g)

Saqqara

Sq19X Hetepet , Saqqara, burial 41 (Firth/Gunn, *Teti pyramid cemeteries*, 59)
Sq18 Aabed (Cairo CG 28108)
Sq23X Nensemekhtuef (*Deutsches Archäologisches Institut, Abteilung Kairo, Rundbrief, September 2007*, 21, fig. 33)

Scheikh Farag

SF1 NN (P. Lacovara, in D'Auria, S.; P. Lacovara; C. R. Roehrig (editors), *Mummies and Magic,* 130-31, no. 63)

Thebes

T1Be Mentuhotep (Steindorff, *Grabfunde des Mittleren Reiches in den Königlichen Museen zu Berlin, I)*
T3Be Sobekaa (Steindorff, *Grabfunde des Mittleren Reiches in den Königlichen Museen zu Berlin, II. Der Sarg des Sebk-o. – Ein Grabfund aus Gebelein*, 1-10, pl. I-II)
T6C Khonsu (Cairo CG 28028)
T7C Nubrediher (Cairo CG 28030)
T10C Senebni (Cairo CG 28029, Lapp, *Typologie*, pl. 34b, Lapp, in Willems (editor), *The World of the Coffins Texts*, 98, pl. 11)
T13C Hemenhotep (coffin lid, Cairo CG 28126)
T4L Queen Mentuhotep (Geisen, *Die Totentexte des verschollenen Sarges der Königin Mentuhotep aus der 13. Dynastie, Ein Textzeuge aus der Übergangszeit von den Sargtexten zum Totenbuch*)
T6L Herunefer (Parkinson, Quirke, in *Studies in Pharaonic Religion and Society in Honour of J. Gwyn Griffths*, 37-51)
T1Lux Ameny (Polz, *Für die Ewigkeit geschaffen, Die Särge des Imeni und Geheset*)
T2Lux Geheset **(**Polz, *Für die Ewigkeit geschaffen, Die Särge des Imeni und Geheset*)

T5NY Nefert (New York MMA 32.3.429, unpublished, Hayes, *Scepter of Egypt I*, 348)
T6NY Ikhet (New York MMA 32.3.430, unpublished: Hayes, *Scepter I*, 347-48, fig. 228)
T7NY Unknown (New York MMA 32.3.431, unpublished: New York, Hayes, *Scepter I*, 348)
T8NY Nemtyemzaf (New York MMA 32.3.428, unpublished: New York, Hayes, *Scepter I*, 348-9)
T1War Amenemhat (Bruyère, *Deir el Médineh (1929)*, 102-105, figs. 46-47)
T2War NN (Bruyère, *Deir el Médineh (1929)*, 104, fig. 48)
T7C Nubrediher (Cairo CG 28030)
T3 Renseneb (Carter, *Five Years*, 54-55)
T33 Mishwep (*L'Egittologo Luigi Vassalli, 1812-1887, disegni e documenti nei Civici Istituti Culturali Milanesi*, Milano 1994, fig. 3)
T34 Teti (Grajetzki, *BMSAES* 5 (2006), 1-12)
T35 Ibiau (Grajetzki, *Die höchsten Beamten*, 136, n.1)
T36 Zatnenna (Tiradritti, In Marée (editor), *The Second Intermediate Period (Thirteenth-Seventeenth Dynasties), Current Research, Future Prospects*, 333, pl. 113)
T37 Unknown (Tiradritti, In Marée (editor), *The Second Intermediate Period (Thirteenth-Seventeenth Dynasties), Current Research, Future Prospects*, 333-335, pl. 114)
T38 Unknown (Tiradritti, In Marée (editor), *The Second Intermediate Period (Thirteenth-Seventeenth Dynasties), Current Research, Future Prospects*, 333, pl. 115)
T39 Ahmose (model coffin, Dolzani, *La Collezione Egiziana del museo dell academia dei concordi in Rovigo*, 11-14, p.l VI-VII)
T40 Khonsu (model coffin, Cairo CG 48404)

unknown
S3 Khnumnakht (Hayes, *Scepter of Egypt I*, fig. 207, Lapp, *Typologie*, 113, figs. 136-37)

Chapter One: The coffin of Zemathor (Aby5)

Material: wood ?
Measurements: not known
Colours: not known
Preservation: small fragments, only recorded in notebooks
See plate I, VIII,

From 1906 to 1909 John Garstang excavated parts of the Abydos cemeteries. These excavations were never published and only minor reports appeared. The objects found were sold to institutions and individuals all around the world, when not left on site. The only known records of these excavations are several notebooks and photographs in the University of Liverpool. There are no tomb cards providing detailed descriptions of the tombs and finds; at least they did not survive or have yet to be located. In the 1980's Steven Snape collected all available material for his PhD including the information of the objects in museums around the world, providing the ground for a database of the excavations and their finds.[3]

Garstang found more than 1000 tombs belonging to almost every period of Ancient Egyptian history.[4] Today, for most tombs it is only possible to reconstruct a list of objects found. In general there is little or no information on the tomb architecture. No map of the excavated cemeteries survived in the records of Garstang. It remains most of the time pure speculation whether a tomb had one or more burials or whether it was reused, especially in cases where objects of different periods are assigned to one tomb group. Garstang must have found many coffins and mentioned them several times. However, the preservation conditions for organic materials are not good in Abydos, by comparison with the excellent conditions in parts of Thebes or several cemeteries of Middle Egypt, such as Meir, Beni Hasan or Asyut. Therefore, coffins at Abydos generally survive only in small fragments. In his first notebook Garstang recorded the fragments of some coffins in sketch drawings. In the later notebooks coffins are mentioned several times, but no further information is provided, beyond a few photographs of New Kingdom examples. It remains an open question whether the latter coffins were found too badly destroyed or whether Garstang no longer took the time to record the fragments excavated. I was not able to locate any coffin or coffin fragments from the 1906 to 1909 seasons. It seems likely that most of them were left on site.

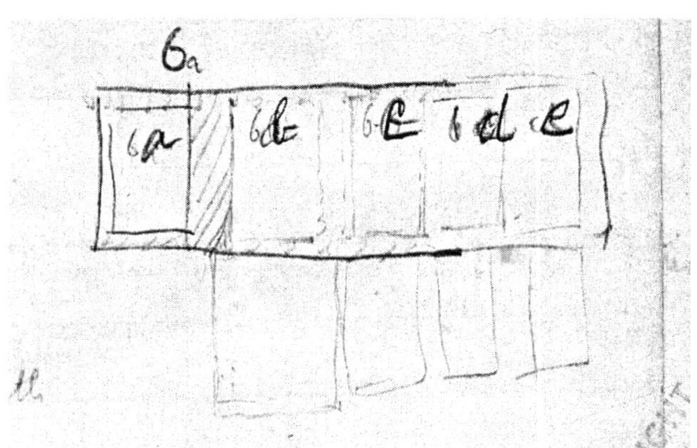

Fig. 1 The plan of the tomb complex as drawn in Garstang's notebook © Liverpool University

The coffin of Zemathor was found at the beginning of the first season, in 1906. The fragments are only preserved in notebook sketches (pl. VIII) with no measurements given. Despite being evidently of small size and with few words on each piece, it is relatively easy to reconstruct the general layout of the coffin as the texts on the fragments are also known from other coffins of the Second Intermediate Period at Abydos. The coffin of Zemathor was probably only decorated on the outside inasmuch as none of the recorded

[3] Snape, *Mortuary Assemblages from Abydos*.

[4] No plan of the excavated area survived, compare Snape, *Mortuary Assemblages from Abydos*, 58, fig. 3 and the plans on p. 407; Kemp, Merrillees, *Minoan Pottery*, 105-108; see also the map in Richards, *Society and Death in Ancient Egypt, Mortuary Landscapes of the Middle Kingdom*, 140, fig. 61. (Garstang worked mainly in the North Cemetery, close to Cemetery E).

inscriptions fit with any known type of inner decoration. The coffin exterior had a horizontal line at the top with about eight or nine vertical columns on the long sides and perhaps two columns on the short ends. An identical layout appears on several other coffins from Abydos dating to the Second Intermediate Period (Aby2, Aby3, Aby4). Between the columns on the long sides were placed small text panels. So far there are yet no other coffins with these text panels and such a high number of columns. In all known other cases the text panels appear on coffins with four columns on the long sides (Li1Li, L9, L10). The columns and horizontal lines bear parts of the text set comprising Coffin Text spells 777-785, as attested on several coffins of the period found at Abydos and Thebes.

From other coffins and the orientation of the hieroglyphs it is clear that the recorded fragments of Zemathor mostly belong to the back side of the coffin. The fragments bear remains of Coffin Text spells 780 to 782 and these spells always appear on the back of other coffins. The hieroglyphs of animals are all depicted without legs and the snakes without their tails. This practice of writing hieroglyphs is typical for the Second Intermediate Period and is first attested at the end of Amenemhat's III reign.[5] In the same way, the word for the falcon god 'Horus' (Hor), in the name Zemathor, is written with the 'street-sign' (Gardiner N31) and not with the Horus falcon, certainly to avoid the falcon and perhaps thereby also to avoid mutilating a divine symbol. A similar writing of Horus is found in the tomb of king Hor (Horus) at Dahshur.[6]

The texts on the panels between the columns were badly preserved. One of them contained the Abydos formula so far mainly known from Middle Kingdom stelae[7]:

Words spoken: your arms are in the neshmet boat on the road of the revered ones, holy is the oar in the night ship, may you sail the day ship.

From the other panels only the lower lines are preserved and without any parallels it is difficult to arrive at a satisfactory translation. I was not able to find any other related or similar text.

The following fragments are not placed in the reconstruction of the coffin on plate I, for the orginal drawings see plate VIII:

no. 5 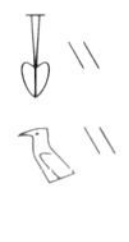 no. 6 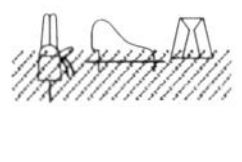 no. 7  no. 11 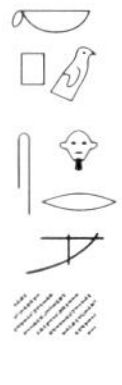 no. 12

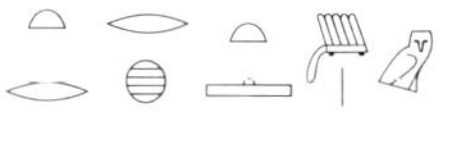

no. 13  no. 14

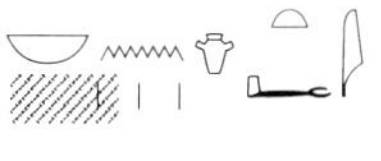

Fragment no. 5 might be part of the name, Zemathor. No. 7 belongs to one of the text panels. Nos. 6, 12, 13 and 14 come from horizontal lines, perhaps again from text panels. No. 11 seems to be a 'speech of god' (a 'mr n-spell', compare pp. 62-63) not to expected on a coffin with CT spells 777 to 785. Perhaps some of the fragments come from a second coffin.

Date: There are problems assigning the coffin fragments to a specific tomb. The drawings of the fragments appear on two pages in Garstang's notebook, next to the description and presentation of the finds and plan of tomb no. 6. It is a tomb complex with five shafts. Four of the shafts had a side chamber at the bottom.

Over the coffin fragments in the notebook is written: 'Frag. of coffin found in several chambers....'. However, there is no coffin mentioned in the list of objects for tomb no. 6, instead there appears the entry:

---

[5] Lilyquist, *Ancient Egyptian Mirrors from the Earliest Times through the Middle Kingdom*, 33-34, n. 377.

[6] de Morgan, *Dahchour I*, 94, 101-102, 104, 106.

[7] Assmann, *Altägyptische Totenliturgien II*, 38-48, Postel, *BIFAO* 103 (2003), 377-420.

'fragments of burned wood, some with inscriptions'. One wonders whether these fragments of burned wood refer to the coffin of Zemathor.

If it is accepted that the fragments come from this tomb, it may be noted that other finds possibly indicate a date for the complex to the time of king Sobekhotep IV or shortly after. In the tomb complex were found two stelae belonging to the 'overseer of the production place' and 'leader of the broad hall' Khonsu. On each stela he bears a different function title. They were most likely produced at different stages of his career. Khonsu is the son of Iimiatuib. The latter is well known from several monuments and datable from these under Sobekhotep II. For a further discussion, see the publication of the stela below.

The name Zemathor (*zmꜣit-ḥr*) is otherwise only once attested in the late Middle Kingdom. At Abydos were found the fragments of a stela showing in front of the stela owner a woman with the double name Zemathor Nebetiunet.[8] A comparable name is Zematmutwer.[9]

The finds in tomb A6:[10]

1. five heads of canopic jars, one now in Manchester, 3996 (pl. IXb)
2. beads of worn necklace, Manchester 4011
3. stela of Khonsu, World Museum, Liverpool 16.11.06.13
4. stela of Khonsu, New York, MMA 21.2.69[11]
5. inlaid eye, Manchester 4009
6. fragment of red faience inlay, Manchester 4010
7. plaster fragments, Manchester 4012 (see below)
8. inlaid eye fragment, Manchester 4013
9. two inscribed limestone fragments, Manchester 4014
10. scarab, London BM 64856 (?)
11. portion of an inscribed jar
12. lid of canopic jar in the form of Isis
13. wooden shabti figure, missing head, inscribed
14. tiny white alabaster kohl pot
15. few gold beads and glaze
16. ceramic vessel, Liverpool Mer. 16.11.06.16 (lost)
17. two cow horns, Liverpool Mer, 16.11.06.1 (lost)
18. very damaged inscribed block (Neg. A.4)

The stela of Khonsu (World Museum, Liverpool 16.11.06.13)
Material: limestone
Measurements: 1.05 x 1.05 m[12]
Colours: hieroglyphs blue, dividing lines red
Plate III, IXa, X

Preservation: the stela was found in good condition, but was damaged in World War II; only parts of the two pilasters framing the central field and the parts of the central field are now preserved in the museum.

The stela consists of three parts. There is a middle panel and there are two framing pilasters. In the middle panel there Khonsu is shown seated on a chair looking to the right. In his left hand he holds a large lotus flower close to his nose. The right arm is stretched out towards the offerings placed in front of him. He wears a broad collar, a bag wig and a long kilt going from the belly to his feet. There is a vessel on a high stand, a drop-shaped tall object on a smaller stand, and, over these, a mat with four objects: two round shapes (bread?), a cut of meat in the middle and some vegetables on top of that. Over the scene are two

---

[8] Peet, *Cemeteries Abydos II*, 113, pl.24.3 (now Dublin, National Museum of Ireland, 1910:337).

[9] Ranke, *PN* II, 313, 24 (only one reference, a woman attested on a Middle Kingdom stela; Cairo CG 20282).

[10] Snape, *Mortuary Assemblages from Abydos*, 189, 405, 407.

[11] Hayes, *Scepter of Egypt I*, 346, fig. 227 (top left).

[12] Further measurements taken from the fragments in the museum: the stela is about 9.5 cm thick; the site pilasters are about 16 cm broad; the text lines in the main field about 4 cm high; those on the pilasters about 5.5 cm wide.

holes (8 cm wide) filled with stone plugs, the function of which is unknown.[13] This stela is framed by two pilasters made of separate pieces of stone each with two columns of inscriptions.

The text over the figure:

An offering which the king gives (to) Osiris, lord of life, ruler of eternity, may he give a good burial in the western desert every day, for the ka of the royal sealer, leader of the broad hall Khonsu[14], true of voice, lord of being revered, begotten of the royal sealer, the overseer of the royal estate Iimiatuib[15], true of voice, born of the king's ornament Id[16].

The text on the right post:

An offering which the king gives (to) Wepwawet-Ra (a), *lord of Abydos, and the gods in the necropolis* (b), *may they give the sweet wind of the North to your nose (of) the member of the elite, foremost of action, the friend, great one of love, the royal sealer, leader of the broad hall, Khonsu, true of voice*

The text on the left post:
An offering which the king gives (to) Osiris, lord of the holy land, and the gods within the broad hall (c), *may they grant the coming to heaven under the gods, having power over the water to the condentment of his heart, for the ka of the member of the elite, foremost of action, beautiful of face in his town, the royal sealer, leader of the broad hall, Khonsu, true of voice*

(a) Wepwawet-Ra is mainly known from Middle Kingdom sources and appears there sometimes as 'lord of Abydos'. Leitz, *Lexikon der ägyptischen Götter und Götterbezeichnungen II*, 346
(b) 'The gods in the necropolis': Leitz, *Lexikon der ägyptischen Götter und Götterbezeichnungen IV*, 465 provides several other example for the Middle Kingdom.
(c) 'The gods in the broad hall'; otherwise only know from the Graeco-Roman Period; according to Leitz, *Lexikon der ägyptischen Götter und Götterbezeichnungen IV*, 460

At least two scarab seals of the 'royal sealer, overseer of the production place' (*ḫtmty-bity imy-r gs-pr*) Khonsu are known.[17] Khonsu is well datable through the evidence of his father Iimiatuib. Iimiatuib is attested on several other monuments: stelae, an offering table, seals and seal impressions.[18] On these monuments he bears two title (strings): 'commander of the ruler's crew' (*ꜣṯw n ṯt-ḥkꜣ*) and 'royal sealer, overseer of the production place' (*ḫtmty bity imy-r gs-pr*)[19]. These most likely represent two different stages in his career. His name is written on a stela in Würzburg. [20] On this object is depicted the 'king's wife' Aja, who also appears in Papyrus Boulaq 18.[21] The papyrus dates perhaps under Sobekhotep (II) Amenemhat or at least around that period. Iimiatuib dates therefore to about the same time. His son Khonsu might be dated around one generation later (20 to 25 years), although there is also the chance that they were in office at about the same time. The stela can therefore be dated within the time frame from Sobekhotep (II) Amenemhat to about Sobekhotep IV or shortly after.

[13] It might be suggested that these plugs hold an upper architrave. However, I am not able to provide any parallel for this.
[14] Ranke, *PN* I, 270, 16.
[15] Ranke, *PN* I, 8, 25.
[16] Ranke, *PN* I, 53, 12; for the title 'king's ornament', see now: Stefanović, *The non-royal regular feminine titles of the Middle Kingdom and Second Intermediate Period: Dossiers*, 85-109.
[17] Martin, *Seals*, nos. 1217, 1218.
[18] Franke, Doss. 23; an additional seal impression of this official: von Pilgrim, *Elephantine XVIII*, 242, no. 207.
[19] For the latter title compare Moreno Garcia, *ZÄS* 126 (1999), 116 – 131; Grajetzki, *Die höchsten Beamten*, 201-202.
[20] Berlev, палестинский сборник, 25 (1974), 26-31.
[21] For discussion of the date of the papyrus, see Ryholt, *Political Situation*, 319.

Some other finds from the tomb complex

Manchester Museum 4012 a-r, 4014 (plate II)
The following fragments were found in the same burial complex. These are small fragments of plaster, decorated with raised relief, most often only parts of single hieroglyphic signs are preserved. Some fragments show some kind of feathers. One small fragment is even partly gilded. The carving of the relief is fine. There are also two small limestone fragments[22].

4012 (?) 4.5 x 2.0
4012A 4.0 x 1.5 cm (partly gilded)
4012B 3.2 x 1.4 cm
4012C 1.1 x 1.0 cm
4012D 1.5 x 2.5 cm
4012E 1.0 x 2.9 cm
4012F (?) 1.0 x 2.0 cm
4012G (?) 1.9 x 3.5 cm
4012H (?) 1.5 x 1.9 cm
4012I (?) 2.6 x 1.0 cm
4012J (?) 2.6 x 1.0 cm
4012K 1.7 x 1.0 cm
4012L (?) 2.0 x 1.2 cm
4012M 1.2 x 1.7 cm
4012N 1.5 x 1.0 cm (shows no signs, but green paint, not depicted)
4012R 1.1 x 1.0 cm
4014 (two limestone fragments)

Fig. 2 The two limestone fragments, Manchester Museum 4014, photo: Grajetzki

The function of these relief fragments remains unknown. However, some of the fragments have a triangular cross section. Therefore, it seems that they come from an uneven surface which was plastered. The un-plastered surface had grooves. These grooves might be the ones between single bricks or between wooden boards. When the object decayed on which the plaster was fixed, the thinner layers of plaster disappeared, while only the thicker parts filling the grooves survived. It remains pure speculation what kind of object was plastered in this way. One option is that a chapel, next to or over the shafts was plastered and decorated. Another option is a wooden coffin which was plastered. However, so far I could not find any other examples of such plastering on a coffin. A loose parallel might be provided by plaster fragments found at two Thirteenth Dynasty mastabas at Abydos-South. However, the latter fragments are thinner and might belong to the covering of a mummy.[23]

The two limestone fragments within this group might come from an entirely different object.

[22] The letters on the fragments in the museum are sometimes not well visible. The problem cases have a question mark.
[23] Landua-McCormack, *Dynasty XIII Kingship in Ancient Egypt*, 355-356.

Chapter Two: Other unpublished or partly published coffins

Sehetepibankh, Abydos, Garstang 1906, tomb 20 (Aby8)

Material: wood (?)
Measurements: not stated
Colours: not stated
Preservation: fragments preserved in notebook sketches

The coffin fragments were found in tomb 20. There is only a sketch drawing preserved. The short captions next to the drawing read:

‘with fragments of coffin.... Plain top’ ?
‘Coffin has usual decoration with gods Osiris Anubis....’

The bigger fragment on the left (see picture below) belongs most likely to the head end of a rectangular coffin. There is a horizontal text at the top and there are two columns under it. The original position of the two columns shown on the right is unknown. From the orientation the left one (labelled 2 on the drawing) might come from the front side, the other (labelled 3) from the back side. Sehetepibankh bears the title ‘lector priest’ (*ẖri-ḥbt*). The coffin dates perhaps to the middle or late Twelfth Dynasty.

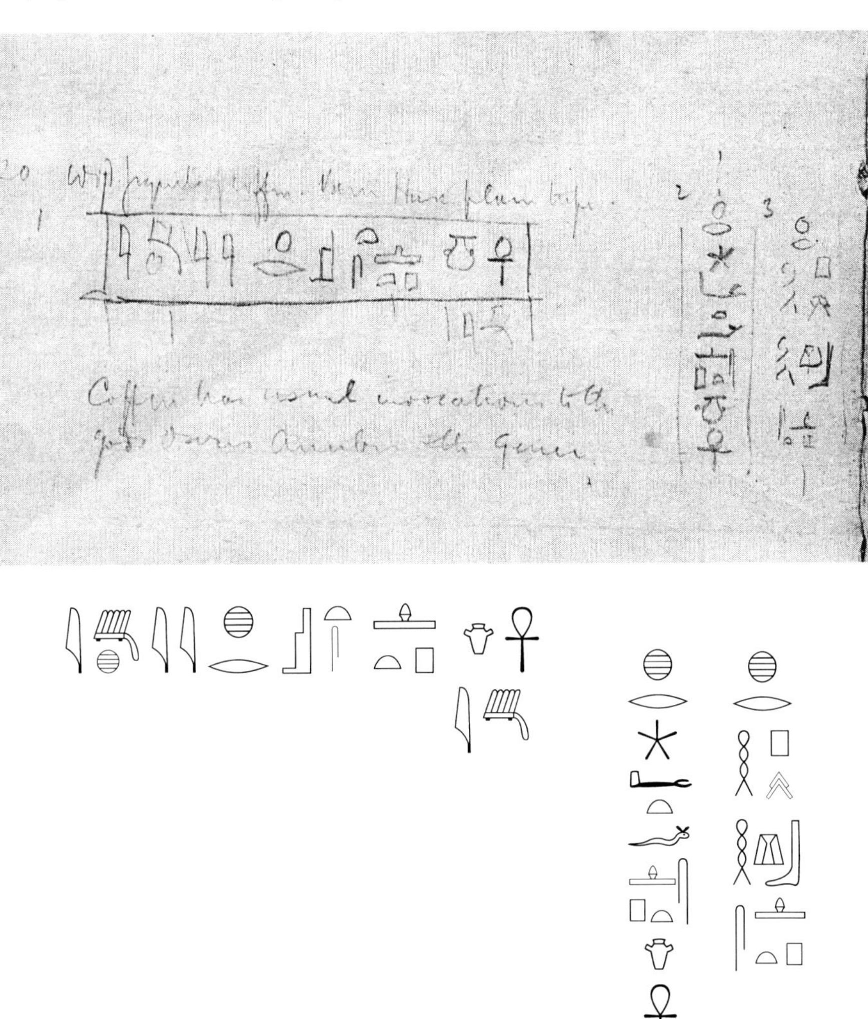

Fig. 3 Inscriptions on the coffin of Sehetepibreankh © Liverpool University (top)

Dedmut, Abydos tomb C.66 (Aby4)

Fragments of coffin and canopic box

Material: wood
Measurements: not stated
Colours: not stated
Preservation: fragments preserved in photographs made at the excavations
Plate V, XIa (coffin), VI, XIb (canopic box)

Bibliography: Peet, *Cemeteries of Abydos II*, 60, fig. 28, pl. XIII, XIV

Thomas Eric Peet excavated between 1911 and 1914 parts of the cemeteries of Abydos for the Egypt Exploration Fund and published his results in several volumes.[24] These publications are of a high standard for their time. Almost all of the tombs found are described and most finds are published as drawing or photographic pictures. Peet discovered also parts of a Middle Kingdom and Second Intermediate Period cemetery. Several burials contained fragments of coffins. At least three of these coffins belong to the Second Intermediate Period. Two of them were fully published; either as drawings or in drawings and photographic pictures (see pp. 42-43). The three coffins are almost identical in style, layout and text programme. The coffin in tomb C.66 was only briefly mentioned and only the parts of inscriptions with the name of the tomb owner and one short end (most likely the foot end of the coffin) were pictured in the publication.

According to the publication, the fragments of two coffins were found in a shaft tomb with one chamber. The only other finds mentioned are 'fragments of white spotted red ware'. In the archive of the Egyptian Exploration Society (London) are two further photographs from the coffin, not previously published. They show fragments of the long sides and three smaller fragments. One of these photographic pictures (pl. XIa) shows fragments of the long sides of the coffin, which were decorated with Coffin Text spells 780 and 783. The hieroglyphs are incomplete. The text bands are framed by a colour pattern, followed by a solid band of one colour. The panels between the columns seems to show a pattern perhaps imitating a high quality wood.

The small fragments on the other photographic picture (pl. XIb) come most likely from a canopic box. This might be the second coffin mentioned in the publication, wrongly identified. On one of the fragments the cloth sign 'menkhet' is visible perhaps combined with a recumbent Anubis jackal. While only the 'menkhet' sign is clearly visible, the jackal can be reconstructed from parallels; indeed, next to the 'menkhet' sign, there is still a dark painted line visible, perhaps the end of the tail of a jackal. The vestige of propably a second 'tail' might indicate two of these jackals were placed back to back. Normally under these groups there appear trees which are visible on better preserved canopic boxes of a similar type.[25] Their remains are perhaps still visible on this fragment. Under the 'menkhet' there is indeed the upper part of some round shaped object detectable. Therefore, the canopic chest shows a typical decoration pattern of Second Intermediate Period canopic boxes.[26] The text columns on the fragments are framed by colour bands and a pattern imitating high quality wood.

The fragments found in tomb C.66 belong to the 'scribe of the temple' Dedmut[27]. His name is written in hieratic on wooden fragments belonging to the canopic box. The main texts on the coffin and canopic box are written in incomplete hieroglyphs.

Beside the style of the coffin, only the pottery, the 'white spotted red ware' provides a clue. This ware is common at the very end of the Second Intermediate Period and the beginning of the New Kingdom.[28]

[24] Naville, *Cemeteries of Abydos I*, Peet, *Cemeteries of Abydos II*, Peet, *Cemeteries of Abydos III*.
[25] Compare the canopic boxes: Berlev, *JEA* 60 (1974), pl. XXVI-XXVII; Winlock, *JEA* 10 (1924), pl. XV.
[26] Compare a full discussion in Lüscher, *Kanopenkästen*, 62-63.
[27] This name seems not to appear in Ranke, *PN*. The name is proposed in the publication, but hard to read on the available pictures.
[28] Seiler, *Tradition & Wandel*, 80-81; Carter, *Five Years*, pl. LXXIV.

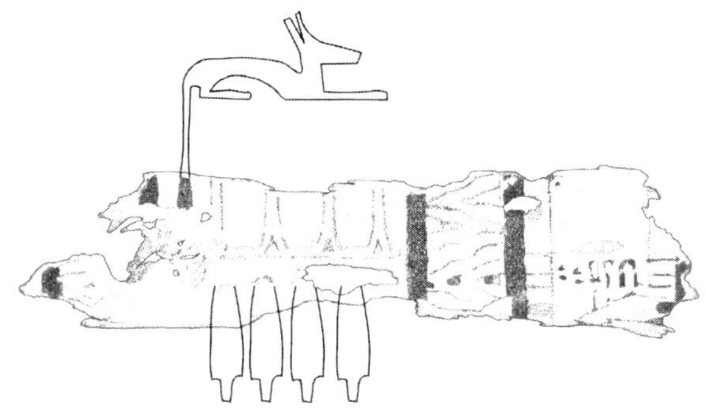

Fig. 4 a The canopic box fragment with the 'menkhet' sign and a reconstruction of a jackal and the trees

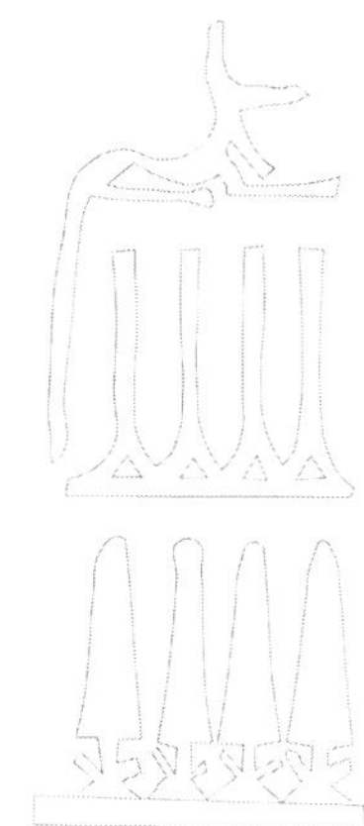

Fig. 4 b Anubis, 'menkhet' and trees on the canopic box of Senebni[29]

The Model coffin of **Nemtyemweskhet** (Aby6)
Plate IV

Abydos, tomb/chapel 321
Liverpool Museum 55.82.114
Material: wood
Measurements: Box: H: 11.7 cm, L: 29.2 cm, W: 12.1 cm; lid: H: 5.5 cm, L: 29.2 cm, W: 12.2 cm.
Colours: background yellow, inscriptions green, wedjat eyes partly black
Preservation: Each side of the model coffin is made from a single wooden board. The bottom board is missing

Bibliography:
Bourriau, *Pharaohs and Mortals*, 93-94, no. 74
Bienkowski, Tooley, *Gifts of the Nile*, 71, fig. 109 (a colour picture)

The wooden model coffin of the 'royal sealer' (*ḫtmty bity*) and 'high steward' (*imy-r pr wr*) Nemtyemweskhet was found in a chapel at about floor level at Abydos[30] and was excavated by John Garstang in 1907 in chapel number 321.From the only published photograph of the excavation showing the object *in situ* it remains unclear whether the model coffin was found under or above floor level. There are no signs that the chapel had a burial chamber, at least nothing like that is attested in the records of Garstang. It was therefore an Abydos offering/memorial chapel.[31] Several stelae were found, some of them still in niches of the walls as can be seen from the excavation photographs. On some of the stela Nemtyemweskhet appears too.[32] The model coffin was placed in an outer undecorated model sarcophagus of limestone. Inside the coffin was found a mummiform figure. The present location of this figure is not known.

The decoration of the coffin follows standard coffins of the late Twelfth Dynasty (Willems type IV). There is a horizontal text line at the top on the exterior and there are four columns under it on the long sides, and two columns under it on the short sides. On the lid there is one text line. The hieroglyphs are incomplete. On the front horizontal line there is the *wn-ḥr* – 'opening of the face' formula.[33] The vertical columns have *imȝḫy ḫr* formulae:

[29] Berlev, *JEA* 60 (1974), pl. XXVII.
[30] Bourriau, *Pharaohs and Mortals*, excavation photograph reproduced on p. 40.
[31] For these chapels see: O'Connor, in *Mélanges Gamal eddin Mokhtar*, 161-177.
[32] Simpson, *The Terrace of the Great God at Abydos: The Offering Chapels of Dynasties 12 and 13*, pl. 29 (ANOC 19).
[33] Lohwasser, *Die Formel 'Öffnen des Gesichts'*; Kees, *Totenglaube und Jenseitsvorstellungen der alten Ägypter*, 260-261.

Top line on the lid

Words spoken, the Osiris, royal sealer and high steward, Nemtyemweskhet[34], *you have gone, that you might become a spirit, you have power as a god, the successor of Osiris.* (a)

Front
Words spoken: Open might be the sight of the royal sealer, high steward Nemtyemweskhet, that he might see the lord of the sky when he crosses heaven.

Columns (front right to left)
Revered before Ptah, Nemtyemweskhet
Revered before Sokar, Nemtyemweskhet
Revered before Geb, Nemtyemweskhet
Revered before Osiris, Nemtyemweskhet

Back side
Word spoken: the royal sealer, high steward Nemtyemweskhet, great is the coming forth of Nemtyemweskhet under the ennead

Columns (left to right)
Revered before Great God, Nemtyemweskhet
Revered before Anubis, Nemtyemweskhet
Revered before Beautiful West, Nemtyemweskhet
Revered before Beautiful Burial, Nemtyemweskhet

head end
Words spoken: may Nemtyemweskhet be raised to the circumpolar stars
(front right to left)
Revered before Nephthys, Nemtyemweskhet
Revered before Mehenet, Nemtyemweskhet

foot end
Words spoken: Geb, lord of the lands is under the ribs of Nemtyemweskhet
(left to right)
Revered before Resnet, Nemtyemweskhet
Revered before the great enead, Nemtyemweskhet

(a) This is pyramid spell 422, paragraph 752b; in the Middle Kingdom the spell also appears on the coffin lids (underside) of the 'governor' Amenemhat from Deir el-Bersheh (B9C, B10C); compare Allen, *The Egyptian Coffin Texts, Volume 8, Middle Kingdom Copies of Pyramid Texts*, 339; pyramid spell 422 was most likely part of a 'Transfiguration' ritual; compare Quirke, in: Grallert/Grajetzki (editors), *Life and Afterlife in the Middle Kingdom and Second Intermediate Period*, 106; The spell conveyc the whish for the deceased to go from his burial place to the gods in heaven, see Assmann, *Altägyptische Totenliturgien III*, 270-71.

Date: The 'high steward' Nemtyemweskhet is well known from several other objects, most importantly several stelae and scarab seals. He is not closely datable, but seems to belong to the Thirteenth Dynasty. One indication is the writing of the title 'royal sealer' (*ḫtmti-biti*) with the red crown and not with the bee.[35] Other indications for this date are the incomplete hieroglyphs on the model coffin, typical for the late Twelfth or Thirteenth Dynasty.[36]

---

[34] Ranke, *PN* I, 69, 19 (reads *ˁn.ti-m-wsḫt*) gives two references for this name. They both refer to this person.

[35] Grajetzki, *Bulletin de la Société d'égyptologie*, 19 (1995), 5-11.

[36] Lilyquist, *Ancient Egyptian Mirrors from the Earliest Times through the Middle Kingdom*, 33-34, n. 377; Miniaci, *RdE* 61 (2010), 113-134.

Hu

In 1898 – 1899 W. M. Flinders Petrie excavated for the Egypt Exploration Fund the cemeteries of Hu, near ancient Hut-Sekhem (Hu, Greek: Diospolis Parva). The results were published shortly after.[37] The publication is of special historical importance because Flinders Petrie developed here the 'sequence dating' which was of fundamental importance for putting Egyptian prehistory in order. However, the series of cemeteries found at Hu contained tombs of almost all periods of Egyptian history, all of which are described to some extent in the book.

The publication is of a relatively high standard for the period. Nevertheless, the tombs are not systematically presented in detail and there is no tomb register, thus leaving many questions open for a modern researcher. Each chapter of the publication is more a summary of the finds than a presentation of the full documentation. Of special interest for the modern researcher is the fact that the notebooks of A. C. Mace, who was working with Flinders Petrie at Hu, have survived. Mace recorded all of the tombs relatively carefully in these notebooks. He made many sketches and supplied short descriptions of the burials and objects found. Mace was mainly working on cemetery Y dating to the Second Intermediate Period. There are not many burial grounds in Egypt of that period published, making this cemetery and the records of Mace especially important. In several of the tombs found, remains of coffins were observed. These fragments were drawn by Mace.

The fragments found at Hu have many points in common with coffins found at Thebes, dating to the Second Intermediate Period. On most of the fragments, the hieroglyphs are incomplete, as common is in that period. Three of the coffins documented at Hu belong to a type with the Nefertem-spell on the front horizontal top line and a spell relating to Anubis on the back. Similar coffins are mainly known from Thebes (see pp. 48-51).[38] The Nefertem-spell appears in the Second Intermediate Period always on coffins with a high number of text columns on the long sides.[39] In these text columns 'speeches of gods' appear. Only on the coffin from tomb 467 are such speeches preserved and even here only in fragments. Whether the coffins at Hu also had a high number of columns must remain an open question, but it seems likely from the parallels at Thebes. The coffin from tomb 467 (Hu4) was decorated on the front side with the 'opening of the face' formula, at Thebes attested on a coffin (T3Be) of the late Twelfth Dynasty.

The coffin from tomb 15 (not from cemetery Y) was decorated on the back side with a hetep-di-nisut formula invoking Anubis. This formula is common on Twelfth Dynasty coffins. The hieroglyphic signs are not incomplete, indicating an earlier date. Whether this coffin still belongs to the Twelfth Dynasty seems an open question. At Hawara, Lisht and Dahshur incomplete hieroglyphs are securely attested for the late Twelfth and early Thirteenth Dynasty. It is not sure whether this also applies for a provincial cemetery.[40]

The coffin from tomb 196 seems to have been decorated with a palace façade, common for coffins of the late Middle Kingdom and still attested in the Second Intermediate Period.

Tomb Hu Y 196 (Hu1)

Plate XIIa

In this shaft tomb were found coffin fragments decorated with a palace façade. The wood of the coffin board was 2 ½ inches (= 6.4 cm) thick. There is also a drawing of the colour scheme of the palace façade although hard to read: white, red, blue, the door, blue. The door in the middle seems to have been white, red, white, red. A further note states: 'columns are framed by black'. The coffin dates most likely to the middle/late Twelfth or early Thirteenth Dynasty.[41] In this period coffins with a palace façade were most common.[42]

---

[37] Flinders Petrie, *Diospolis Parva: the cemeteries of Abadiyeh and Hu, 1898-9*; the coffins are only briefly mentioned on p. 51.

[38] CG 28030, Hayes, *Scepter of Egypt I*, 347-49, Grajetzki, *BMSAES* 5 (2006), 4.

[39] Willems, *Chests of Life*, 116-117.

[40] Miniaci, *RdE* 61 (2010), 113-134

[41] Bourriau, in, *Sitting beside Lepsius*, 71.

[42] Willems, *Chests of Life*, 163-164.

Tomb Hu Y 219 (Hu2)

Plate XIIb, XIIIa

The tomb, which seems to have been a simple shaft tomb without chamber, contained the remains of two coffins. The drawings of the inscriptions are placed on two facing pages. On the left page most hieroglyphic groups belong to columns. Here the copies of the inscriptions are marked as coming from one or the other of the coffins (one above the other) (plate XIIb). On the right page (plate XIIIb) it is not possible to distinguish the origin of the fragments. However, most of the fragments come from one text line and are most likely from one coffin. Only two fragments (a, b) come from other text lines.

The largest group of fragments belongs to the horizontal line on the front (1) as can be seen from the orientation of the writing and from parallels. One fragment belongs to the back side (2), one to the lid (3) and several smaller fragments belonging evidently to the vertical columns. There is no further information on any other finds in the tomb.

Fig. 5 Coffin from tomb Hu Y 219; the hieroglyphs in typescript, transcribed from the notebook.

Fig. 6 Reconstruction; front side (d, f, g, c, e)

The Nefertem- spell (pyramid text spell 249 § 266, b, c):
[ḏd mdw ẖꜥ NN m nfr-]tmw m sšn r šrt nt rꜥ pri.f m ꜣẖt rꜥ nb wꜥb nṯrw n mꜣ.n.f ẖꜥ nb ỉỉ.n [*NN* …]

[*Words spoken: may NN appear as Nefer]tem as lotus at the nose of Ra, may he go forth from the horizon, every day, and at the sight of which the gods purify himself, Osiris NN come…*

back side (2) (reconstruction following coffin Cairo CG 28030)

This is a spell common in the late Middle Kingdom to the Second Intermediate Period (p. 63). It appears always on the back (right, west) side of the coffin.

Fig. 7 Coffin from tomb Hu Y 219; notebook drawing and hieroglyphs in typescript; text fragment from back of coffin

[ḏd mdw ꜥwi inpw tpi ḏw.f] ***<u>nb tꜣ-dsr ḥꜣ</u>*** *[ꜣst-irt NN di.f ẖnm sw zmit imntt m ẖn.s ẖm nfr nb ḥtpw imi iz n ẖrt-nṯr di.f iwꜥ ꜣst-irt NN nḥḥ ḏt]*

[Words spoken: may the arms of Anubis, on his mountain,] lord of the holy land be around [NN, may he cause that he is united with the western desert in the beautiful shrine of the lord of offerings in the tomb of the necropolis, may he cause that NN is inheriting for all eternity]

lid (3) part of the Nut formula (Pyramid text 368 (638))

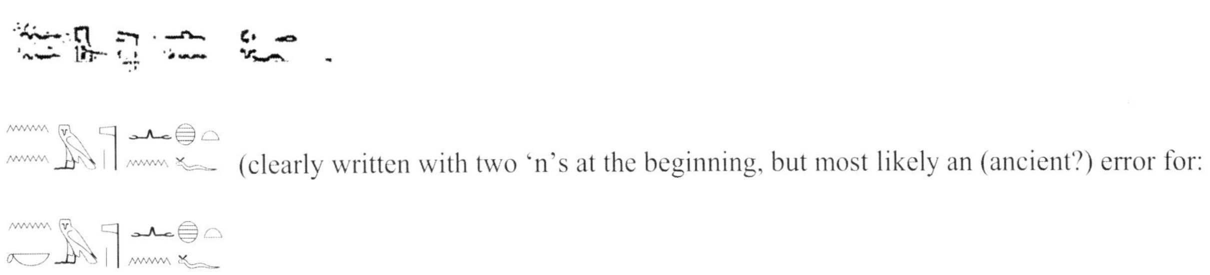

(clearly written with two 'n's at the beginning, but most likely an (ancient?) error for:

Fig. 8 Coffin from tomb Hu Y 219; notebook drawing and hieroglyphs in typescript; text from lid of coffin

Tomb Hu 15 (Hu3)

Two inscriptions are drawn in the notebook. There is one column with an *imꜣḫ ḫr* formula, perhaps to be read as: *imꜣḫ ḫr tf[nwt]*. From the orientation the column was on the back side.[43] There were wedjat eyes on the front. The other inscription in the notebook shows a hetep-di-nisut formula invoking Anubis and certainly once again placed on the back side of the coffin. This type of text was no longer common on Second Intermediate Period coffins. The hieroglyphs of the inscriptions on this coffin are not incomplete, pointing to a date in the Twelfth Dynasty. In this case the title and name and title of the coffin owner are preserved: the wab-priest Ib[44]. The coffin and the tomb date most likely to the late Twelfth Dynasty or early Thirteenth Dynasty.[45]

The long inscription on the back side

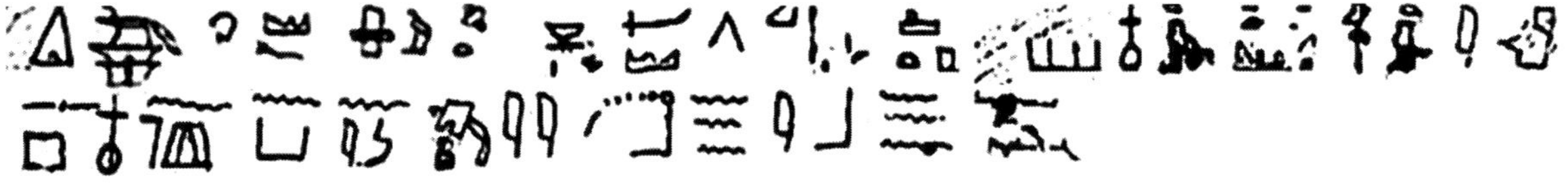

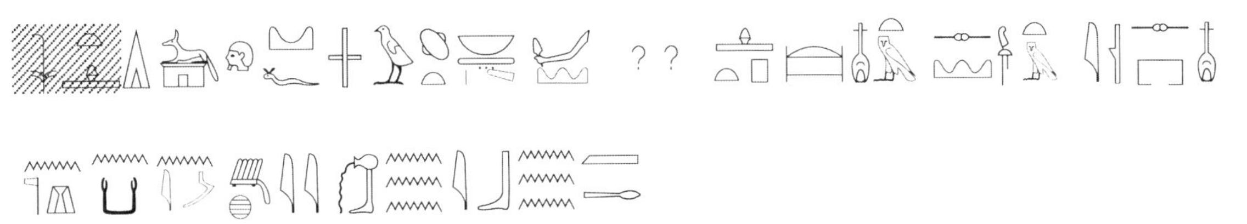

Fig. 9 Coffin from tomb Hu 15; notebook drawing and hieroglyphs in typescript; text fragment from back of coffin

ḥtp di niswt inpw tpi ḏw.f imi-wt nb tꜣ ḏsr … ḥtp ḳrst nfrt m zmit imntt m iz nfr n ẖrt-nṯr n kꜣ n imꜣḫii wꜥb ib mꜣꜥ ḫrw

[43] Willems, *Chests of Life*, 138-39.

[44] The name does not appear in this writing, in Ranke, *PN*.

[45] Bourriau, in, *Sitting beside Lepsius*, 55.

[An offering that the king] gives to Anubis on his mountain, the one in the place of embalming, lord of the secret land... a beautiful burial in the western desert in the beautiful tomb of the necropolis, for the ka of the revered one, the wab priest Ib, true of voice

revered before Tef[nut]

Fig. 10 Coffin from tomb Hu 10; notebook drawing and hieroglyphs in typescript; column

Tomb Hu Y 467 (Hu4)
Plate XIIIb
The tomb is a simple shaft. Several fragments of inscriptions were recorded. From the orientation of the signs most fragments seem to come from the front of the coffin. Of particular interest is the short phrase *ḥrt m ḥtp wp f* (a). These words have parallels in the 'opening of the face' formula (compare p. 61). The hieroglyphic signs are complete. This is so far the only coffin from Hu with the 'opening of the face' formula. The coffin might date to the late Twelfth or early Thirteenth Dynasty.

Fig. 11 Coffin from tomb Hu Y 467; hieroglyphs in typescript; text fragment from front of coffin

Part of the horizontal text can be reconstructed as (b + c + a):

The placement of fragment b at the front is just a guess with the suggestion that is part of the coffin owner's name. A gap followed where the end of the name might have appeared and . The might be a misunderstanding on the part of Mace for .

Tomb Hu Y 480 (Hu5)[46]
Plate XIVa
The fragments found in this tomb belong again to a coffin decorated with the Nefertem-spell (p. 63-64) at the front and the Anubis formula (p. 61) at the back.

Front side
This is again a part of the Nefertem-spell[47].

Fig. 12 Coffin from tomb Hu Y 480; notebook drawing and hieroglyphs in typescript; text fragment from front of coffin

back side
The text is part of the Anubis formula.

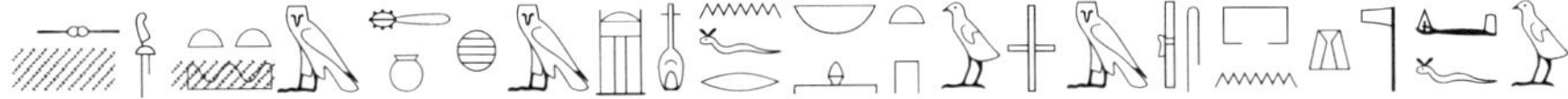

Fig. 12 Coffin from tomb Hu Y 480; notebook drawing and hieroglyphs in typescript; text fragment from back of coffin

There are several other smaller fragments recorded. Four of them are presented here in my typescript, for the others I was not able to provide parallels, compare plate XIVa.

a. Words spoken by Nebet-hut: I came …
b. … [you are happy with it] today, Osi[ris …]
c. [Words spoken by] Neith: I came …
d. …coming of

Fig. 13 Coffin from tomb Hu Y 480; hieroglyphs in typescript; text fragment from the coffin

[46] Bourriau, in, *Sitting beside Lepsius*, 85.
[47] Compare CG 28030.

Tomb Hu Y 511 (Hu6)
Plate XIVb
The coffin found in this tomb belongs again to the type with the Nefertem-spell on the front.

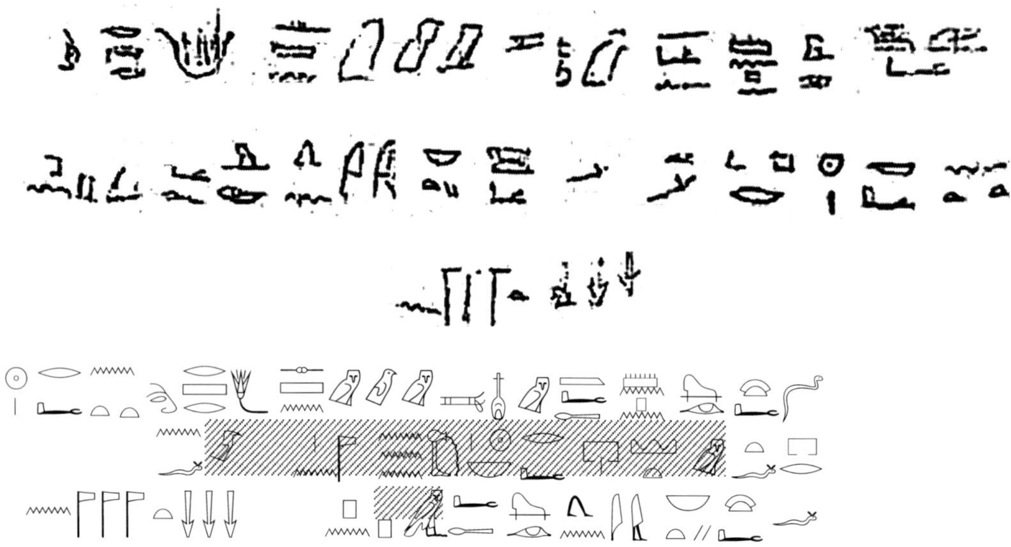

Fig. 14 Coffin from tomb Hu Y 511; notebook drawing and hieroglyphs in typescript; text fragment from front of coffin

The spell on fig. 14 is to a greater part preserved even including signs *mn pn* – *this NN* – as replacement for the name of the coffin owner.

Fig. 15 Coffin from tomb Hu Y 511; notebook drawing and hieroglyphs in typescript; text fragment from head end: 'Isis'spell[48]

Fig. 16 Coffin from tomb Hu Y 511; notebook drawing and hieroglyphs in typescript; text fragment from foot end, 'Nephthys' spell[49]

[48] The spell appears on several coffins of the late Middle Kingdom and Second Intermediate Period: Thebes CG 28030, model coffin CG 48404, king Hor, perhaps Abydos: Grajetzki, *SAK* 34 (2006), 210.
[49] Thebes: CG 28030, Abydos: Grajetzki, *SAK* 34 (2006), 208.

Tomb Y 217 (Hu7)

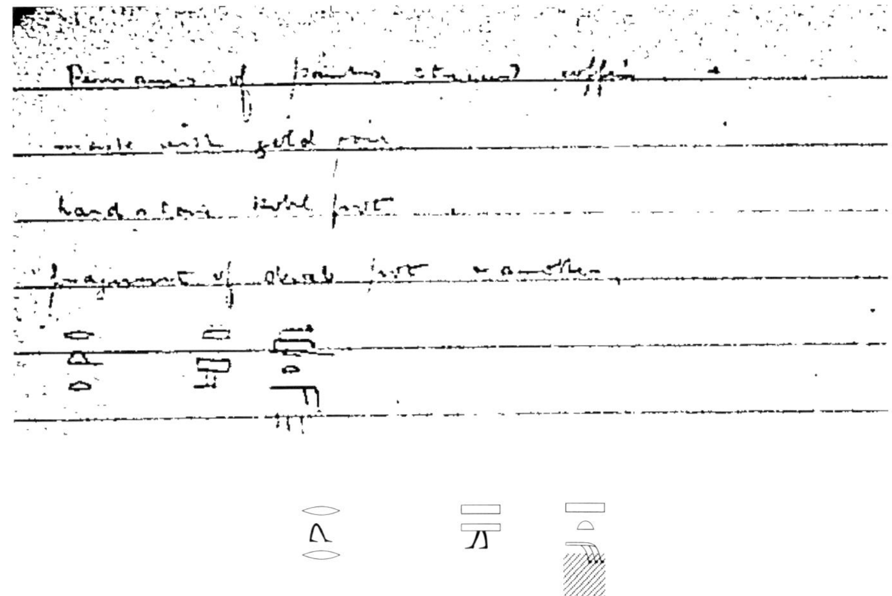

Fig. 17 Coffin from tomb Hu Y 217; notebook drawing and hieroglyphs in typescript; text fragment from the coffin

Only three short fragments, most likely from columns, are recorded, perhaps dating to the Twelfth Dynasty.[50] The captions on the notebook page mentions that the coffin was stuccoed.

Hawara

The cemeteries of Hawara are best known for the pyramid of Amenemhat III and his 'labyrinth'. Next to the royal funerary monument, there must have been a big cemetery for the officials of the ruler, little of which is preserved. Most of the tombs are looted and reused in the Late Period for crocodile burials. The date of the few burials found is hard to establish. While the cemetery might have started at the same time as the king built his pyramid around his 20th year[51]; it is an open question whether the cemetery was still used on a larger scale in the Thirteenth Dynasty.

Zatrenenutet (Haw1)
Material: wood and stuccoed
Colours: yellow background, inscriptions in blue
Preservation: poor condition when found, left on site

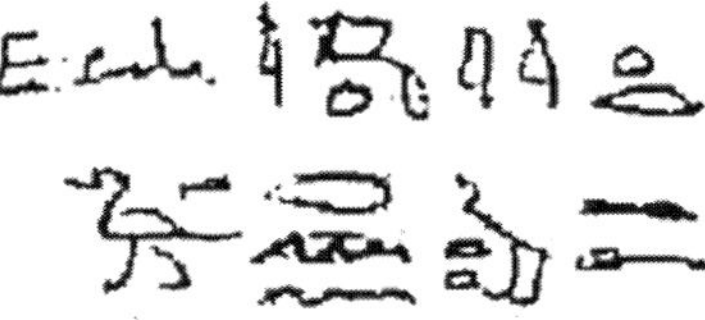

Fig. 18 notebook drawing: inscription on the coffin of Zatrenenutet

[50] Bourriau, in, *Sitting beside Lepsius*, 73 (Middle Kingdom).
[51] Arnold, *Senwosret III*, 117.

The tomb of Zatrenenutet[52] was discovered undisturbed and contained a set of objects and two burials. There was the body of Zatrenenutet and the body of a child, both placed in the same coffin. The coffin was found largely destroyed by ants. It was made of 'stuccoed wood', with two eyes on the east side with the 'usual formulae'.[53] In the Petrie notebooks there is further information that there was at least an *im3ḫy ḫr* formula on the coffin (on the east side). The notebook also provides the writing of the name. The tomb was dated by the pottery to the end of the reign of Amenemhat III.[54]

[52] Ranke, *PN* I, 290, 23 ('daughter of Renenutet').
[53] Petrie/Wainwright/Mackay, *The Labyrinth, Gerzeh and Mazghuneh*, 36.
[54] Bourriau, Patterns of change in burial customs, 19.

Chapter Three: Coffins of the late Twelfth and Thirteenth Dynasty and Early Second Intermediate Period

Saqqara

The cemeteries of Saqqara were used in all periods of Egyptian history, including those of the late Middle Kingdom and Second Intermediate Period.

Hetepet, Saqqara, burial 41(Sq19X)[55]
The coffin of Hetepet was found in her undisturbed tomb. It was a rectangular coffin with a vaulted lid and raised ends. The outside of the coffin was covered with pitch or resin. The interior had been plastered or painted white. There were texts in vertical columns of hieroglyphs in red and black. The excavators only recorded the name of the coffin owner: Hetepet(i).

The coffin type seems similar to the four coffins of women found next to the pyramid of Amenemhat II at Dahshur and to the middle coffin of Senebtisi from Lisht. The date of the coffin of Hetepet is hard to estimate. Five pottery vessels found in the tomb are vaguely similar to a pottery vessel found in the tomb of king Hor. [56] The deceased was richly adorned with jewellery: a girdle of eight silver cowry shells, a necklace of large flat silver shells, gold lions and strings of carnelian, garnet and amethyst beads.

Aabed (Sq18) [57]
The coffin of Aabed was found by Loret in the area of the Teti pyramid. The coffin is relatively closely datable because it contained a dagger[58] of king Apophis (here with the throne name Nebkhepeshre), the last Hyksos ruler known from contemporary sources.[59] The text programme of the coffin is close to Middle Kingdom coffins. It is decorated on the long sides with a horizontal line and four columns. The horizontal lines contain hetep-di-nisut formula invoking Osiris. The four columns on each side are contain *imakhu-kher* formulae. On one of the short ends is shown Isis with a short caption: 'words spoken by Isis'. On the long sides there are further depictions. On the front is shown a mummy on a bed. On the back is shown Anubis with the caption: 'Words spoken by Anubis'. On the long sides at the head end there is on either side a single wedjat eye. There are also a checkerboard pattern in the middle field between the columns. Altogether the coffin shows a mixture of Middle Kingdom (text) and late Second Intermediate Period (vignettes) elements.

Nensemekhtuef (Sq23X)
The coffin is so far only known from a photographic picture in a short summary of the season in 2006 in Saqqara, by the German Archaeological Institute.[60] It was found in the subterranean galleries of the Second Dynasty king Ninetjer. The published photograph shows part of the lid. A middle column is visible. There are also vertical columns with *imakhu-kher* formulae. In the fields between the columns there are panels with (most likely) religious texts. The hieroglyphs are incomplete. The ornamental hieroglyphs are well painted in different colours. The hieroglyphs in the panels are blue. The closest parallel for this coffin are those of Amenhotep (Da6X) from Dahshur and Senebhenaf (Aby7) from Abydos.

---

[55] Firth/Gunn, *Teti pyramid cemeteries*, 59.
[56] Firth/Gunn, *Teti pyramid cemeteries*, 59, fig. 66; the vase in the tomb of king Hor: de Morgan, *Fouilles à Dahchour I*, 98, fig. 228. The vessel in the tomb of king Hor is much slimmer and the region connecting neck with the body is slightly different . However, the vessels are in general of the shape; similar vessels are not common in the late Middle Kingdom compare the vessel depicted in Engelbach, *Harageh*, pl. XXXIX, 63M; Engelbach, R., *Riqqeh and Memphis VI*, pl. XXXII, 60b-f.
[57] Ranke, *PN* I, 60, 10.
[58] Daressy, *ASAE* 7 (1906), 115-120.
[59] Beckerath, *Untersuchungen*, 127-130, 275; Ryholt, *Political Situation*, 385-87 (File 15/5, 19).
[60] Dreyer, in *Deutsches Archäologisches Institut, Abteilung Kairo, Rundbrief, September 2007*, 21, fig. 33 http://www.dainst.org/medien/de/daik_rundbrief_2007.pdf (retrieved 10/04/2010).

Dahshur

Dahshur is one of the key sites for late Twelfth and Thirteenth Dynasty coffins. In this period it was one of the main burial grounds for the kings, the royal family and the court officials. Many of these people are also known from other sources and therefore well datable. The main published excavations are those of de Morgan in 1894 and 1895. His extremely successful operation led to the discovery of several undisturbed burials of royal women. He also found the well preserved burial of the Thirteenth Dynasty king Awibre Hor. All these burials contained decorated coffins.

Further excavations have taken place since the 1970s by the German Archaeological Institute, by the Metropolitan Museum, New York and by a Japanese mission. Only the Japanese mission has published several coffins important for this study.

Zatip (Da1X)[61]
The coffin of Zatip[62] was found in her undisturbed tomb at Dahshur (tomb no. 22). The coffin was poorly preserved, but G. Daressy was able to copy the inscriptions, most likely painted on the interior. No further decoration is published. Therefore it is impossible to assign her coffin to a particular type. It is possible to reconstruct the arrangement of the texts presented in the excavation report.[63] Following that, the coffin was decorated with the Pyramid Text spells 247 to 258 (plate VII).[64] The burial of Zatip was found close to the pyramid of Senusret III. Therefore, her tomb might date under this king or slightly later.

Ita (Da2X), **Itaweret** (Da4X), **Khnumet** (Da3X), **Zathathormeryt** (Da1C).
These are the coffins of four women, three with the title 'king's daughter'. Their burials, all intact, were found in two galleries (each with two tomb chambers) next to the pyramid of Amenemhat II at Dahshur. Their coffins are identical in design. They are simple rectangular boxes with wedjat eyes as only decoration on the outside. The lid is vaulted. The edges of the boxes were covered with gold foil which is decorated with parallel lines. The inside of the coffins had almost identical inscriptions with pyramid spells. The coffins were placed inside of sarcophagi. Inside the coffins were anthropoid coffins.[65] The tombs date perhaps under Amenemhat III (compare p. 96-97).

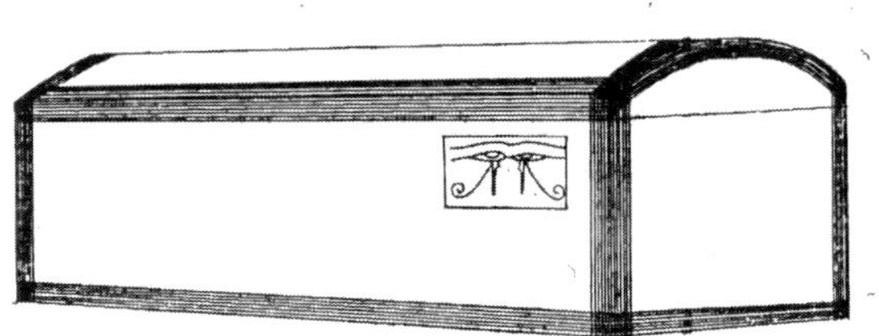

Fig. 19 The coffin of Ita (Da2X)[66]

These four coffins form a unique set. The closest parallels are the coffin of Hetepet (Sq19X) from Saqqara and the middle coffin of Senebtisi (L5) from Lisht.

---

[61] de Morgan, *Fouilles à Dahchour I*, 36, fig. 73.
[62] Ranke, *PN* I, 285, 20.
[63] Some of the fragments drawn by Daressy join, with perhaps just a few signs missing in between. However, there are problems with the biggest fragment (lower right on pl.XX). Paragraphs 264 a/b to 270 a join perfectly with the fragments above. 259a to 263a only join if we assume that Daressy failed to copy one line. The missing line is marked 'a' on the reconstruction.
[64] The same sequence appears in the Middle Kingdom also in the burial chamber of Siese in Dahshur and in the burial of Senusret-ankh at List: Allen, *Occurrences of Pyramid Texts*, 72; Carrier, C. *Textes des Pyramides de l'Égypte Ancienne, Tome VI, Annexes*, 4118-4141.
[65] Discussion of the anthropoid coffins: Mace, Winlock, *The Tomb of Senebtisi at Lisht*, 47-48.
[66] de Morgan, *Fouilles à Dahchour II*, 50, fig. 109.

Senu (Da1)[67]

The coffin of the 'commander' (*ꜣṯw*) Senu was found at Dahshur in his undisturbed tomb. Over the head of the deceased there was a feathered mummy mask.[68] The tomb is not yet fully published, but it seems that there was little burial equipment. In exhibition catalogues the tomb is dated to the late Twelfth or Thirteenth Dynasty.

The coffin is painted yellow with blue inscriptions. It has on the horizontals bands offering formulae and on the vertical columns simple *imakhu-kher* formulae. The coffin style and its inscriptions are very much in the tradition of the Twelfth Dynasty. The feathered mummy mask seems to point to a later date. It recalls the rishi coffins and the mummy mask of Nubherredi[69] found in her Theban coffin (T7C).

Awibre Hor (Da4C)

The coffin of Hor was made of wood with the inscriptions in gold foil. De Morgan and his team were only able to save fragments of the gold leaf, but not the coffin itself. However, the general appearance of the coffin is shown in a reconstruction of the tomb. It is decorated with four vertical columns on the long, and two on the short sides.[70] The horizontal top line on the front shows the *wn-ḥr*/'opening of the face' formula. The columns are decorated with 'speeches of gods'. The horizontal line on the back is not preserved. The hieroglyphic signs of animals are incomplete. The legs of birds are missing, the ends of snakes and for some signs the heads. The king's name Hor is written phonetically. Most likely the artist composing the text did not want to write the Horus falcon incomplete to avoid mutilating of a divine symbol.

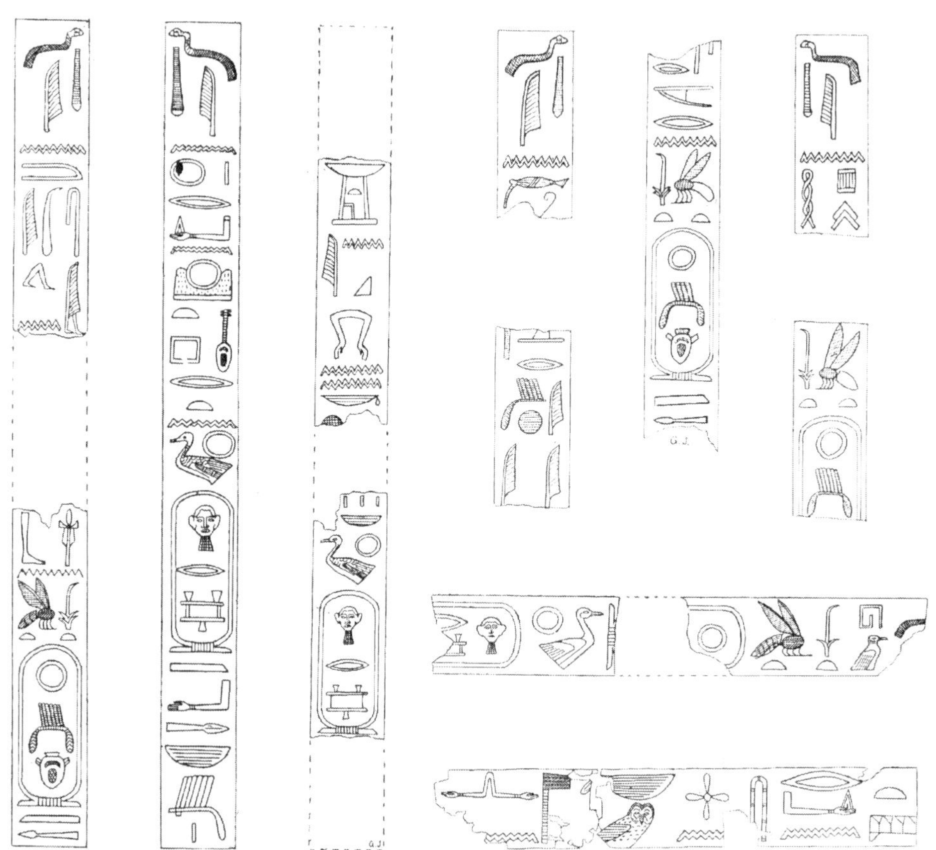

Fig. 20 The inscribed gold foil on king Hor's coffin as published by de Morgan

[67] Yoshimurra, *Excavating in Egypt*, 192-193, 228 (dated to Thirteenth Dynasty), no. 248; Yoshimura, *Excavating in Egypt for 40 years* (2008), 30, no. 47 (dated to the late Twelfth to Thirteenth Dynasty).

[68] Yoshimurra, *Excavating in Egypt*, 194-197, 228, no. 249; Yoshimura, *Excavating in Egypt for 40 years* (2008), 31, no. 48.

[69] Cairo CG 28109.

[70] A reconstruction of the texts: Grajetzki, *Bulletin of the Egyptian Museum* 2 (2005), fig. 2 on page 77 (in the reconstruction the right column on the front should be reversed).

Nubhetepti-khered (Da2C)
The burial of the 'king's daughter' Nubhetepti-khered was found next to those of king Hor. The burial contained a similar coffin to that of the king. However, the gold foil was better preserved than those of the king, making it possible to reconstruct most of its decoration.[71] The decoration of the coffin is almost identical to the one of king Hor.

Zatsobek (Da3C)[72]
The fragments of gold foil belonging to the 'lady of the house' Zatsobek were found at Dahshur, but seem not to have been recorded in the excavation report of de Morgan from which they come. They are now in Cairo. However, there is one tomb briefly mentioned and shown with a small drawing on which a coffin which seems to fit the fragments of Zatsobek. The tomb contained a wooden box coffin inside which was found an anthropoid coffin. The rectangular coffin showed one horizontal and four vertical columns on the front side. On it there is a canopic box and next to it an anthropoid coffin with a gilded face.[73]

The texts on the coffin are similar to those on the coffin of king Hor and the 'king's daughter' Nubhetepti-khered with spells of gods in the columns and pyramidion spells in the horizontal lines.[74] The fragments are only published in typescript hieroglyphs and there are problems reconstructing the arrangement of the texts. There are indeed three columns naming children of Horus, orientated to the right (Amset - arm, Duamutef – left leg, Qebehsenuef – right leg). For the Thirteenth Dynasty, there is no coffin known where one of the children of Horus appears on the short end of the coffin (in the columns). Therefore, from the orientation it must be concluded that all three columns were placed on the left (front) side of the coffin, if the texts are published correctly.

Amenhotep (Da6X)

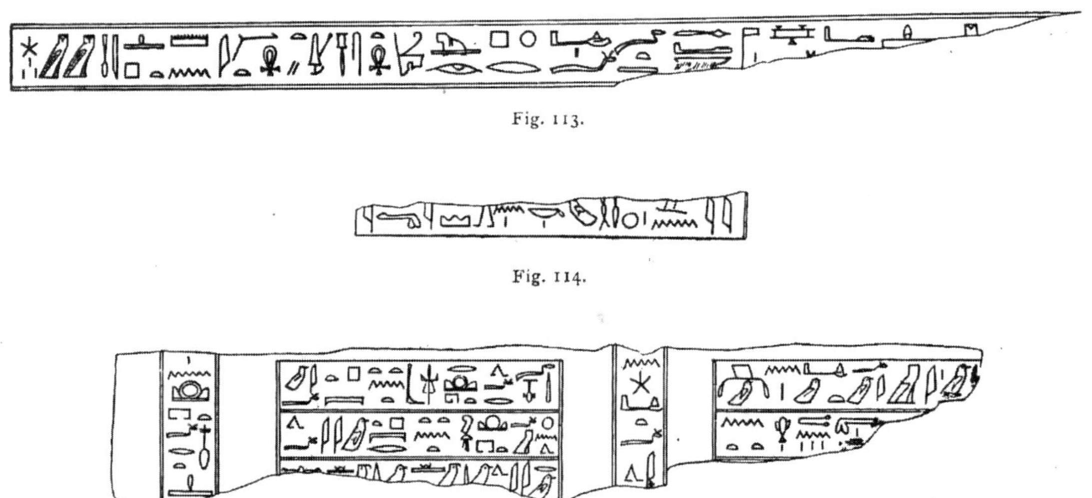

Fig. 21 The coffin fragments of Amenhotep[75]

The burial of the 'royal sealer' (*ḫtmti-biti*), 'sole friend' (*smr-wʿti*) and 'treasurer' (*imi-r ḫtmt*) Amenhotep was found next to that of queen Keminub (Da5X) at Dahshur. His tomb contained an outer sarcophagus and the fragments of a wooden inner coffin which was inscribed. The fragments of a dark coffin ('couleur sombre') belong to the lid, the front side and one single text end, perhaps from the head end or the back of the coffin.[76] The front side bears the remains of vertical columns and blocks of text in between. Although only two of the spells of gods are preserved, it seems certain that they belong to the standard text

[71] Grajetzki, *Bulletin of the Egyptian Museum* 2 (2005), fig. 3, on page 78.
[72] Cairo CG 28105.
[73] Da3C; de Morgan, *Dahchour II*, 102-103, fig. 151; Cairo CG 28105.
[74] A reconstruction: Grajetzki, *Bulletin of the Egyptian Museum* 2 (2005), 73, n. 8.
[75] de Morgan, *Dahchour II*, 70, fig. 113-115.
[76] de Morgan, *Dahchour II*, 70.

programme (compare p. 61-66) of the Thirteenth Dynasty. On the lid appears a formula placing the deceased among the stars. The texts in the three partly preserved panels seem to be without parallels. The closest parallel for his coffin is the one of Senebhenaf (Aby7) from Abydos.

The second panel:
Words spoken: may he arrive at the eastern horizon of the sky, may he settle down in the western horizon of heaven, may he go, may he go, may he be healed, may he be healedl, may he not ...

The 'treasurer' Amenhotep is also known from several scarabs.[77] One of the scarabs has back type 8,[78] while all the others have back type 6. Back type 6 is typical for the middle of the Thirteenth Dynasty. Back type 8 dates later. There are four royal names connected with back type 8, mentioning the following kings: Khahetepibre, Wahibre, Merneferre and Sheshi.[79] Furthermore, the title 'royal sealer' of Amenhotep is written not with a bee, but with a red crown. This writing of the title appears on seals more often only from the time after Sobekhotep IV.[80] From this slight evidence it might be proposed that Amenhotep and his coffin date somewhere after Sobekhotep IV, most likely in the reigns of Khahetepibre Sobekhotep to Merneferibre.

Keminub (Da5X)

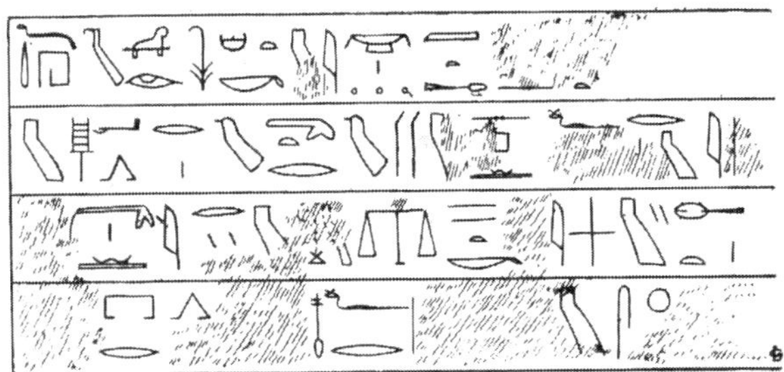

Fig. 116.

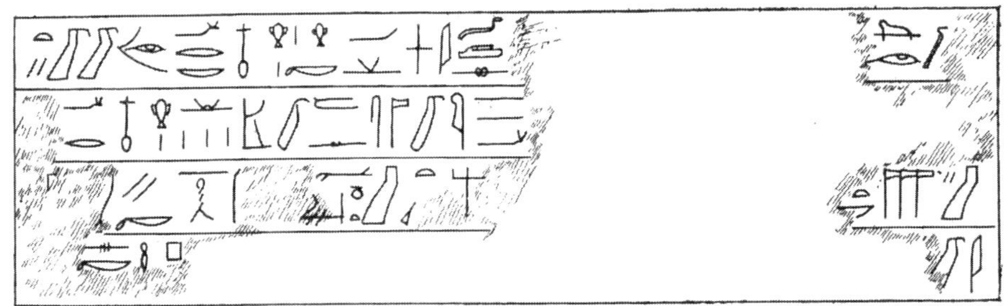

Fig. 22 The text panels found in the tomb of queen Keminub

[77] Martin, Seals, nos. 189-192.
[78] Martin, Seals, no. 190.
[79] Martin, Seals, 6.
[80] Grajetzki, *BSEG* 19 (1995), 5-11.

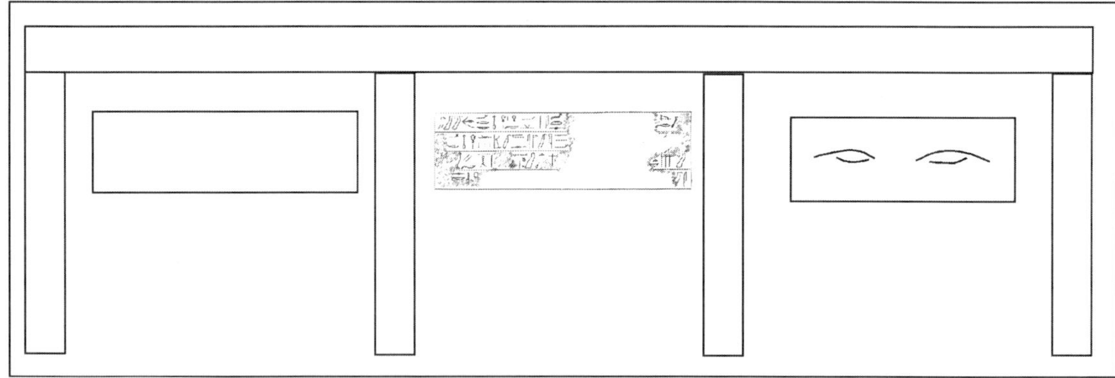

Fig. 23 Reconstruction of the coffin of Keminub

The burial of queen Keminub was found next to the pyramid of Amenemhat II at Dahshur. It contained the remains of the coffin[81] which is described as made from one piece of wood. It was decorated with inscriptions that were painted on the coffin. Two panels of texts were published, both with four lines, one oriented to the left, and the other one to the right. One of the panels shows the mummy mask spell from Book of the Dead chapter 151[82], the other one the heart scarab spell Book of the Dead chapter 30b. The only clue for dating this tomb is the writing of the hieroglyphs on the coffin. The animals are incomplete, common only after the Twelfth Dynasty.[83] Next to the queen in the same gallery was buried the 'treasurer' Amenhotep (Da6X), who is datable into the second half of the Thirteenth Dynasty as argued above. This might give a further clue as to the dating of queen Keminub and her coffin, as they were buried side by side in the same gallery and are therefore perhaps close in date.[84]

Lisht

Lisht was the royal cemetery of the early Middle Kingdom. The pyramids of Amenemhat I and Senusret I were built here. Around these pyramids developed important cemeteries. They were still used in the Thirteenth Dynasty even for people of high social status. The cemetery was the target of a French mission in 1894/1895. Later an American team excavated here from 1906 to 1934 and again from 1988 on. The French excavators published a final report to the standards of the day, while little of relevance for this sudy is published from the later work. The exception is the important tomb of Senebtisi. Lisht is the find place of some key coffins of the late Middle Kingdom and Second Intermediate Period.

Senebtisi (L4/L5)
The tomb of the 'lady of the house' Senebtisi was found almost untouched and is one of the key tombs of the late Middle Kingdom. The tomb was a simple shaft tomb and Senebtisi was buried in a set of three coffins. The outer one was made of wood and decorated with one horizontal text line on each side at the top and four columns of texts on the long and two columns on the short sides. On the north east side there were two wedjat eyes. This is the common decorative scheme on most Middle Kingdom rectangular coffins. The coffin was badly preserved so that only parts of the inscriptions could be copied. The horizontal texts at the top are too destroyed to provide any idea of their contents. However, it seems, that they are so far without parallels. They are not offering formulae or spells known from other coffins. In the columns are found the 'speeches of gods'. For the column at the head end, on the front side was a formula mentioning Ra. A Ra spell is known from several late Twelfth Dynasty and Second Intermediate Period coffins (see page 64).

The middle coffin had as its only inscription a single text line on the lid with a Nut formula. The outside of the middle coffin is decorated with wedjat eyes and the edges with gold leaf. The gold leaf is decorated

[81] Da5X; de Morgan, *Dahchour II*, 70, figs. 116-117.
[82] Lüscher, *Totenbuch Spruch 151*, 52-53.
[83] For the dating: Janosi, Keminub - eine Gemahlin Amenemhets II.? In, *Zwischen den beiden Ewigkeiten Festschrift Gertrud Thausing*, M. Bietak [ed.], 94 – 101.
[84] de Morgan, *Dahchour II*, 70-71, figs. 116-117.

with lines. The lid is vaulted. The coffin is similar to those of the women found next to the pyramid of Amenemhat II at Dahshur (compare p. 24).

The inner coffin was anthropoid and was already heavily destroyed when found.[85]

The dating of the tomb of Senebtisi is disputed. In the excavation report it was placed at the beginning of the Twelfth Dynasty. B. Williams argued that the tomb dates rather to the Thirteenth Dynasty.[86] His argument is based on the outer coffin with the vaulted lid, which he places after king Awibre Hor whose coffin had a flat lid and the assumption that vaulted lids were introduced at a later time. C. Lilyquist prefers a late Twelfth Dynasty date, arguing that there is no reason to believe that rounded and flat lids could not have existed at the same time.[87] K. Ryholt assumed that Senebtisi is the grandmother of the kings Neferhotep I, Zahathor and Sobekhotep IV and placed the tomb to about the reign of these kings. One argument is the similarity of her burial equipment to those of other royal burials, such as Nubhetepti-khered and king Awibre Hor.[88] J. Bourriau and Do. Arnold date the tomb via a marl C jar to the 'reign of Amenemhat III or a little later.'[89] However, Ryholt makes the point that this is too vague as it relies on a single vessel type.[90]

In terms of coffin type there are two indications for a dating. The text programme on the outer coffin shows 'speeches of gods'. They are not standardized as in most examples of the Thirteenth Dynasty. This observation points to the Twelfth Dynasty. The hieroglyphs are not complete, as in many examples of the Thirteenth Dynasty. Both features might indicate a late Twelfth Dynasty date, but it must be admitted, we do not know very much about the extent to which different coffin types were used at about the same time. An early Thirteenth Dynasty date seems also possible.

Fig. 24 The outer coffin of Senebtisi

[85] Mace, Winlock, *The Tomb of Senebtisi at Lisht*, 36-47.
[86] Williams, *Serapis* 3 (1975-1976), 41-55.
[87] Lilyquist, *Serapis* 5 (1979), 27-28.
[88] Ryholt, *Political Situation*, 83-84.
[89] Bourriau, Patterns of change in burial customs, 17-18.
[90] Ryholt, *Political Situation*, 84.

Sesenebnef[91] (L1Li/L2Li)

The tomb (shaft and one chamber) of Sesenebnef contained two wooden coffins, a canopic box with four canopic jars and a set of staves and weapons inside the coffins.[92]

The coffins were found in a bad condition and only the texts were copied by the excavators. From the outer coffin it was possible to draw the outside decoration; from the inner coffin the inside decoration was copied and published. The inner coffin of Sesenebnef is one of the few examples of a coffin after the Twelfth Dynasty with an inner decoration.

The long sides of the outer coffin are decorated with four vertical columns and a horizontal line at the top. The space between the columns is filled with panels of long religious texts written in columns. The hieroglyphic signs of animals are incomplete. The inner decoration shows lines of text, but also unique friezes of objects (mainly jars and linen). Many of the Coffin Texts on his outer coffin are already very close, or even identical, to several chapters of the Book of the Dead.[93] Several of the texts found here are so far not attested anywhere else.

The canopic box found in the burial provides an important clue for an initial dating of the tomb group. It is decorated on the vertical columns with *imakhu-kher* formulae. On the horizontal line appears a text also known from the canopic boxes of king Hor and Nubhetepti-khered.[94] In the tomb was found a set of weapons and staves, typical for 'court type burials' (see below p. 92-94). 'Court type burials' are so far only attested for the late Twelfth and early Thirteenth Dynasty. A further point is perhaps a depiction on the inside of the inner coffin. Here are shown on the left side an hieroglyphic West and an East sign with an arm holding a bowl. These symbols with arms are popular on stelae in the first part of the Thirteenth Dynasty.[95] The coffin most likely dates within this time frame. The incomplete hieroglyphs point rather to the late Twelfth or Thirteenth Dynasty.[96] The inscriptions on the canopic chest might indicate a date into the early Thirteenth Dynasty.[97]

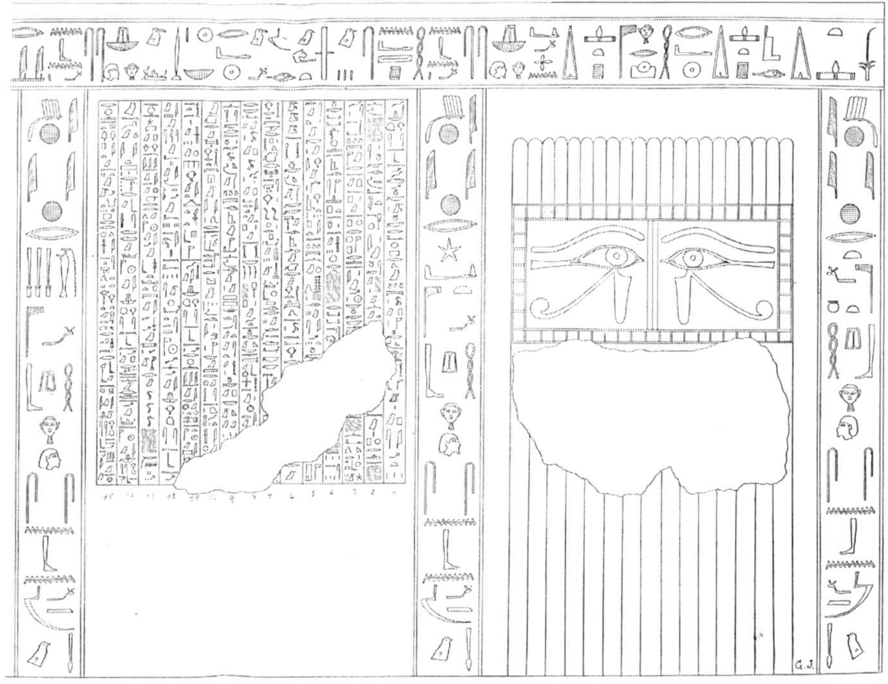

Fig. 25 The front side of Sesenebnef's outer coffin (right and middle panel[98])

[91] Ranke, *PN* I, 320, 14 (Ranke gives only this person as the reference for the name).

[92] Gautier/Jéquier, *Mémoire sur les Fouilles de Licht*, 74-79, fig. 97 (the staves).

[93] Lapp, *SAK* 13 (1986), 143; Gestermann, in: Backes, Munro, Stöhr, *Totenbuch-Forschungen, Gesammelte Beiträge des 2. Internationalen Totenbuch-Symposiums 2005*, 110-111.

[94] Lüscher, *Kanopenkästen*, 29.

[95] Grajetzki, *Two treasurers*, 61-62.

[96] Willems, *Chests of Life*, 105, especially note 208.

[97] Compare for the dating in general Allen, in *World of the Coffin Texts*, 15.

[98] Gautier/Jéquier, *Mémoire sur les Fouilles de Licht*, XVII.

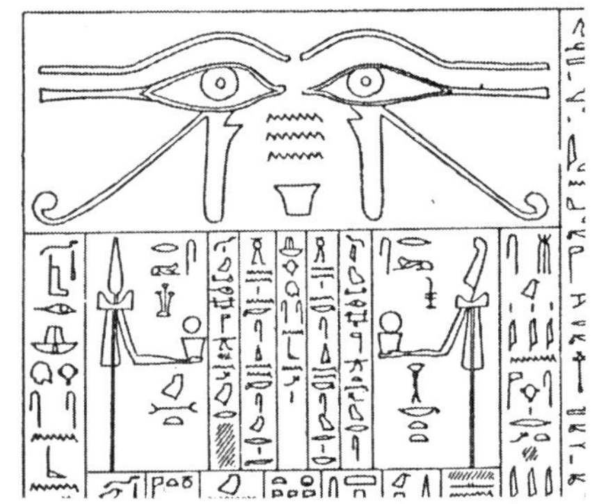
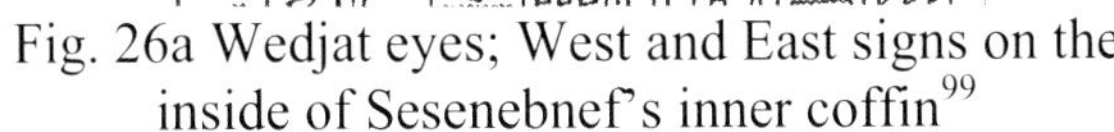

Fig. 26a Wedjat eyes; West and East signs on the inside of Sesenebnef's inner coffin[99]

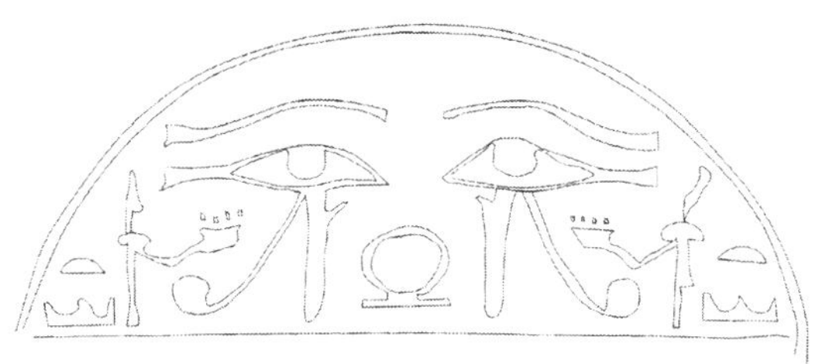

Fig. 26b The lunette of stela Roanne 163[100], datable around Neferhotep I or shortly before

Zay (L9), **NN** (L10)
The coffin of the 'army scribe' Zay was found in a shaft close to the pyramid of Amenemhat I. The coffin is not yet published, although J. P. Allen provides a short description. The coffin is decorated according to Willems type IV, but has between the columns panels topped with a carvetto cornice. Each panel contains four lines of texts.[101] A second, similarly decorated coffin was also found near the pyramid of Amenemhat I. The name of its owner is lost.[102]

Bener (L6)
The model coffin of Bener was found at the pyramid complex of Senusret I at Lisht. The model coffin is decorated according to Willems type IV. The lid is vaulted. There are four floor battens. The texts on the long horizontal lines are the *wn-ḥr* formula and the *ʿwi*-Anubis formula. The columns have *ḏd-mdw* formulae. With the model coffin was found a vessel which has its parallels in other tomb groups which are datable to the late Twelfth and early Thirteenth Dynasty. Inside the model coffin was found a shabti inscribed with the shabti-spell.[103]

Wahneferhotep (L7)
The model coffin of Wahneferhotep was found near the pyramid complex of Senusret I at Lisht. The coffin is again decorated with Willems type IV. The lid is vaulted. There are four floor battens. The texts on the long vertical lines are the 'opening of the face' formula and the *ʿwi*-Anubis formula. The columns have *ḏd-mdw* formulae combined with *imakhu-kher* formulae. With this model coffin were found three beakers and three bowls used as lids. According to Do. Arnold the beakers indicate a date in the advanced Thirteenth Dynasty or even beyond.[104]

Debehni (L11)
The coffin of Debehni is so far not yet fully published. From the few references given it was decorated with inscribed gold foil and had pyramid spell 588 on the lid.[105] The wood of the coffin did not survive.[106]

---

[99] Gautier/Jéquier, *Mémoire sur les Fouilles de Licht*, pl. XXIII.
[100] Grajetzki, *Two Treasurers of the Late Middle Kingdom*, 64.
[101] Allen, in *World of the Coffin Texts*, 6.
[102] Allen, in *World of the Coffin Texts*, 6.
[103] L6; Arnold, *Pyramid of Senwosret I*, 34-37, 147-49.
[104] L7; Arnold, *Pyramid of Senwosret I*, 37-40, 147-49.
[105] Allen, *The Egyptian Coffin Texts, Volumne 8, Middle Kingdom Copies of Pyramid Texts*, 389.
[106] Bourriau, P. der Manuelian (editor*), Studies in Honor of William Kelly Simpson, Vol.I*, Boston 1996, 110-111.

Hawara

Bebut (Maz1)[107]
Material: wood
Colours: inscriptions in green
Measurements: 43 x 185.4 cm (17 x 73 inches, measurements taken from the notebook)
Preservation: poor condition when found, left on site

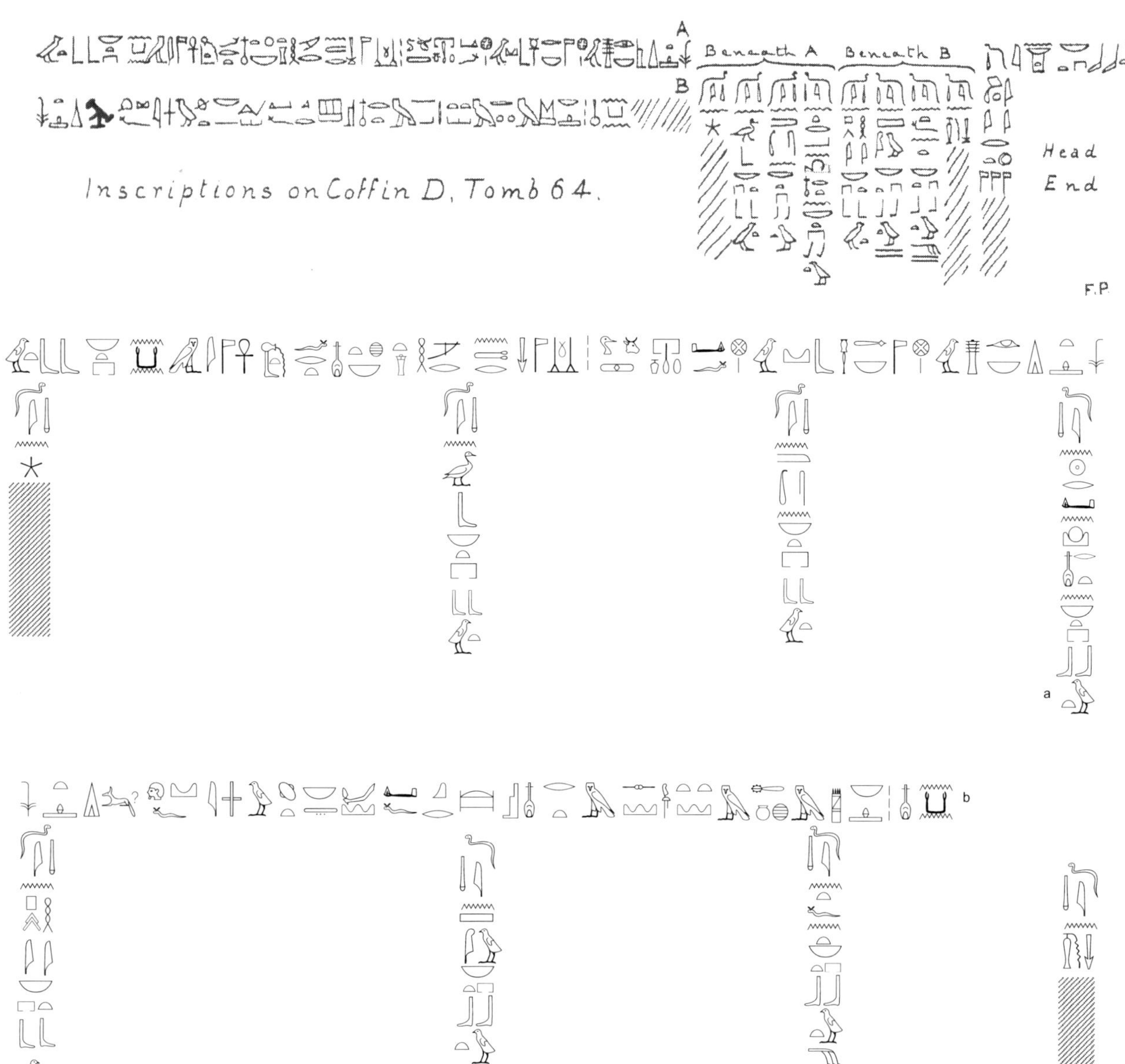

Fig. 27 Coffin of Bebut from Hawara; as published and with typeset hieroglyphs

The coffin of the 'lady of the house' (*nbt-pr*) Bebut[108] was found by Flinders Petrie at Hawara in a shaft tomb (no. 64) with one chamber. Tomb 64 contained three coffins, two undecorated ones belonging to children and another inscribed coffin for an adult. There was only one vessel in the burial: a large beer

[107] Petrie/Wainwright/Mackay, *The Labyrinth, Gerzeh and Mazghuneh*, 35, pl. XXXVII.
[108] Ranke, *PN* I, 96, 9 ('die Perücke (?)' – 'the wig').

jar.[109] The jar has parallels in the late Twelfth Dynasty.[110] In one of the uninscribed coffins were found two beads with a shell and a scarab with a ring.

The coffin was found in bad condition; only the inscriptions could be copied by the excavators. It was a rectangular coffin with four columns on the long and two columns on the short sides. On the front there were two wedjat eyes painted in a rectangular panel.[111] There is the impression that the modern copist of the inscriptions did not understand all of the signs. From parallels it is fairly easy to reconstruct the original text programme. The following inscriptions are garbled in the copies: On the front, at the head end (here labelled a), there can be reconstructed the formula: '*Words spoken by Ra, I have given a beautiful horizon for NN'*. This is a 'speech of a god' (compare p. 64), common at this position on many coffins of this period and the Thirteenth Dynasty. The horizontal line at the back is also garbled in the preserved copies, but has a close parallel on the coffin of Zatimpi from Harageh (Ha3).

All vertical columns on the long sides (four on each) are introduced by 'Words spoken by GOD NN'. Most of the time the title and name of Bebut follows, only at the head end a different spell follows. On the short head end there are *imakhu-kher* formulae.

Date: Second part of the reign of Amenemhat III or slightly later?

Neferuptah: Middle coffin (Haw2)
The tomb of the 'king's daughter' Neferuptah was excavated in 1956.[112] It was found intact but suffered heavily from incoming water. Remains of three coffins were found. There was the outer sarcophagus in granite. A rectangular wooden box placed in it and there were the remains of an inner anthropoid coffin. From the middle coffin only the inlays of the wedjat eyes and the gilded bands of inscriptions survived. The latter were published without any attempt to reconstruct them.[113] However, it is indeed possible to reconstruct the inscriptions on the coffin of Neferuptah. The coffin seems to have its closest parallel with the sarcophagus of queen Hatshepsut of the Eighteenth Dynasty.[114] The hieroglyphs are incomplete.

Text 1. The Nut spell appears on the lids of the coffins in the Middle Kingdom. On the coffin of Neferuptah it is different to the version of the Nut spell found on the New Kingdom sarcophagi of Hatshepsut, and seems instead closer to the version found on the Middle Kingdom coffins with Nut directly after Dd mdw and the personal pronoun 'she' in 'she will not die' at the end of the spell.[115]

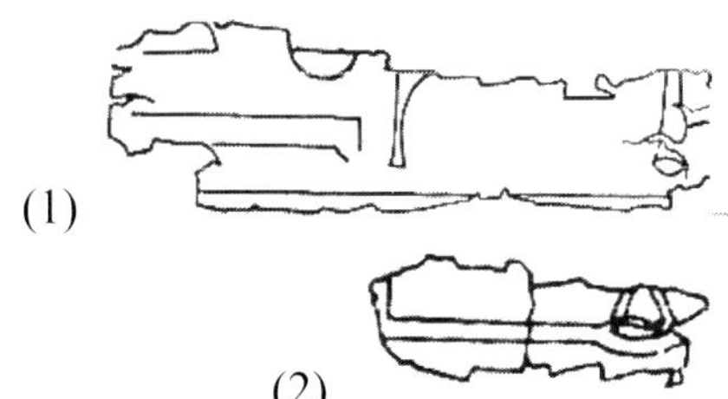

Fig. 28a Coffin of Neferuptah: fragments from the lid

[109] Petrie/Wainwright/Mackay, *The Labyrinth, Gerzeh and Mazghuneh*, 35, pl. XXXV, 100.
[110] Aston, *Tell el-Dab'a XII, A Corpus of Late Middle Kingdom and Second Intermediate Period Pottery*, 289.
[111] The eyes are drawn in the sketch of the notebook, but do not appear in the publication.
[112] Excavation report: Farag/Iskander, *The Discovery of Neferwptah.*
[113] Farag/Iskander, *The Discovery of Neferwptah*, 49-53, figs. 30-32.
[114] Grajetzki, *GM*, 205 (2005), 55-66; the numbering follows Hayes, *Royal Sarcophagi of the XVIII Dynasty*, 186-204; compare von Falck, *SAK* 34 (2006), 125 – 140 for the origin of texts on New Kingdom royal sarcophagi.
[115] Compare: Mace, Winlock, *The Tomb of Senebtisi at Lisht*, pl. XIX.

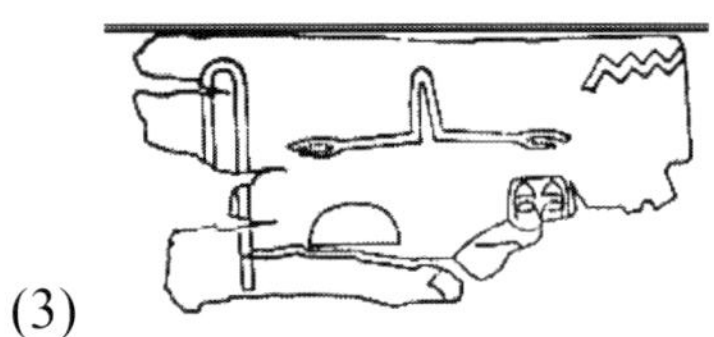

Fig. 28b Coffin of Neferuptah: fragment from the lid

Words spoken by Nut (1: ḏd mdw in nwt): you have been made a spirit, you have been powerful in the body of your mother Tefnut, at your birth, she has caused (2: di) the king's daughter Neferuptah, true of voice to be a god, lord of eternity, she unites the king's daughter Neferuptah, true of voice for life stability and health, she may not die (3: n mwt.s) eternally.

Text 17 The spell (fig. 29) is completely preserved. It is also known from the sarcophagi of Hatshepsut both as king's wife and as ruling queen, and from other royal sarcophagi of the early Eighteenth Dynasty. It has not previously been identified on Middle Kingdom coffins.[116]

ḏd mdw inḳ.n iwf.ṯ ḥn.n ꜥwt.ṯ ꜥnḫ n mwt.ṯ

Words spoken: we envelop your flesh, we order your limbs. Live! May you not die!

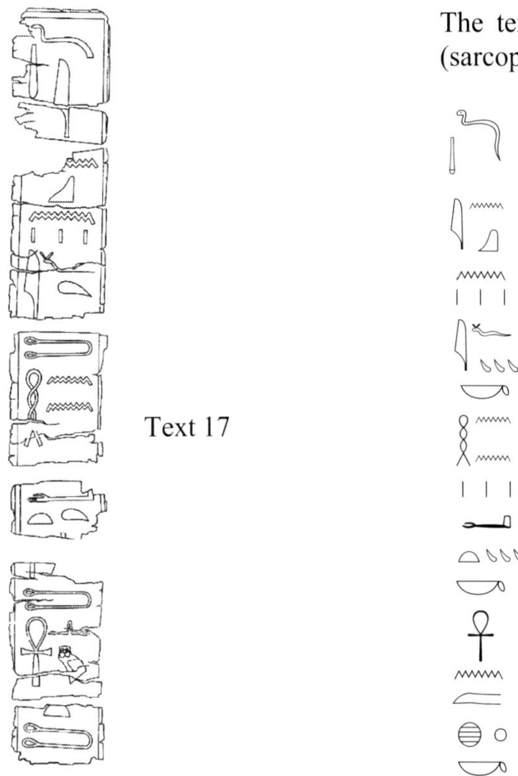

The text on the sarcophagus of Hatshepsut (sarcophagus C, reworked for Thuthmosis I):

Fig. 29 Coffin of Neferuptah: fragment from the lid

Text 25. This is the most interesting spell in the group, as previously known only from the sarcophagus of Hatshepsut as king's wife,[117] where it appears as the horizontal line on the front side. From the orientation of the fragments of Neferuptah it seems plausible that the spell had the same position on her coffin. The key element is the ꜥḥꜥ-sign (Gardiner P6) behind the name:

[116] Hayes, *Royal Sarcophagi*, 175.
[117] Hayes, *Royal Sarcophagi*, 70, 175.

*[ḏd mdw in gb zꜣt-niswt nfrw-ptḥ sṯz ṯn n mwt].**ṯ nwt nḏr**(1) [s im.t] **inḳ.s ṯn** (3)[zꜣt-niswt] **nfrw-ptḥ ꜥḥꜥ** (3)[.i m nw ṯn zꜣt-niswt nfrw-ptḥ ꜥꜣ ib.ṯ nḏ.n ṯn ḥr nṯr.]*

Words spoken by Geb: the king's daughter Neferuptah, raise yourself to your mother Nut, that she may take hold of you, that she may embrace you. King's daughter Neferuptah, I stand up as one who tends you. King's daughter Neferuptah, your heart swells, for Horus the god has rescued you.

The diagnostic fragments:

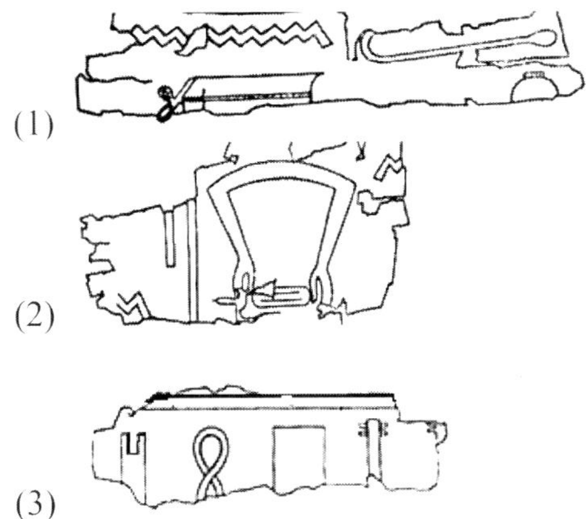

Fig. 30 Coffin of Neferuptah: fragment from the front (?) side

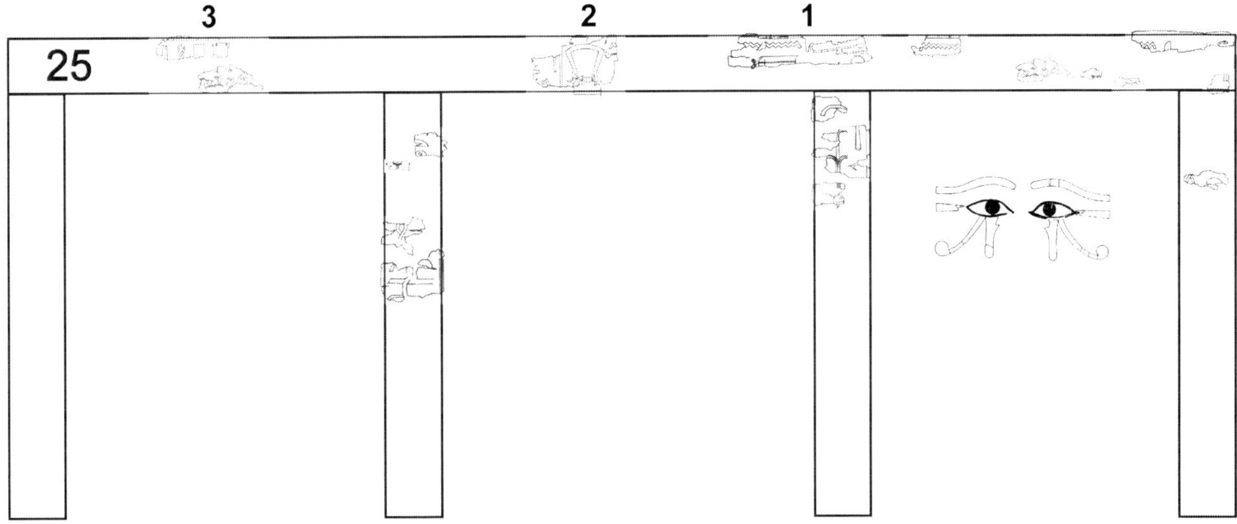

Fig. 31 Coffin of Neferuptah, reconstruction of the front

The text on the sarcophagus of Hatshepsut:

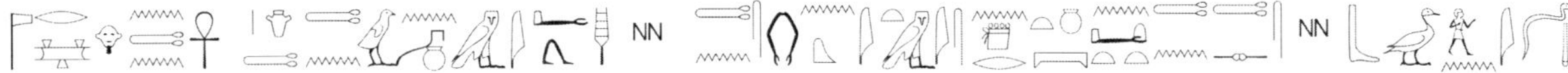

Text 35. The spell appears as the vertical top line on the back side on the sarcophagus of Hatshepsut. The reconstruction of this spell seems possible as it is the only instance on the Neferuptah and Hatshepsut coffins where *ꜥnḫ.ti im* appears.

The diagnostic fragments:

Fig. 32 Coffin of Neferuptah, fragments from the back (?)

Reconstruction of the back side:

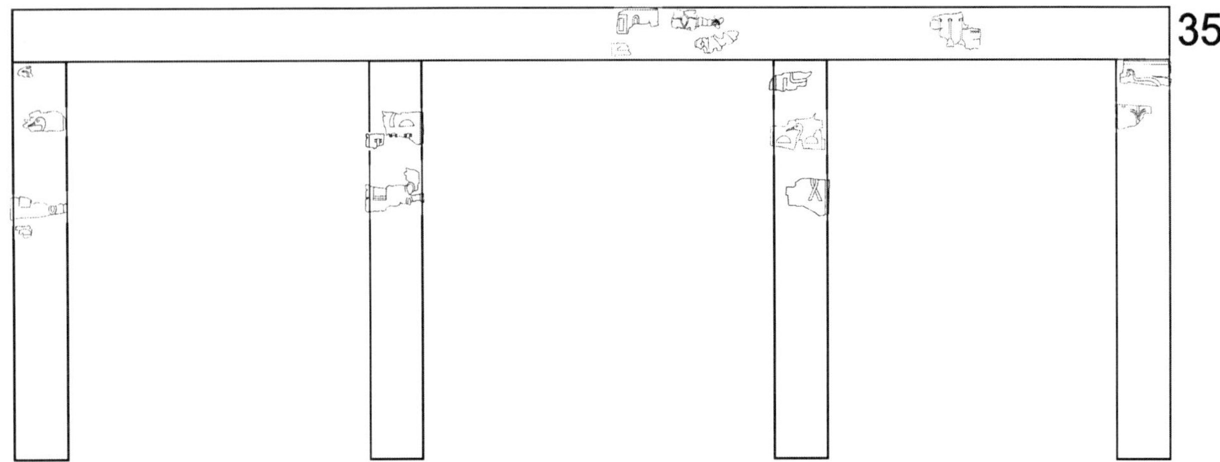

Fig. 33 Coffin of Neferuptah, reconstruction of the back

The text on the sarcophagus of Hatshepsut:

[*ḏd mdw in nwt ip.n.i zꜣt-niswt nfrw-ptḥ*] ***ꜥnḫ.ti im***.[*ṯ sk dr sdb.ṯ zꜣt-niswt nfrw-ptḥ ꜥnḫ.ti rdi.n n.ṯ ḏḥwti nṯrw.*]

Words spoken by Nut: I have counted the king's daughter Neferuptah, may she live! May you not perish. May any obstacle to you be removed. King's daughter Neferuptah may you live. Thoth has given to you the gods.

The reconstruction of the following texts is no more than a guess. The reconstructions are possible, but there are no diagnostic fragments of the texts preserved, leaving other options open for a reconstruction:

Head end:

Text 13: (vertical) [*ḏd mdw zꜣt-niswt nfrw-pt*]***ḥ*** [*jn*]***k*** [*ꜣst ink nbt-*]***hwt***.

Words spoken: king's daughter Neferuptah. I am Isis. I am Nephthys.

Text 14: (column) [*ḏd mdw zꜣt-niswt nfrw-ptḥ ii.n.n*] ***ṯ***[*s.ṯ*]***n ꜥnḫ*** [*ib.ṯ.*]

Words spoken: king's daughter Neferuptah we have come that we may raise you up, that your heart may live.

Foot end :

Text 23: (column) [*ḏd mdw z3t-niswt nfrw-ptḥ*] ***ii***.[*n.i nḏr.i*]***im***[.*ṯ*.]

Words spoken: king's daughter Neferuptah, I have come that I may take hold of you.

All other fragments are either not diagnostic or bear single words (*imnw, pḥti*)[118] which do not have, to my knowledge, any parallels in the outer decorations of Eighteenth Dynasty royal sarcophagi or late Middle Kingdom/Second Intermediate Period coffins.

Neferuptah can be dated from her appearance on several monuments in connection with Amenemhat III. She was most likely his daughter. In his pyramid at Hawara a burial was prepared for her[119], but she was never placed there. Perhaps the king died earlier, the pyramid was closed and she had to be buried somewhere else. This means the burial dates to the final decade of the Twelfth Dynasty, or to the very early Thirteenth Dynasty. Her coffin must belong to this general period.

Lahun

Lahun is a modern town at the entrance to the Fayum. In Egyptology the name refers to the pyramid and pyramid town of Senusret II. There is also a large cemetery near these places.

Zathathoriunet (tomb no. 8) (La1)
The tomb of Zathathorinuet is well known for the jewellery found in a niche in the burial chamber. Her tomb was excavated near the pyramid of Senusret II. Otherwise the tomb was found looted. However, in the sarcophagus of the tomb were still found the remains of gold foil decoration.[120] Zathathoriunet was buried under Amenemhat III. With some reservation it can be assumed that her coffin was similar to those of the royal ladies buried next to Amenemhat II at Dahshur (Da1C, Da2X, Da3X, Da4X).

tomb no. 7 (La2)
In tomb no. 7 at Lahun was found gold foil which is decorated with parallel lines.[121] There were also found fragments of blue glaze. In the publication it is argued that this comes from the inlaid inscriptions of a coffin.[122]

tomb no. 10 (La3)
In tomb no. 10 at Lahun was found gold foil which is decorated with parallel lines.[123]

Harageh

Harageh is the modern name given to a chain of cemeteries over the southern half of a desert outcrop called Gebel Abusir at the entrance to the Fayum. Here, there are several burial grounds dating to the late Middle Kingdom and Second Intermediate Period.[124] The Middle Kingdom cemeteries seem to have started under or shortly after Senusret II, and may be linked to the rise of the pyramid town of Lahun, not far away. Whether Harageh is one of the burial grounds of the pyramid town is an open question. The exact chronology of the cemetery is disputed and there are almost no fixed dates. It has often been assumed that the cemetery flourished especially in the late Twelfth and perhaps Thirteenth Dynasty.[125] However, there is some evidence that the cemetery was in decline already in the Thirteenth Dynasty. It was certainly used

[118] Farag/Iskander, *The Discovery of Neferwptah*, 51, fig. 31.
[119] Petrie, *Kahun, Gurob, and Hawara*, 15.
[120] Brunton, *Lahun I*, 14, 18.
[121] Brunton, *Lahun I*, 16.
[122] Brunton, *Lahun I*, 14.
[123] Brunton, *Lahun I*, 14.
[124] Richards, *Society and Death in Ancient Egypt, Mortuary Landscapes of the Middle Kingdom*, 90-98.
[125] Kemp, Merrillees, *Minoan Pottery*, 26-30, compare the datings Bourriau, Patterns of change in burial customs, 18-19.

into the New Kingdom, but on a smaller scale. For the coffins it can be observed that none of them has inscriptions with incomplete hieroglyphs, which is well attested at the nearby sites at Hawara and Lisht. It might be argued that the incomplete hieroglyphs started at the royal court and reached lower levels of society only later, as the evidence from Dahshur might indicate (coffin of Senu, Da1). However, cylinder beads were found at Harageh, some of them with royal names.[126] The royal name cylinders might already date to the Thirteenth Dynasty, but it seems strange that none of the Thirteenth Dynasty kings appears on those at Harageh, while at least royal scharabs are common at other Thirteenth Dynasty sites and cemeteries[127]. Scarabs with the names of Thirteenth Dynasty kings and their known officials are also absent. With due reservation it seems that all decorated coffins so far found at Harageh date to the late Twelfth Dynasty.

Senusretankh (Ha1)

Fig. 34 The coffin of Senusretankh (front)

The coffin of Senusretankh was found in a shaft tomb (no. 250) at cemetery S at Harageh.[128] The burial was disturbed but still contained the well preserved coffin, an inscribed wooden canopic box[129], perhaps a mummy mask and some pottery. The coffin is decorated on the long side with offering formulae along the top, with four coloumns below containing the 'speeches of gods'. The decoration is painted and simple.

Three vessel types were found in the tomb: 2e4, 7j2 and 41j.[130] They all have their parallels in the levels at Tell el-Dab'a attributed to the late Twelfth Dynasty.[131]
Date: end of Twelfth Dynasty?

Harageh tomb 219 (Ha8)[132]
Tomb no. 219 was found disturbed. It had a shaft with two chambers, one on the South, the other on the North. According to the tomb card, there was found one vessel, type 67y and some glazed beads. On the back of the tomb card part of a coffin inscription is recorded. The short fragment of a column comes perhaps from the back of a coffin, assuming the copy of the inscription is not reverted. It is a 'speech of a god': *Gb: ii.n.i ...Geb: I have come ...* The fragment is therefore evidence for another coffin with 'speeches of gods' for Harageh.

---

126 Engelbach, *Harageh*, pl. XX, nos 9, 13 – 26, 28-33 (Senusret II, Senusret III and Amenemhat III).
127 Ryholt, *Political Situation*, 346 (19); 349 (9); 353 13/31 (2), 254 (1, 6, 7), 355 (8)
128 Ha1; Engelbach, *Harageh*, 23-24, pl. LXX; Grajetzki, *Bulletin of the Egyptian Museum*, 72, fig. 1.
129 Engelbach, *Harageh*, 26, pl. LXIV; compare Lüscher, *Kanopenkästen*, 31, 69, 104 (52).
130 Engelbach, *Harageh*, pl. LIX.
131 Aston, Tell el-Dab'a XII, *A Corpus of Late Middle Kingdom and Second Intermediate Period Pottery*, 288 n. 1214 (type 2), 289 n. 1231 (type 7) and 28n. 1239 (type 41); Kemp, Merrillees, *Minoan Pottery*, 44, fig. 20
132 The tomb is not published in the excavation report and is only known from its tomb card, now in the Petrie Museum; for the coffin: Grajetzki, *Harageh,* 46.

Fig. 35 Fragment of coffin from tomb Harageh 219

Harageh tomb 128 (Ha9),[133]
In an almost undisturbed tomb was found a coffin in bad condition. The coffin was 'unpainted', but had texts on the outside. It is only known from descriptions of the excavators. There were 'four or five' columns beginning with 'Words spoken by'.[134] The other burial goods were pottery vessels.

Zatimpi (Ha3) [135]
From this coffin only a board was found.[136] The board contains the Anubis spell also known from pyramidia of the late Middle Kingdom:

Fig. 36 Fragment from the coffin of Zatimpi

ḏd mdw ꜥwi inpw tpi ḏw.f ḥꜣ ꜣst-irt zꜣt-impi ẖnmw zmit imntt m ẖnw ḫm nb-ḥtp nfr imi.s di.s w jwꜥ zꜣt-impi … ḥḥ ḥr ḏd ꜥnḫ.ti ḏt

Words spoken: the arms of Anubis, first on his mount are around the Osiris Zatimpi, the western desert enfolds her in the chapel of the lord of offerings so that the one who is inside her is well … for always and ever, may she live eternally

Date: end of Twelfth Dynasty?

Scheikh Farag

NN (SF1)
This is a fragment of a foot board with the figure of a woman facing right with her arms raised. There are two columns with *ḏd-mdw* formulae and 'speeches of gods'. The only partly preserved texts seem to be garbled. The fragment dates perhaps to the very end of the Second Intermediate Period or even to the early New Kingdom.[137]

Abydos

Abydos is one of the most important cemeteries of the Second Intermediate Period. There have been several excavations[138], many of them found coffin fragments. Organic preservation is not good at Abydos. Therefore few coffins are well preserved.

---

[133] Engelbach, *Harageh*, 16.
[134] *ḏd mdw in*; see tomb card.
[135] Ranke, *PN* I, 286, 5.
[136] Engelbach, *Harageh*, 24-25, pl. LXV, 2 (the tomb number is not recorded).
[137] Lacovara, in D'Auria, S.; P. Lacovara; C. R. Roehrig (editors), *Mummies and Magic*, 130-31, no. 63.
[138] Richards, *Society and Death in Ancient Egypt, Mortuary Landscapes of the Middle Kingdom*, 138-145.

Nakht(i) (Aby1)
The sarcophagus of Nakht was found by J. Garstang in tomb 252 ('cemetery E') at Abydos. The sarcophagus belongs to the 'controller of the phyle' (*mti n zꜣ*) Nakht.[139] It is made of limestone. There are few parallels for decorated stone coffins of the late Middle Kingdom.[140] Each of the long sides has a horizontal line of text and below five columns. On the front horizontal line there is the *wn-ḥr* formula. On the back there is an offering formula. The columns contain the *ḏd-mdw* formulae, without 'speeches of gods'. On the short ends are shown standing women with raised hands. The number of vertical lines on the long sides is remarkable. The sarcophagus has five instead of the usual four. However, in general it is an exact copy of a wooden coffin.

The sarcophagus belongs perhaps to the end of the Twelfth or the beginning of Thirteenth Dynasty, but at the moment it is impossible to provide an exact date. In the burial was found a shabti of Nakht.[141]

Senebhenaef (Aby 7)
The fragments of the coffin of Senebhenaef were found in Abydos tomb D25 and are only preserved in small fragments.[142] It is possible to reconstruct the coffin to a certain extent. It was a rectangular box decorated on the long sides with vertical columns bearing the 'speeches of gods'. Between the columns were text panels, one which is partly preserved. On the short ends were depictions of two female figures, one is preserved.

Fig. 37 The coffin of Senebhenaf, front (top) and short ends; reconstructions

[139] Brussels, E5277: Garstang, *El Arabah: A Cemetery of the Middle Kingdom*, pl. VI-VII; M.-P. Vanlathem, *Oudegyptische lijkkisten en mummies - Cercueils et momies de l'Égypte ancienne*, Bruxelles 1983, 12-13 ; F. Lefebvre et B. Van Rinsveld, L'Égypte. *Des Pharaons aux Coptes*, Bruxelles 1990, 245; *Museumstukken als figuranten in een stripverhaal - ...Quand la BD s'inspire des objets du Musée (Exposition),* Bruxelles 1996, 16.

[140] Montet, Les constructions et le tombeau d'Osorkon II a Tanis, pl. XLVII; Bosticco/Rosati, *Aegyptus* LXXXIII, 2003, 15-52.

[141] Garstang, *El Arabah: A Cemetery of the Middle Kingdom*, pl. VI, XIV.

[142] Preliminary publication of the coffin in colour: Grajetzki, *Ancient Egypt Magazine* 5/6 (June/July 2005), 16-19; full publication: Grajetzki, *SAK* 34 (2006), 205-216, pls. 5-8. The fragments are now in the Ashmolean Museum, Oxford (E 1952 a-o, E 1953).

There are some additional observations to make on the publication of the coffin. The background colour of the whole coffin was most likely black as indicated by two fragments with that colour beyond the text column. However, on one fragment[143] a red border is visible beside the text column. This border has parallels on a coffin found at Abydos even though the coffin had overall a different background colour.[144] Therefore, it does not mean that this part of the coffin had a red background. Some columns were just framed with a red line.

In the publication, the coffin of Senebhenaef is reconstructed with four columns on the long sides. However, according to the published reconstruction, this would make the coffin about 1.7 m long. Whereas coffins of the period are more than 2 m long. It might be wondered whether the coffin had five columns, similar to the coffin of Senebni from Thebes (Cairo CG 28029; T10C) or the coffin of Nakht from Abydos (Aby1). The coffin of Senebni has on the front eight columns, but five of them are highlighted with a special background, better drawn hieroglyphs and a colour pattern border of the columns.[145] The remaining three columns are rather simply painted. The overall decoration is therefore a coffin with five main columns on the front and three additional, 'lesser' columns. In the case of Senebhenaf it might be argued that the simple columns were replace by the panels with texts.

The text programme on the coffin of Senebhenaef with 'speeches of gods' in the columns and text panels on the outside is close to the coffin of the 'treasurer' Amenhotep (Da6X) found at Dahshur. Both coffins are perhaps not very much apart in date.

With the coffin of Senebhenaef were found two clay canopic jars[146], armlets[147], a beard inlaid with faience, perhaps from a mummy mask or anthropoid inner coffin.

Some fragments are decorated slightly differently to the other coffin fragments. They have a different background colour and the columns for the texts are wider. These wooden fragments belong perhaps to a canopic box.

The two spells of the preserved text panel are the later Book of the Dead chapters 33 and 149 (parts in red are underlined):

<u>*Spell for expelling all snakes*</u>
O Rerek, go with the legs of Shu because you have eaten a mouse, the abomination of Ra; and you have crunched the bones of a putrefied cat.

<u>*First mound*</u>
O Osiris, Mouth of Nekhen, Senebhenaef, true of voice, it is the west of the gods, where one lives of...

There are only a few clues for a dating. Senebhenaf, Ibia (his mother) and Zaamun[148] (his father) are typical names of the later Thirteenth Dynasty and Sixteenth Dynasty.[149] The close relation to the coffin of the 'treasurer' Amenhotep (Da6X) might rather point to the advanced Thirteenth Dynasty. There are almost no decorated canopic jars known from the Sixteenth and Seventeenth Dynasty, indicating an earlier (or even later?) date. At least on one short end, two female figures seem to be depicted. One is lost but can be reconstructed from the available space and from parallels. The female figure is shown with raised arms, in adoration. This arm position is sometimes found on the feet of rishi coffins.[150] This point might rather

---

[143] Grajetzki, *SAK* 34 (2006), 206, [E 1952e].
[144] Peet, *Cemeteries of Abydos II*, pl. XIII, 5 (Brussels, E 5277).
[145] Lapp, *Typologie*, pl. 34b.
[146] Ashmolean Museum Oxford, E 354; London, BM EA 32709 (I am grateful to Marcel Maree for this information).
[147] Manchester Museum 4077-80 (information kindly provided by Janine Bourriau).
[148] The father bears the title *wr mdw šmʿw*; a person with this title and same name appears on stela Cairo CG 20188.
[149] Senebhenaef is the name of a vizier, father of queen Mentuhotep, who was the wife of king Djehuty, who dates to the Second Intermediate Period (Habachi, *SAK* 11 (1984), 113-26). Ibiau is the name of a Thirteenth Dynasty king (Ryholt, *Political Situation*, 353-54 (File 13/32)). Several high officials bear the name Ibiau, they all date to the Thirteenth or Sixteenth Dynasty: Grajetzki, *Die höchsten Beamten*, 30 (I.35- vizier), 122 (IV.15 – 'overseer of troops'), 136 (V. 18 – 'overseer of fields'), 166 (IX.5 – 'controller of the broad hall'), 187 (XII.5 – 'deputy treasurer'). Ibiau as a woman's name, see Ranke, *PN* I, 19, 4; The name Zaamun is also common in this period, compare: Franke, Doss. 512-517.
[150] Lüscher, *Totenbuch Spruch 151*, 105, figs. 38-39.

indicate a later date of the coffin, although it might be argued that this type of figure was introduced earlier and so far no earlier parallels are known. Indeed the figures on rishi coffins are always kneeling, while the one on the Senebhenaf coffin is standing, similar to the figures of Thirteenth and Sixteenth Dynasty coffins.[151]

Sobekhotep (Tomb X3) (Aby2)

The coffin fragments of 'commander of the ruler's crew' (*3ṯw n ṯt ḥk3*) Sobekhotep were found by Thomas Eric Peet on the 15th December 1908 in a shaft tomb.[152] The coffin belonged originally to a person whose name and titles are hard to read but ended with …iri. The coffin is of the type with Coffin Text spells 777 to 785. Only the two long sides are published. They show a horizontal line and a high number of columns beneath. The background colour of the coffin was white, the hieroglyphs were painted in light blue with details painted in black. The lines of hieroglyphs were framed by a colour band.

In the tomb were found several pottery vessels, including fragments of white spotted ware.

The coffin was reused and is therefore most likely earlier than the other finds in the tomb; whether this means a few years or much earlier remains unknown. The pottery of the tomb is best comparable with vessels from Thebes dating to the late Seventeenth and early Eighteenth Dynasty.

For the pottery see:

Peet, Cem, Abydos II, p. 61 (b), compare Seiler, *Tradition & Wandel*, 86-89, Falttafel 6

Peet, Cem, Abydos II, p. 61 (c), compare Seiler, *Tradition & Wandel*, 150-51, Falttafel 4

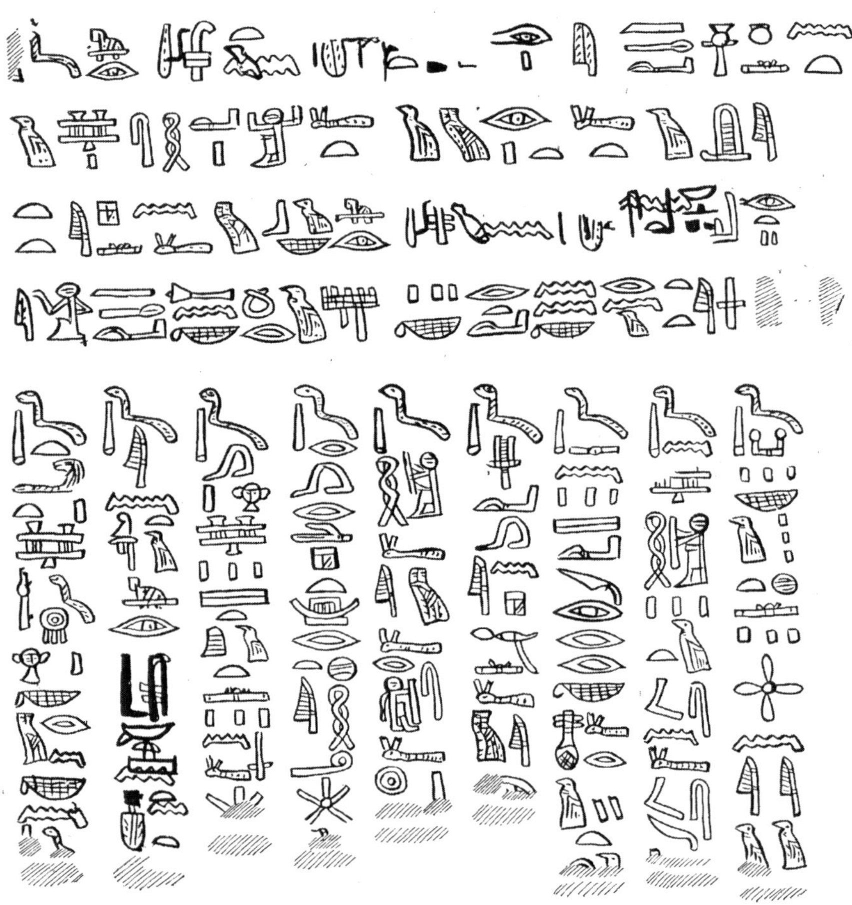

Fig. 38 The inscriptions on the back side of Sobekhotep's coffin[153]

[151] Lüscher, *Totenbuch Spruch 151*, 103-107.

[152] Peet, *Cemeteries of Abydos II*, 61, pl. XIII, 4, pl. XXXVI; date taken from the tomb card stored in the EES.

[153] Peet, *Cemeteries of Abydos II*, pl. XXXVI

Amenemhat (Tomb Z 2a) (Aby3)
The coffin fragments of the 'commander of the ruler's crew' (*ꜣṯw n ṯt ḥkꜣ*) Amenemhat were discovered on the 31st December 1908, in a rectangular shaft with two chambers.[154] All objects of the burial were found in the North chamber. The coffin was only found in small fragments, but seems to be similar to the one of Sobekhotep (Aby2) from tomb X3, decorated with the set of Coffin Texts 777 – 785.

Other objects found in the tomb chamber:
gold foil
two red dishes[155]
white spotted dish (compare for a late 17th Dynasty date: Seiler, *Tradition & Wandel*, 80-81)
inlaid eye
alabaster vase, 6,5 cm
few beads of blue glaze
a drop-shaped pendant of glazed rock crystal

Thebes

Thebes was the royal burial ground of the Upper Egyptian state (Sixteenth and Seventeenth Dynasty) of the Second Intermediate Period. Many coffins of the period found belong to people of the royal court or highest state officials. Herbert Winlock excavated parts of Second Intermediate Period cemeteries of this period. Very little of these excavations has so far been published.

Sobekaa (T3Be)
The coffin of Sobekaa is today in the Egyptian Museum of Berlin.[156] It was found at Thebes although the exact findspot and circumstances of the find are not known. It was discovered by teams working for Giovani Athanasi in 'the small temple of Isis'. It remains uncertain which temple he was referring to.[157]

The coffin of Sobekaa is in some ways a transitional coffin. It is decorated on the outside with a palace façade and four columns on the long and two on the short sides. The front horizontal line contains the *wn-ḥr* /'opening of the face' formula. The columns contain 'speeches of gods'. Unlike most other coffins with these speeches, the coffin also has an inside decoration. It seems to date to a time when the new text programme for the coffin exterior started to develop and existing inside decorations were still in use. H. Willems dates the coffin to the end of the Twelfth Dynasty.[158]

Ameny (T1Lux), **Geheset** (T2Lux)
The coffins of Ameny and his wife Geheset were found in 2004 in Drah Abu el-Naga, Thebes.[159] It is a set of two coffins, an outer and an inner one. The outer one was produced for Ameny and later given to Geheset, who is called in a dedication inscriptions, 'his beloved wife'. The inner coffin was originally made for Geheset.

The coffin of Ameny is most likely a copy in wood of a limestone sarcophagus. At the top of each outer wall it has a horizontal line of text. There are two columns on each side with *imakhu-kher* formulae placed at the corners. The inscriptions are incised on a raised back ground. The whole outside is painted white, evidently copying limestone. The decorative scheme in this form is not found on other wooden coffins of the Middle Kingdom, but has a parallel in the granite sarcophagus of Amenyseneb, now in Florence, which is also decorated on the front side with a text line at the top and columns at the edges.[160] The sarcophagus of Amenyseneb displays some additional features, such as wedjat eyes and a matting pattern, but the

---

[154] Peet, *Cemeteries Abydos II*, 62, 122, fig. 88, 123, fig. 89; the date is recorded on the tomb card, preserved in the EES.
[155] One of the bowls: Cambridge Fitzwilliam E. 22.1910: J. Bourriau, *Umm el-Ga'ab, Pottery from the Nile Valley before the Arab Conquest*, Cambridge 1981, 58, no. 102.
[156] Berlin no. 45; Steindorff, *Grabfunde des Mittleren Reiches in den Königlichen Museen zu Berlin, II. Der Sarg des Sebk-o. – Ein Grabfund aus Gebelein*, 1-10, pl. I-II.
[157] See the discussion Willems, *Chests of Life*, 114.
[158] Willems, *Chests of Life*, 114-115.
[159] Polz, *Für die Ewigkeit geschaffen, Die Särge des Imeni und Geheset.*
[160] Bosticco/Rosati, *Aegyptus* LXXXIII, 2003, 15-52.

arrangement of texts is comparable to Ameny's coffin and also does not relate to wooden coffins of the late Twelfth Dynasty. The inside of Ameny's coffin is fully decorated with Coffin Texts and friezes of objects.

The inner coffin (T2Lux) of the tomb group was from the beginning made for Geheset and shows at the front four columns, a horizontal text line, the pair of wedjat eyes and a false door under the eyes. It is Willems' coffin type IVba.[161]

The dating of both coffins is a problem. The tomb group has been dated by the pottery to the Thirteenth Dynasty.[162] Especially the inner decoration of the outer coffin of Ameny seems to point to the Twelfth Dynasty. The inner coffin of Geheset seems also more typical for the Twelfth Dynasty, although the new finds at Dahshur, such as the coffin of Senu (Da1), might indicate that type IV and its subtypes were still widely used in the Thirteenth Dynasty.

Amenemhat (T1War)[163]

The burial of a *smsw h3iit* ('elder of the hall') Amenemhat was found at Deir el-Medineh. It was a simple shaft tomb with a small chamber. It was heavily disturbed and contained next to the burial of Amenemhat coffins of the New Kingdom.[164] From the rectangular coffin of Amenemhat only the short ends survived. They belong to a coffin with vaulted lid and one horizontal and two vertical lines as decoration on the short ends. The texts are simple *imakhu-kher* formulae. The hieroglyphs are complete. The background colour is orange/brownish with dark dots, perhaps imitating some hard stone.

The dating of this coffin and of Amenemhat himself is a problem. The name Amenemhat appears on three objects in the tomb, each one connected with a different title. On the coffin fragments he is *smsw h3iit*, on a piece of cartonnage he appears as *wr mdw šmʿw*. On a stone fragment he bears the vizier's titles. Here the name is only partly preserved. The titles *smsw h3iit* and *wr mdw šmʿw* are typical titles of the late Middle Kingdom and Second Intermediate Period.[165] There are also several officials with the name Amenemhat and these titles known from the Middle Kingdom and Second Intermediate Period.[166] The name Amenemhat is common and therefore any identification with another person of the same name seems very unsafe. The burial of a vizier at Thebes seems only likely at a time the royal court moved to Thebes, which is certainly not the Twelfth or early Thirteenth Dynasty. However, it is also possible that in the late Middle Kingdom the office of the vizier was already divided. In this case Amenemhat could be a southern vizier of the late Twelfth or early Thirteenth Dynasty. Finally it is also possible that Amenemhat was a vizier at the residence near Lisht and was buried for unknown reasons at Thebes. Therefore, the dating of the coffin fragments remains highly uncertain. Any period between the late Twelfth and early Eighteenth Dynasties seems possible. The style of the coffin is more typical for the late Twelfth and early Thirteenth Dynasty.

---

161 Willems, *Chests of Life*, 160-61.

162 Seiler, in Polz, *Für die Ewigkeit geschaffen*, 98-99.

163 Bruyère, Deir el Médineh (1929), 102-104, figs. 46-47; the fragments are now in Prague (Naprstek Museum, Prague P1424) and not in Warsaw.

164 Bruyère, *Deir el Médineh (1929)*, 105: 'fragments des plusiers androids du Nouvel Empire'.

165 Quirke, in: Silverman, Simpson, Wegner, *Archaism and Innovation: Studies in the Culture of Middle Kingdom Egypt*, 305-316.

166 Franke, Doss., 80; A *wr mdw šmʿw* Amenemhat: Petrie, *Season*, pl. VII, 159; Habachi, *Elephantine IV, The Sanctuary of Heqaib, Text*, 102, no. 85 (the same person and the same mother is mentioned); another example: Seipel, *Götter Mensche, Pharaonen*, no. 69.

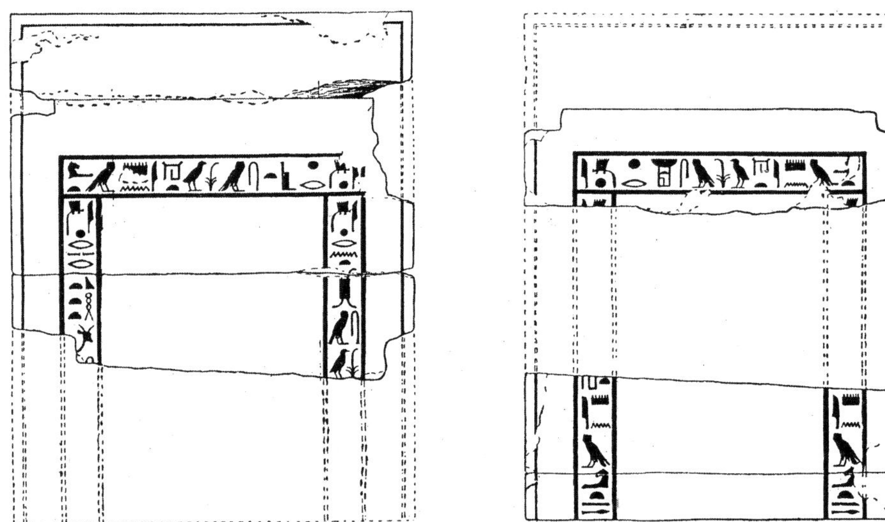

Fig. 39 The fragments of Amenemhat's coffin (Bruyère, *Deir el Médineh (1929)*, 103, fig. 46)

NN (T2War)[167]
From this coffin only the upper part of a short end survived. It was found in the same tomb as the coffin of Amenemhat (T1War). The fragment shows a horizontal line at the top and two columns under it. In the middle there is the depiction of a female figure with raised arms. The text lines have 'speeches of gods'. Only the one in the horizontal line is fully preserved: 'Words spoken by Nephthys: I have come to embrace you, Osiris'. There is no name preserved. In the publication the fragment is assigned to a canopic box. However, there are so far no canopic boxes with the picture of a standing goddess known.[168] This image is typical for coffins of the late Middle Kingdom and Second Intermediate Period. It seems therefore more likely that the fragment belongs to a coffin.

Fig. 40 Short end of the coffin (Bruyère, *Deir el Médineh (1929)*, 104, fig. 48)

Mishwep (T33)
The coffin of a person, perhaps named Mishwep was found by Luigi Vassalli in Thebes.[169] The coffin is only preserved in drawings. It is a rectangualr coffin with one horizontal line on the top of each of the long

[167] Bruyère, *Deir el Médineh (1929)*, 104, fig. 48.
[168] Lüscher, *Kanopenkästen*, 53.
[169] Tiaretti, *L'Egittologo Luigi Vassalli, 1812-1887, disegni e documenti nei Civici Istituti Culturali Milanesi*, fig. 3; Tiradritti, In Marée (editor), *The Second Intermediate Period (Thirteenth-Seventeenth Dynasties), Current Research, Future Prospects*, pl. 111, 112.

sides and four columns under that. The horizontal lines contain simple offering formulae, the columns *im3ḫw ḫr* formulae. This is typical for a Twelfth Dynasty coffin. There are some features indicating a later date for this example. Above the horizontal line, the coffin is decorated with three bands of an elaborate pattern; there is a band of spirals, and above that two bands of patterns, quite similar to the mat patterns found on late Second Intermediate Period coffins. The inscriptions on the coffin are quite garbled. The mat pattern only found on coffins of the second half of the Second Intermediate Period indicates an advanced date for the coffin closer to the middle or second half of the Second Intermediate Period (compare p. 94-95).

Mentuhotep (T4L)[170]

Today the coffin of queen Mentuhotep is lost. Wilkinson copied its inscriptions in 1832 at Thebes. The coffin was perhaps already seen and described by Passalacqua between 1822-1825. He brought a canopic box with the name of the queen to Berlin from his excavation at Thebes.

The outside of the coffin is decorated with the Coffin Texts spells 777-784 in several columns. The lid has the shape of a per-wer shrine only known from one Middle Kingdom coffin.[171] There is no inscription recorded belonging to the lid of queen Mentuhotep's coffin. Several panels on the inside bear long religious texts, some of them are Coffin Texts, and others are early versions of the Book of the Dead.

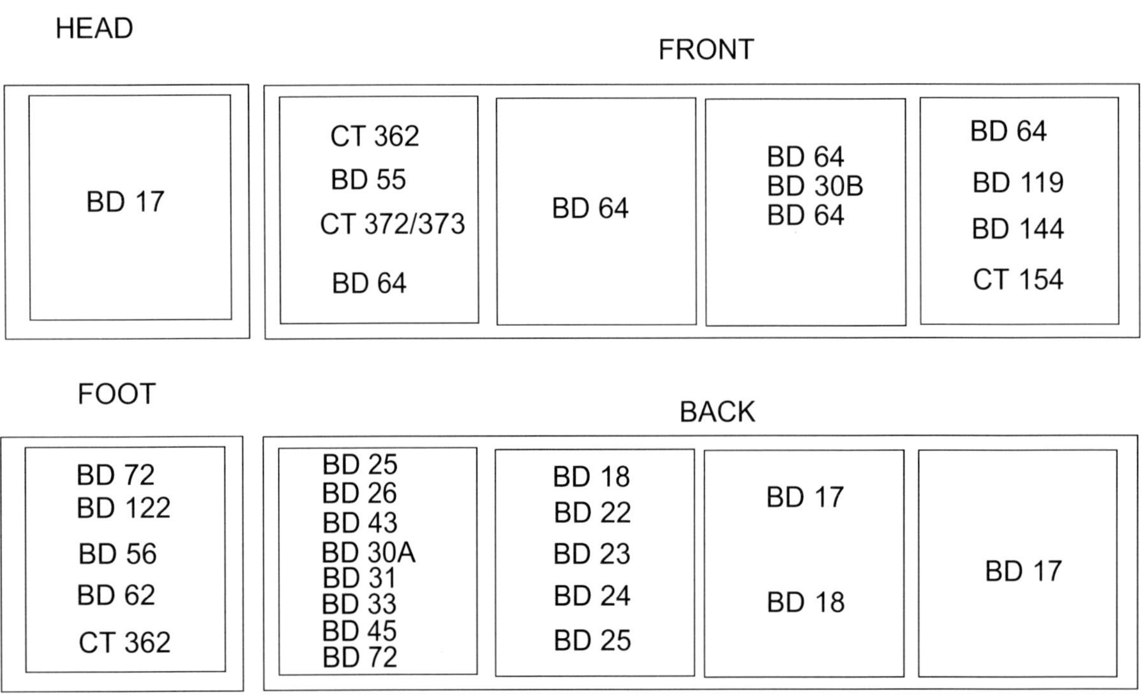

Fig. 41 The Texts on the inside of Mentuhotep's coffin

S. Quirke summarises the arrangement of these texts as following. At the head and at the back are the Book of the Dead chapters 17 and 18 making sure that the deceased becomes Ra and 'true of voice'. On the front there is Book of the Dead chapter 64 in two versions, one long and a short one. It secures the possibility 'to go out in the day'. Here is also placed the Book of the Dead chapter 30B making sure that the heart is not speaking against the queen in the judgement of the dead. [172] Furthermore, Book of the Dead chapter 72 at the foot end of the back and on the back secures the eternal food supply.

For the dating of the coffin there are three indicators. There is her royal husband, king Djehuty, the style of the canopic box and the dating of the family of the queen.

---

[170] Geisen, *Mentuhotep.*

[171] The other example is the outer coffin of the 'steward' Mentuhotep (T1Be).

[172] Quirke, *Journal of Ancient Near Eastern Religions* 5 (2005), 232-34.

1. Queen Mentuhotep had a canopic box belonging originally to king Djehuty, dedicated by him to the queen. The date of this king within the Second Intermediate Period is not known for sure and is therefore not that much help. All his monuments were found in Upper Egypt, implying that he was an Upper Egyptian king reigning at a time when the unity of the country had already fallen apart. A date of late Thirteenth, Sixteenth or even Seventeenth Dynasty is equally likely. As queen Mentuhotep was buried in Thebes it seems likely that her husband was also buried there. In the Middle Kingdom queens were always buried close to their husband or at least in the royal cemeteries. For the Second Intermediate Period there is less evidence. There are only six burials of 'king's wives' known:

a. The fragment of a canopic jar belonging to the 'king's wife' Seneb... (rest of the name is lost) was found at the pyramid complex of king Khendjer at Saqqara. She was most likely the wife of Khendjer and perhaps buried in the small pyramid next to that of her husband.[173]
b. The burial of the 'king's wife' Keminub (Da5X, compare pp. 27-28) was found next to the pyramid of king Amenemhat II at Dahshur. The queen belongs to the Thirteenth Dynasty, when Dahshur was still used as royal burial ground.[174]
c. The burial of queen Mentuhotep at Thebes, wife of king Djehuty.
d. Nubkhaes, wife of king Sekhemre-shedtawy Sobekemzaf was buried within the pyramid of her husband at Thebes.[175]
e. Queen Sobekemzaf was perhaps buried at Edfu. She was the wife of Nubkheperre Intef who had a pyramid at Thebes. She is so far the only exception before the New Kingdom. However, this case is disputed.[176]
f. Teti-sheri, dating to the end of the Seventeenth Dynasty was most likely buried at Thebes. Her mummy wrappings were found in the Cachette of Deir el-Bahari.[177]

2. The canopic box of queen Mentuhotep is stylistically similar to the boxesof Khonsu and Senebni found at Thebes. [178] These two people are datable under king Sewahenre. A staff with the name of that king dedicated to Senebni was found in the tomb of Khonsu and Senebni (compare p. 48). The position of king Sewahenre within the Second Intermediate Period is uncertain, but his monuments were found only in Upper Egypt[179], similar to king Djehuty. Both kings might have reigned fairly close together, though whether this means that they belonged to the same dynasty remains unknown.
3. Queen Mentuhotep is the daughter of the vizier Senebhenaf, perhaps related to a well known family. An 'overseer of fields' Senebhenaf was perhaps the son of a vizier Ib-iau. It had been argued that these two officials with the name Senebhenaf were identical. Furthermore, the vizier Ibiau is often identified with the 'overseer of the compound' Ib-iau, who is well datable under king Ibiau. This identification is possible, as the career from an 'overseer of the compound' to a vizier is otherwise also attested.[180] Altogether, the evidence of this family was often taken to date the queen about three generations after the Thirteenth Dynasty king Ib-iau.[181] This seems possible, but there are too many uncertainties about that dating. The connection of all the people involved is not really proven. Furthermore, it is possible that Senebhenaf was appointed vizier when his daughter became queen. This means that she is datable just 20 years after king Ibiau.

Taking the evidence together there is little evidence for dating queen Mentuhotep and king Djehuty. They are floating around, unanchored, between the late Thirteenth Dynasty and Seventeenth Dynasty.[182]

[173] G. Jéquier: *Deux pyramides du Moyen Empire*, Cairo 1933, 28, fig. 1; compare Ryholt, *Political Situation*, 221.
[174] Compare Ryholt, *Political Situation*, 81-82.
[175] Ryholt, *Political Situation*, 270-71.
[176] Ryholt, *Political Situation*, 269; Polz, *Der Beginn des Neuen Reiches*, 38-42.
[177] PM I (2), 662.
[178] Lüscher, *Kanopenkästen*, 60-61; Dodson, *The Canopic Equipment of the Kings of Egypt*, 38.
[179] Ryholt, *Political Situation*, 359 (File 13/c).
[180] For a person called Bebi Sobekaa, Ryholt, *Political Situation*, 260.
[181] Geisen, *Mentuhotep*, 2-3
[182] Quirke, *Journal of Ancient Near Eastern Religions* 5 (2005), 229-30.

Nubherredi[183] (T7C)

The coffin of the 'king's ornament' Nubherredi (Cairo CG 28030) is one of the key coffins of the Second Intermediate Period. It was found in 1895 at Deir el-Bahri or following the dealer in Gebelein.[184] The coffin is the best preserved and best published Second Intermediate coffin with 'speeches of gods', and therefore important for reconstructing other less well preserved coffins with the same text programme. The coffin is black with yellow inscriptions. On the short ends are depicted Isis and Nephthys. Parts of the coffin are gilded. The front horizontal line shows the Nefertem-spell. On the back there is the Anubis spell. The front shows seven columns, the back eight of them. They contain the 'speeches of gods'.

Hemenhetep (T13C)

This is the vaulted coffin lid belonging to the 'commander of the ruler's crew' Hemenhetep (Cairo CG 28126). The lid is decorated with three horizontal lines with Pyramid text spells: 368 (638a-b), 252 beg (272-273a), 353 (275a-d). The coffin box of Hemenhotep is in Chicago and unpublished, but has the same decoration programme as the coffin of Nubherredi (T7C).

Senebni (T10C) and **Khonsu** (T6C)

The coffins of Senebni[185] and of Khonsu[186], perhaps his wife, were discovered before 1888 at Qurna. The coffins and objects found with them, are a key group for the Second Intermediate Period, as they are connected with a royal name and well preserved. The objects so far known from this tomb group were sold to Cairo and Moscow. These are two coffins, two canopic boxes and a staff with the name and titles of Senebni and the Second Interemediate Period king Sewahenre, a viscera, an uninscribed staff and a piece of linen.[187]

The coffins are similar on style and text programme. They are both black painted with high vaulted lids. The outside of both coffins is decorated with Coffin Texts spells 777 – 785. The coffin of Senebni is partly gilded and at the bottom, all around decorated with a palace façade, similar to the facades found on the lower parts of late Twelfth Dynasty sarcophagi.[188] This type of decoration might be taken from there.

The date of this tomb group rests heavily on the dating of king Sewahenre who appears on some monuments with the birth name Senebmiu. All monuments of the king were found in Upper Egypt, but none of these objects provides any clue for a more precise dating. The name of the king is not securely preserved in the Turin Canon. In line VIII, 27 appear the remains of a name ...nre.[189] Von Beckerath identified this king with Sewahenre.[190] However, this attribution of the remains in the Turin Canon with king Sewahenre is far from certain. The first part of the Turin Canon for the Thirteenth Dynasty is quite well preserved. There, there is no room for Sewahenre. This king dates therefore most likely to the late Thirteenth Dynasty or Sixteenth Dynasty, to a time when the royal court had already moved to Thebes. This might indicate that Senebni was in office at a time, when the king ruled from and most importantly was buried at Thebes. Furthermore, the outside decoration of both coffins is similar to the coffin of queen Mentuhotep, indicating a date not too far apart. The queen was also buried at Thebes, again showing that the court had moved to Thebes, where the king and his court was buried, although the burials of these kings have yet to be found.[191]

Teti (T34, model coffin)

The model coffin of Teti in the British Museum comes from the Robert Hay collection. The provenance of it is unknown, but Thebes seems to be most likely as the decorative and text scheme of the coffin is so far only attested at Thebes.[192] Indeed, the model coffin is a small version of a Theban black coffin with a similar text programme. On the front horizontal line, there is the Nefertem-spell, on the back there is the

---

[183] Ranke, *PN* I, 191, 19 (only one reference).

[184] Compare the discussion in Willems, *Chests of Life*, 117, n. 280.

[185] T10C; Cairo CG 28029.

[186] T6C; Cairo CG 28028.

[187] Berlev, *JEA* 60 (1974), 106-113.

[188] Arnold, *The Pyramid Complex of Senwosret III at Dahshur, Architectural Studies*, 36-37

[189] Ryholt, *Political Situation*, 71, fig. 10.

[190] Beckerath, *Untersuchungen*, 258 (XIII 41).

[191] compare Ryholt, *Political Situation*, 160.

[192] Grajetzki, *BMSAES* 5 (2006), 1-12.

Anubis formula. The columns have 'speeches of gods'. The texts most often break off in the middle, evidently for reasons of limited space on this small object type. On the lid there are three text lines. One of them is Pyramid Text spell 253 (275a-c).

Fig. 42 The model coffin of Teti

Ahmose (T39)[193]

The model coffin of the 'king's son' Ahmose comes perhaps from Thebes although an exact provenance is not known. It is decorated on the long sides with horizontal text lines and two columns. The vaulted lid has three text lines. The short ends are undecorated. On the lid there is a hetep-di-nisut formula and a djed-

[193] Dolzani, *La Collezione Egiziana del museo dell academia dei concordi in Rovigo*, 11-14, p.l VI-VII.

medu formula naming Qebehsenuef. The horizontal texts on the long side show djed-medu formulae; the columns imakhu-kher formulae. The general background of the coffin is black. Ahmose bears the title 'king's son'. One wonders whether he is identical with a king's son of the same name being the son of king Seqenre Djehuti-aa.[194] The whole coffin layout and the inscriptions are close to Twelfth Dynasty coffins. The black background has parallels in the Second Intermediate Period at Thebes (T6C, T7C, T10C).

Fig. 43 the model coffin of Ahmose; from Whelan, *Mere Scraps of Rough Wood?, 17th – 18th Dynasty Stick Shabtis in the Petrie Museum and other Collections*, 44, fig. 26, 3

Khonsu (T40, Cairo CG 48404)
The model coffin of *z3b r3-nḫn* Khonsu is made of terracotta. It has a vaulted lid with three text lines. They contain Pyramid Text spell 253 (275a-c). On the right side are two wedjat eyes and the Nefertem-spell in the horizontal line and a 'speech of a god' spread over four columns. On the left side is the *ˁwi*-Anubis spell going over the horizontal line and three columns. On the short ends appear spells mentioning Isis (head end) and Nephthys. In its text programme the model coffin of Khons is similar to those of other coffins from Thebes (T7C, T34). The smaller number of columns might relate to the more limited space on a model coffin. Although no findspot is recorded, Thebes seems to be a likely place of origin.

Nemtyemzaf (T8NY; New York Metropolitian Museum, MMA 32.3.428)
The coffin of the wab-priest Nemtyemzaf is so far unpublished.[195] It is a black coffin with nine columns on the front side. One of these columns is placed under the wedjat eyes, which are placed within a box. At the head end are wedjat eyes within a painted false door. The lid is vaulted and has three lines. On the foot end are two columns and a standing goddess with raised arms. On the horizontal line on the front side is the Nefertem-spell and the columns have 'speeches of gods'. The text programme of this coffin seems to be almost identical to that of Nubherredi (T7C).

Nefnefert[196] (T5NY; New York Metropolitian Museum, MMA 32.3.429)
The coffin of the 'king's ornament' Nefnefert is so far not published. It is a black coffin with eight columns on the front side. At the head end (of the front side) are wedjat eyes within a painted false door. The lid is vaulted and had three lines. On the foot end are two columns and a standing goddess with raised arms. On the horizontal line of the front side is the Nefertem-spell and the columns have 'speeches of gods'. The text programme of this coffin seems to be almost identical to the one of Ikhet. (T6NY).

[194] Miniaci, 'Il potere nella 17a dinastia: il titolo "figlio del re"e il ripensamento delle strutture amministrative nel Secondo Periodo Intermedio', In Pernigotti, Sergio ; Marco Zacchi (eds), *Il tempio e il suo personale nell'Egitto antico : Atti del quarto Colloquio, Bologna - 24/25 settembre 2008*, 114, no. 10.
[195] I am grateful to Gianluca Miniaci and Paul Whelan for providing me with photographic images of this and the following coffins in the Metropolitian Museum, New York.
[196] Perhaps a misspelling of Nefert.

Ikhet (T6NY; New York Metropolitian Museum, MMA 32.3.430)
The coffin of the wab-priest Ikhet is so far only published in one photographic image.[197] It is a black coffin with eight columns on the front side. At the head end (of the front side) are wedjat eyes within a painted false door. The lid is vaulted and has three lines. On the foot end are two columns and a standing goddess with raised arms. On the horizontal there is the Nefertem-spell and the columns have 'speeches of gods'. The text programme of this coffin seems to be almost identical to the one of Nubherredi (T7C). So far as can be judged from the published photograph, the texts are complete and not garbled versions of older texts as stated by Hayes.[198]

NN (T7NY; New York Metropolitian Museum, MMA 32.3.431)
The coffin is so far unpublished. The space for the name of the coffin owner is left blank. The front side of the coffin is decorated with eight columns containing 'speeches of gods'. The horizontal line at the top bears the Nefertem-spell. The lower part of the coffin is all around decorated with a palace façade, similar to the one of Senebni (T10C). The 'speeches of gods' are partly garbled, breaking off before their proper ending, in most cases this would include the name of the coffin owner.

Herunefer (T6L)[199]
Only the upper part of a short end from the coffin of the 'king's son' Herunefer is preserved. On the inside it bears Book of the Dead chapter 17 in hieratic as on the interior on the coffin of queen Mentuhotep (T4L). Herunefer was the son of a king Mentuhotep. There are several kings with that name in the Second Intermediate Period

Renseneb (T3)
The coffin is only known from a description: 'bitumen coating ... had had bands of yellow hieroglyphs along its sides and ends... and certain of the hieroglyphs were of the mutilated type'.[200]

Ibiau (T35)
The coffin is only published in a short description, mentioning that these are fragments of a black painted, varnished coffin with numerous columns of yellow closey spaced hieroglyphs,.[201]

Zatnenna (T36)[202]
The coffin of the 'lady of the house' (*nbt-pr*) Zatnenna was recorded by Luigi Vassalli while he was working in Thebes (1862-63). The long side is decorated with one horizontal line at the top and four columns beneath. The horizontal lines contain an offering formula. The columns contain imakhu-kher formulae. On the short ends there is only one horizontal line with a standing female figure under that. The lid is vaulted with one text line down the middle. The ends are raised. The coffins shows on both head end panels (between the columns) wedjat eyes over a checkerboard pattern. On each side of the coffin is shown next to the panel Anubis, lying on a shrine or box. The third panel shows on both sides no figure but seems to show a painted pattern imitating wood. The coffin is in many ways a transitional type. The hieroglyphs are complete, but the hetep-di-nisut signs show the order more typical for the Second Intermediate Period.[203] Wedjat eyes on both coffin sides are more typical for the late Second Intermediate Period, as are the figures of Anubis painted on a middle panel on the exterior. The coffin was found in the same tomb as T37 and therefore perhaps dates to the early Eigtheenth Dynasty.

[197] Hayes, *The Scepter of Egypt I*, 347-48, fig. 228.
[198] Hayes, *The Scepter of Egypt I*, 348.
[199] Parkinson, Quirke, in *Studies in Pharaonic Religion and Society in Honour of J. Gwyn Griffths*, 37-51.
[200] Carter, *Five Years*, 54-55.
[201] Grajetzki, *Die höchsten Beamten*, 136, n. 1 (following letter from J. P. Allen).
[202] Tiradritti, In Marée (editor), *The Second Intermediate Period (Thirteenth-Seventeenth Dynasties), Current Research, Future Prospects*, 333, pl. 113.
[203] Franke, *JEA* 89 (2003), 39-57.

NN (T37)[204]

The coffin was also recorded in the work of Luigi Vassalli at Thebes. This coffin is in some ways exceptional. On the long sides it is decorated with a horizontal band at the top and five columns. Instead of text, the band at the top and the columns just contain colour bands; only one on each side contains an imakhu-kher formula, but does not name the coffin owner. On each long side, at the head end are two wedjat eyes upon a shrine. In the panels next to that are shown sandals, offerings on a table and a mirror. The short ends show standing figures of Isis and Nephthys. They are both identified with short captions. The lid of the coffin was vaulted. With the coffin were found cartouches of several kings of different periods. The last king mentioned is Ahmose. Therefore the coffin belongs to the very beginning of the Eighteenth Dynasty, perhaps even under that king.[205]

NN (T38)[206]

This coffin side was also recorded in the work of Luigi Vassalli at Thebes. Of the coffin Vassali recorded only one sidel, most likely the left outer side. It is decorated with seven columns. There is no horizontal line, but that might just be missing and was not preserved. The columns bear inscriptions, but they are not legible in the copies. The hieroglyphs are complete, albeit the copies show only one living animal, a bird (with legs). Between the columns there a palace façade over a checkerboard pattern. As it was found in the same tomb as T37 it therefore perhaps dates to the early Eighteenth Dynasty.

Gebelein

Gebelein was an important place in the Second Intermediate Period. Several stelae of the period were found there, although little is known about the Second Intermediate Period cemeteries.

NN (G1)

The coffin (Cairo CG 28031) is decorated on the front with four panels, on the back with six. There are no inscriptions between these panels unlike most of the other coffins of this period. On the front is a small further panel with wedjat eyes and the beginning of a Hetep-di-nisut formula under it. Only on the short ends are there texts in two columns and a horizontal band. The texts are garbled and basically not understandable. It is hard to provide a date for the coffin. The arrangement of panels recalls coffins from Thebes (T6C, T7C, T10C). This coffin might be contemporary: late Thirteenth or Sixteenth Dynasty?

NN (G2)

The coffin (Cairo CG 28031) is decorated with a high number of columns (seven at the front) including the 'speeches of gods'. The speeches are partly garbled. Although on the long sides there is a horizontal line for a text band, no inscription was placed there. The coffin is furthermore decorated with checkerboard patterns, perhaps a degenerated palace façade. On the front are the wedjat eyes with a short column beneath, including a Hetep-di-nisut formula. For the date see G1.

Qubbet el-Hawa/Elephantine

Qubbet el-Hawa, near Elephantine is the main cemetery for the ruling class of the Old and Middle Kingdoms. There are only few remains of the Second Intermediate Period.

---

[204] Tiradritti, In Marée (editor), *The Second Intermediate Period (Thirteenth- Seventeenth Dynasties), Current Research, Future Prospects*, 333-335, pl. 114 (Coffin T 100.2).

[205] Tiradritti, In Marée (editor), *The Second Intermediate Period (Thirteenth- Seventeenth Dynasties), Current Research, Future Prospects*, 335. The cartouches might be faience plaques (I am grateful to Stephen Quirke for discussing this point); for similar plaques, see Brunton, G., R. Engelbach, *Gurob*, pl. XXI, 82 (6); Downes, *The Excavations at Esna*, 62, 233 (3); Petrie, Flinders, W.M., *Scarabs and Cylinder with Names*, pl. X 7.9; XIII (second line, right); XXV (18.5.1) .

[206] Tiradritti, In Marée (editor), *The Second Intermediate Period (Thirteenth- Seventeenth Dynasties), Current Research, Future Prospects*, 333, pl. 115 (Coffin T 100.6).

Neferhesut (A1X)

The coffin of Neferhesut was discovered in 1910 by J. Clédat on Elephantine. It is not yet published. Following H. Willems, who provides a short description, it dates to the Thirteenth Dynasty. The coffin is on the outside decorated with a palace façade and text columns. On the short ends are shown Isis and Nephthys. On the outside there is also Coffin Text spell 397 (or at least a related text) and on the long side are also shown objects, similar to a frieze of objects ('des armes et autres objets'; according to Clédat).[207]

Nebetneheh (A2X)

The coffin of the 'lady of the house' Nebetneheh was in poor condition when found in tomb QH 34 at Qubbet el-Hawa.[208] There is only a hand copy of the inscriptions and a short description preserved.

The coffin was decorated on the long sides with at least six and on the short side with two columns. The hieroglyphic signs are incomplete. They are light blue and outlined in black on a yellow background. In this respect the coffin is almost identical to examples found at Abydos and Thebes. The background colour of the coffin was red with black and white spots.

From the texts only parts of the columns could be copied. The coffin was decorated with 'speeches of gods' most of which can be identified from parallels on other coffins from Thebes. The coffin dates perhaps to the Thirteenth Dynasty.

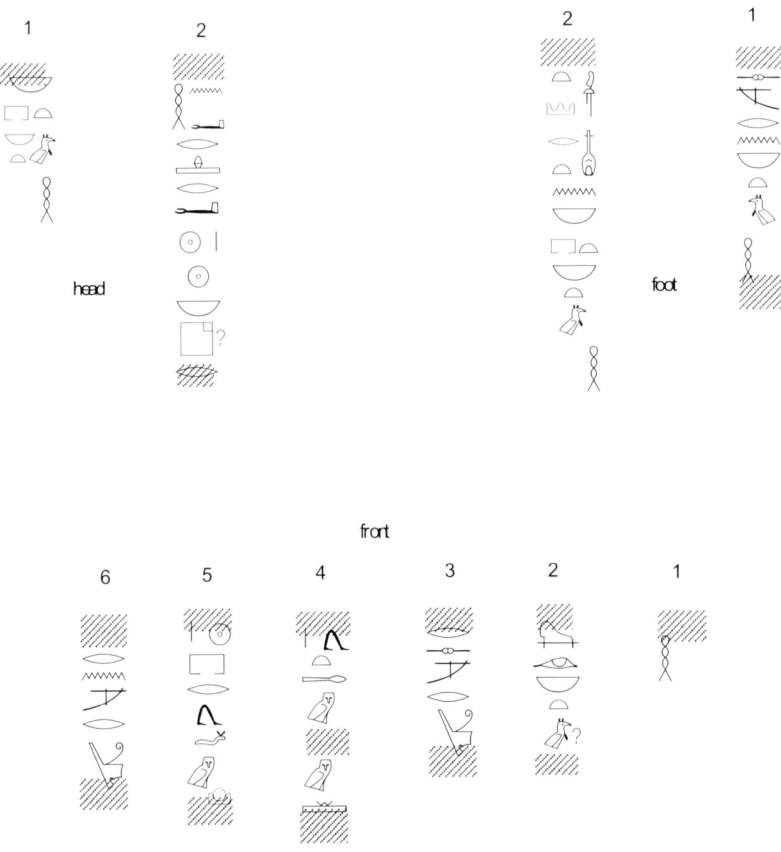

[207] Willems, in J. van Dijk (editor), *Essays on Ancient Egypt in Honour of Herman te Velde*, 356-57, note 47.

[208] Edel, *Die Felsgräbernekropole der Qubbet el-Hawa bei Assuan, I. Abbteilung Band 1*, 436 (for the hand copies of the inscriptions).

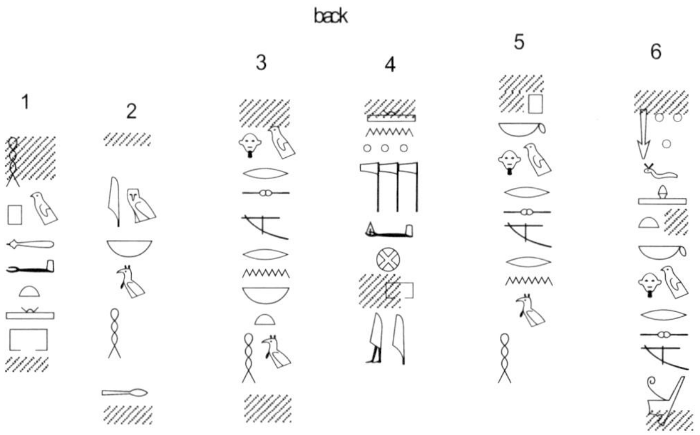

Fig. 44 The texts on the coffin of Nebetneheh

Mirgissa

Mirgissa was a Middle Kingdom fortress town in Nubia. There are important, well excavated and published cemeteries of the Second Intermediate Period.

NN (Mi1)[209]

In the Nubian cemetery of Mirgissa were found several decorated coffins and coffin fragments.[210] These coffins are not consistent in style and there is the impression that at least the decorated examples were imported from several places in Egypt. While most of the coffins seem to date to the Twelfth Dynasty, there is one coffin board (Tomb 117), coming from a foot end and most likely dating to the Thirteenth Dynasty. The fragment shows two columns with 'speeches of gods'. The hieroglyphs are incomplete. In the middle of the panel is the depiction of a female figure.

Unknown provenance

Khnumnakht (S3)

The coffin of Khnumnakht (Metropolitian Museum New York, MMA15.2.2ab[211]) is decorated on the front side with wedjat eyes and a false door beneath. Here, there is one horizontal line with an offering formula and ten columns. Four of these columns have a buff/pink background colour and brightly painted hieroglyphs, just like the horizontal line at the top. They are therefore in a certain way highlighted. They contain *imakhu-kher* formulae. The other columns have a dark blue or buff/pinkish background, but the hieroglyphs are monochrome. The hieroglyphs on the buff/pinkish background are dark blue, the hieroglyphs on the dark blue background are buff/pinkish. These columns all contain 'speeches of gods'. On the back there appears the same pattern, without the wedjat eyes, but with thirteen columns. On the head end is the image of a goddess, most likely Isis as she is mentioned in the horizontal line at the top. On the foot end there are just texts, three *imakhu-kher* formula and in the middle a 'speech of good', in this case by Nephthys.

This coffin is in many ways a transitional type. The high quality painting and the IV type of the ornamental texts are similar to Twelfth Dynasty coffins. A new feature are the additional text columns between the ornamental texts. The coffin most likely dates – on typological grounds - to the end of the Twelfth Dynasty.

---

209 Vercoutter, *Mirgissa II*, fig. 61g.

210 Tomb 117, short end with painted figure, Vercoutter, *Mirgissa II*, 159, fig. 61g, Vercoutter, J., *Mirgissa II, Les necropolis, Part 2,* 292, fig. 13, 2; Tomb 117, no. 57, fragment with two columns, Vercoutter, *Mirgissa II*, 160; Tomb 130 (C4): coffin decorated with Coffin Texts on the inside, Vercoutter, *Mirgissa II*, 187, fig. 78a, Vercoutter, J., *Mirgissa II, Les necropolis, Part 2,* 291, fig. 12a; Tomb 130 (C5), coffin Willems type IV with funerary procession painted on the outside, Vercoutter, *Mirgissa II*, 187, fig. 77c; Tomb 131 coffin Willems type IV with goddess on the short end, Vercoutter, *Mirgissa II*, 198, fig. 82, Vercoutter, J., *Mirgissa II, Les necropolis, Part 2,* 291, fig. 12b.

211 The coffin is not yet fully published; for pictures see Hayes, *Scepter of Egypt I*, 318, fig. 207 (also in colour on the cover of the 1990 reprint; it is assign to Asyut).; Lapp, *Typologie*, 113, figs. 136-37; Lapp assigns the coffin to Meir.

Chapter Four: Late Second Intermediate Period – early Eighteenth Dynasty

Thebes

Rediamun

The coffin remains of the 'royal sealer' and 'overseer of fields' Rediamun were found in a shaft tomb with two chambers in the Assasif. From the coffin itself, only small fragments of inlays survived; all the wood had perished when it was found. However, the coffin left imprints in the sand of the tomb chamber providing some information. The coffin was 78-79 cm wide and about 2.2 m long. The height is unknown. It was placed on at least 8 wooden beams. The outer head end left an impression in the sand and was decorated most likely with a palace façade framed on the left by a *zꜣ*-sign and on the right by a djed pillar. There were remains of inlaid wedjat eyes, a shen ring and further inlays, perhaps coming from a palace façade under the eyes. There was also a fragment of gold foil, perhaps belonging to a rishi coffin.[212]

In the tomb were found some pottery vessels, some smaller objects and the gilding from a canopic box providing the name of the tomb owner. The pottery seems to provide a date into the second half of the Second Intermediate Period.[213]

Thebes, Carter excavation tomb 37/7[214]

The coffin was found in a large Middle Kingdom tomb at Thebes. The tomb was reused at the end of the Second Intermediate Period and early Eighteenth Dynasty as a mass burial place. There were found undecorated and decorated coffins, of anthropoid and rectangular shape. Coffin no. 37/7 was painted yellow and had its design in red, green, dark blue and white. Only a photo of the front side is published. At the head end there is a single wedjat eye, in the middle there are three panels of a degenerated palace façade and at the food end an Anubis jackal is shown lying on a shrine. According to the description in the publication Isis and Nephthys are depicted on the short ends. They are placed on neb signs on a white background. The coffin contained the mummy of an old man.

Thebes, Carter excavation tomb 37/59[215]

The colouring of the coffin was similar to 37/7 of the same tombs. There is again only a photographic picture of the back side published. In the upper half is a mat pattern, the lower half of the coffin decoration is separated into four panels. At the head end there is a wedjat eye, in the next panel a plant, in the next a boat or ship and in the last again a plant. According to the publication four bodies were found in the coffin as well as scarabs of Thutmosis I and Thutmosis II.

Fig. 45 Coffin 37/59 in the Cairo, Egyptian Museum (© Gianluca Miniaci)

---

[212] Graefe, *Das Grab des Padihorresnet*, 62-63, pl. 31bc, 32a, 115 (Kat. 536-539), 118 (Kat. 540).

[213] Graefe, *Das Grab des Padihorresnet*, pl. 134, no, 156-59, compare: Bourriau, in: Oren (editor), *The Hyksos*, fig. 18

[214] Carter, *Five Years*, 70-1, pl. LX.

[215] Carter, *Five Years*, 81, pl. LX, a line drawing of the back side: Ikram/Dodson, *Mummy*, 206, fig. 262D.

Thebes, Carter excavation tomb 37/63[216]

The coffin seems to be in several ways typologically the earliest one found in tomb 37. On the front at the head end are two wedjat eyes. The rest of the side is decorated with patterns incorporating a palace façade and a mat/checkerboard design. At the ends there Isis and Nephthys are shown standing with raised arms. Inside the coffin were found two mummies, that of a man and that of a woman. The coffin might still date to the end of the Seventeenth Dynasty.

Fig. 46 Two views of coffin 37/63, Egyptian Museum Cairo (© Gianluca Miniaci)

Tomb 'M'

In this Middle Kingdom tomb in the Assasif, several badly damaged coffin fragments were found, dating from the Middle Kingdom to the Late Period. The following fragments belong to the Second Intermediate Period or early New Kingdom.

1. Board with the remains of a female figure.[217]
2. Board with an empty column and a checkerboard pattern.[218]
3. Board with a figure of a woman with raised arm.[219]
4. Board with the figure of a woman sitting on a nub (gold)-sign.[220]
5. End piece of a coffin lid, decorated with the two wedjat-eyes. The back side of the piece shows the coffin had a vaulted lid.[221]

---

[216] Carter, *Five Years*, 82-83, pl. LX, a line drawing: Ikram/Dodson, Mummy, 206, fig. 262A.
[217] Graefe, *Die Doppelgrabanlage 'M' aus dem Mittleren Reich*, 75-76 (005), 0-Taf. 1.
[218] Graefe, *Die Doppelgrabanlage 'M' aus dem Mittleren Reich*, 76 (006), 0-Taf. 2.
[219] Graefe, *Die Doppelgrabanlage 'M' aus dem Mittleren Reich*, 76-77 (007), 0-Taf. 2.
[220] Graefe, *Die Doppelgrabanlage 'M' aus dem Mittleren Reich*, 77 (008), 0-Taf. 2.

6. Fragments of wood, decorated with a row of triangles which are filled with black stripes.[222]
7. Three wooden fragments with a column decorated with crosses and horizontal lines.[223]

Beni Hasan

John Garstang found in tomb 287 a simply decorated coffin. Only two pictures of the coffin are published. The coffin had a vaulted lid with two straight end beams. In the middle of the front side there is just one vertical line. The text is hardly visible on the published photo and partly destroyed, but seems to read: [*im3ḫw ḫr*] *dw3*-[*mwt*].*f 3st-irt*. The outer edges of the front side are decorated with a colour pattern.[224] The date of the coffin and the tomb is uncertain. However, the coffin seems not to fit into the pattern of other Middle Kingdom coffins. A date into the late Seventeenth Dynasty or even early New Kingdom seems to be more likely. The objects found in the tomb confirm this date. There are two occupation phases visible. One belongs to the Middle Kingdom and is attested by pottery and wooden models. The second phase belongs to the second half of the Second Intermediate Period. The tomb equipment consists of furniture (a low chair) and musical instruments,[225] which are not very typical for Middle Kingdom burials, but common in the Eighteenth Dynasty. For the pottery Garstang notes: 'and five not corresponding with any … type but of XII to early XVIII Dyn, style.'[226]

Saqqara

Saqqara is quite rich in rectangular coffins, dating to the Second Intermediate Period and early New Kingdom. However, a great proportion of them are only published as descriptions and not as drawings or photographs.

I. A Second Intermediate Period coffin was found at the funerary temple of Pepy II at Saqqara South.[227] One side of the coffin is published as a drawing. At the top there is a checkkerboard pattern, under which are four rectangular panels. In the left outer one is a painted triangle; in the right outer one, is a single wedjat eye.

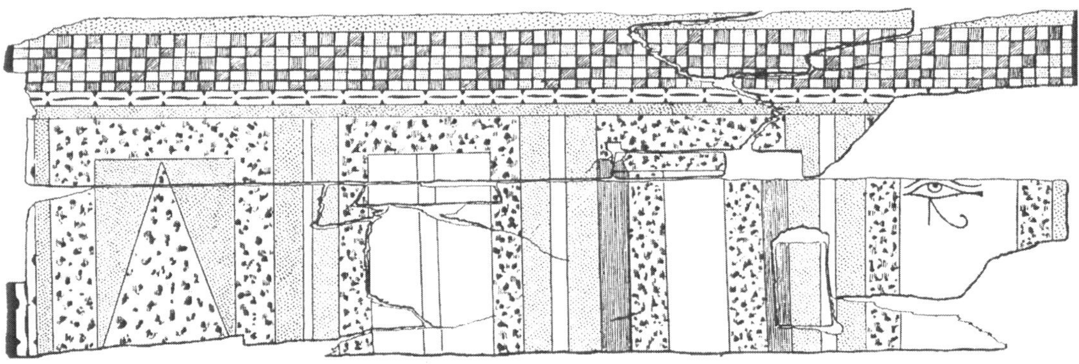

Fig. 47 Coffin found in the funerary temple of Pepy II

II. An early Eighteenth Dynasty coffin is only known from the description of the excavators: 'rectangular wooden coffin, much decayed painted with vertical bands of black, white red white black chain patterns,

[221] Graefe, *Die Doppelgrabanlage 'M' aus dem Mittleren Reich*, 78 (010), 0-Taf. 3.
[222] Graefe, *Die Doppelgrabanlage 'M' aus dem Mittleren Reich*, 78-79 (012), 0-Taf. 4.
[223] Graefe, *Die Doppelgrabanlage 'M' aus dem Mittleren Reich*, 81 (026a-c), 0-Taf. 4.
[224] Hoffmeier, Coffins of the Middle Kingdom, 86, pl. 1; Garstang, *Burial Customs,* 181, fig. 189.
[225] Garstang, *Burial Customs,*119, fig. 113; 123, fig. 118, 154, fig. 153.
[226] Garstang, *Burial Customs,* 222 (tomb list).
[227] Jéquier, *Pepi II*, 44, fig. 34.

black lines on blue, black chain'. A scarab with the name of Amenhotep I provides the dating of the tomb to the early Eighteenth Dynasty.[228]

III. A rectangular coffin was found as an intrusive burial within the mastaba of the Old Kingdom vizier Khentyka Ikhekhi. It is also only published in a short description: '… a rectangular wooden coffin, dated to the early New Kingdom … On the side of the coffin was painted a black figure of the Anubis jackal on the sledge'. There were three objects placed with the burial; a forked staff, a small pot and a reed kohl-tube. Finally there was a dom-nut.[229]

[228] Firth/Gunn, *Teti pyramid cemeteries*, 68.
[229] James, *The Mastaba of Khentika called Ikheki*, 3.

Unprovenanced

Petrie Museum UCL 380364, 55168

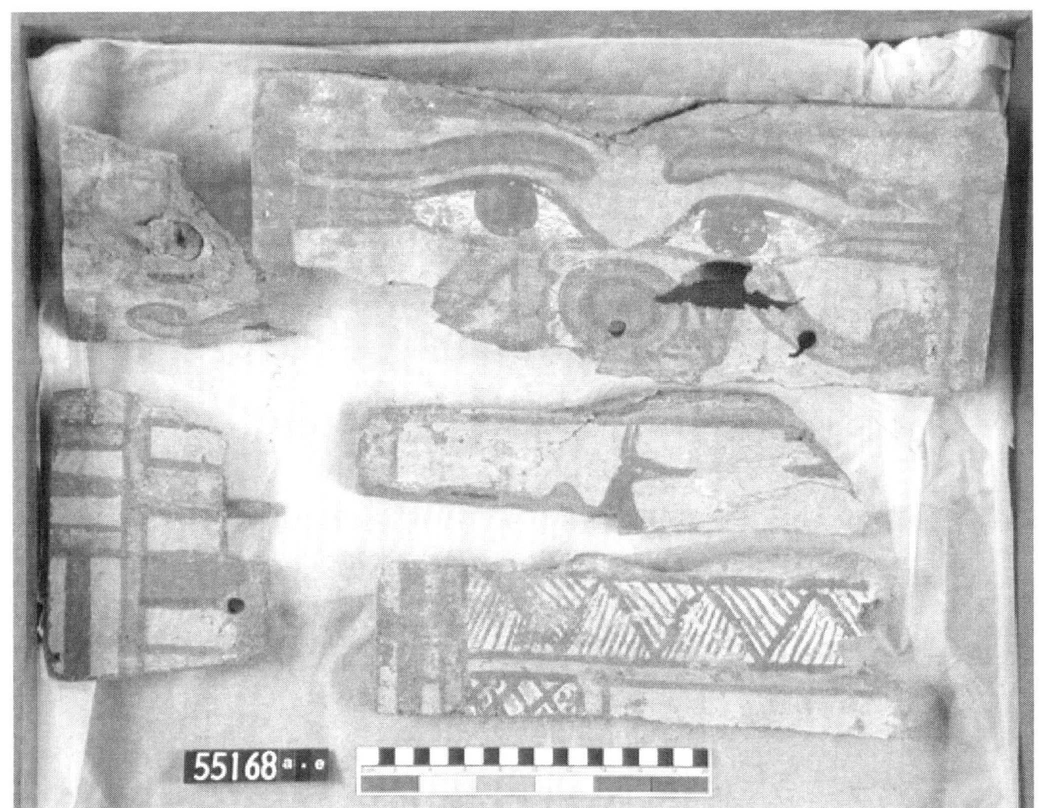

Fig. 48 Fragments in the Petrie Museum of Egyptian Archaeology (top), © UCL; bottom: detail showing the corner of the fragment with the wedjat eyes, photo: Grajetzki; the fragment with the eyes is 41 cm long

In the Petrie Museum of Egyptian Archaeology are several unprovenanced fragments of a typical late Second Intermediate Period/early New Kingdom coffin. The larger fragments (UC 38036), belong to a long side and are already published.[230] The long side shows a series of five panels decorated with a degenerated palace façade and checkerboard pattern. The borders are framed by a colour band (blue, green, red and yellow, the latter is the background colour of the coffin).

---

[230] Stewart, *Mummy Cases & Inscribed Funerary Cones in the Petrie Collection*, London 1986, 3, no. 2, pl. 2.

One of the unpublished pieces joins with the right edge of the big fragment. The other three unpublished fragments are hard to place. Two fragments belong to a panel with wedjat eyes, and one further fragment shows patterns different to the one found on the long side. It has a row of triangles with a striped decoration within the triangles. A similar pattern was found on a coffin fragment at Thebes.[231] The last of the three fragments shows the remains of two jackals.

The biggest piece with the two wedjat eyes is an end piece with the corner on either side. Therefore, the piece must come from the short end of the coffin and was most likely placed at the head end.[232] This is confirmed by the colour pattern visible on the corner of the fragment. The colour pattern is identical to the colour pattern framing the largest fragment. The placing of the two eyes at the head end has so far only one parallel on a fragment found at Thebes.[233] The placement of the two other fragments is pure speculation. The jackals might belong to the foot end of the coffin, or they might have decorated a panel on the other long side. The placement of the last fragment is also unclear, but belongs perhaps to the other long side of the coffin, indicating that this side was decorated in a totally different manner. A second option is that it belongs to the lid of the coffin.

With due reservation it might be argued that these fragments come from Thebes. At least all of the parallels for certain patterns come from there (compare the fragments from Tomb 'M', p. 56-57).

Fig. 49 Reconstruction of the fragments in the Petrie Museum

[231] Graefe, *Die Doppelgrabanlage 'M' aus dem Mittleren Reich*, 78-79 (012), 0-Taf. 4.

[232] Although, it must be admitted, that there is no real proof for that.

[233] Graefe, *Die Doppelgrabanlage 'M' aus dem Mittleren Reich*, 78 (010), 0-Taf.3.

Chapter Five: the main text programmes

On coffins of the late Middle Kingdom and Second Intermediate Period were found three text programmes.

(1) Some coffins are still decorated following Middle Kingdom patterns. On the long horizontal lines appear offering formulae and on the columns imakhu-kher formulae.
(2) In the late Middle Kingdom appear 'speeches of gods', some of them are also attested on pyramidia of the same period.
(3) At Abydos and Thebes were found coffins decorated with Coffin Text spells 777 to 785.

Finally there are some coffins with longer religious texts. They appear additionally to the texts just mentioned. These appear on the outside of the coffins in panels and sometimes even on the inside. Coffins with interior decoration are especially rare.

Speeches of gods

Several of the spells known from the late Middle Kingdom and Second Intermediate Period coffins are also known from the royal pyramidia of the same period.[234] These spells appear not only there and on coffins, but are known from a wide range of objects, including mastabas (which sometimes seem to copy coffins). Other spells are not known from the pyramidia. In general the pyramidion spells seems to refer to the cosmic aspect of the deceased, while other spells refer to the hourly vigil.

In the late Twelfth Dynasty the texts in the columns show a great variation. In the Thirteenth Dynasty certain certain text patterns are visible all around the whole country.

I. The horizontal line on the long sides, pyramidia spells:

1. *wn-ḥr* (opening-of-the-face) – formula[235]:

NN

Hapyankhtifi (M2NY)[236], Khakheperreseneb/Iy (M20) (Meir, about Senusret III ?)[237], Hor (Da4C), Nubhetepti-khered (Da2C), Sobekaa (T3Be), Sesenebnef (L2Li), Zatsobek (Da3C); perhaps Hu4; Bener (L6); Wahneferhotep (L7)

The 'opening-of-the-face' is known from pyramidia and appears on their east side, which is the same side as it appears on the coffins.

2. Anubis formula

NN NN

Hapyankhtifi (M2NY)[238], Khakheperreseneb (M20), Nubhetepti-khered (Da2C), Nubherredi (T7C), Hu2, Hu5, Teti (T34), Khons (T40), Zatimpi (Ha3)

[234] Lapp, *Typologie*, 226-228.
[235] Lohwasser, *Die Formel 'Öffnen des Gesichts'*; Vernus, *RdE* 28 (1976), 124-127; Willems, *Chests of Life*, 168.
[236] The spell appears on the coffin inside.
[237] Kamal, *ASAE* 14 (1914), 75-78.
[238] The spell appears on the coffin inside.

Words spoken: may the arms of Anubis, on his mountain, who is in his embalming place be around NN, may he cause that he is united with the western desert in the beautiful shrine[239] *of the lord of offerings in the tomb of the necropolis, may he case that NN is inheriting for all eternity*[240]

The Anubis spell is also known from the royal pyramidia of the late Middle Kingdom. It appears there on the Western, (i.e. back) side.[241] It is placed in the same position on coffins. The Anubis spell is known from coffins found in the North and in the South, from Thebes to Dahshur[242]. The spell replaced the offering formula of the Twelfth Dynasty where on the back Anubis was invoked. In the late Twelfth Dynasty these offering formulae (for example Sobekaa - T3Be; Bebut - Maz1) with Anubis are already close to the Anubis formula expressing the same wish (*may he cause that he is united with the western desert in the beautiful shrine*), with just a different opening.

II. Pyramidia spells on the short ends

1. *Geb, Lord of the Lands is below the torso and Osiris below the feet of NN*[243]

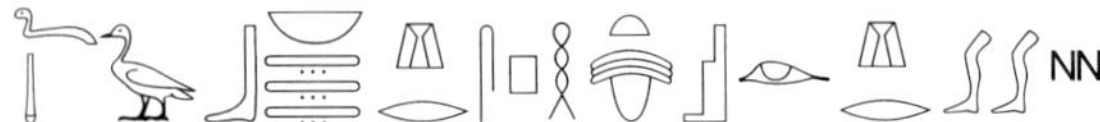

Bener (L6), Wahneferhotep (L7), Sobekaa (T3Be), Ikhet (T6NY), Nefert (T5NY), NN (T7NY), Nemtyemweskhet (Aby6)

The spell always appears on the top horizontal line at the foot end. Willems summarizes the contents that the body of the deceased is supported by the earth god Geb and by Osiris. [244] The spell appears several times, but not on all coffins with 'spells of gods'. On pyramidia the spell appears on the south side.[245]

2. *The ba of NN is elevated to the heights of Orion, when he (Orion) unites with the Dat. He makes NN firm on top of the stars*[246]

NN NN

Bener (L6), Wahneferhotep (L7), Sobekaa (T3Be), Nefert (T5NY), Ikhet (T6NY), NN (T7NY), Teti (T34), Zatsobek (Da3C), Nemtyemweskhet (Aby6)

The spell has the following variation:

Words spoken by Ra, I have fixed NN among the stars

NN

Head end, left: Nubherredi (T7C), Nefert (T5NY), Ikhet (T6NY)

The spell and its variations appear on the short ends of the coffin on the head (North) end. In this position it appears on the pyramidia too.[247]

---

[239] The text writes instead of or .
[240] This is the version on T7C.
[241] Lapp, *Typologie*, 227-228.
[242] Willems, *Chests of Life*, 169.
[243] Willems, *Chests of Life*, 169.
[244] Willems, *Chests of Life*, 169.
[245] Lapp, *Typologie*, 227-228.
[246] Willems, *Chests of Life*, 169.
[247] Lapp, *Typologie*, 227-228.

III. Pyramidia spell: The mr n-spells

1. *Words spoken by the beautiful west (or beautiful horizon): you are happy with it today NN*

Front, foot end: Nubherredi (west) (T7C); Amenhotep (horizon)(Da6X)

2. *Words spoken by the Mehyt: you are happy with it today NN*

Head end, right: Nubherredi (T7C), Ikhet (T6NY), T7NY

3. *Words spoken by the (all) gods: you are happy with it today NN*

Foot end, left side: Nubherredi (T7C), Mi1 (Mi1), Nefert (T5NY)

4. *Words spoken by the beautiful west: you are happy with it today NN*

back, foot end: Nubherredi (T7C)
unknown position: Zatsobek (Da3C)

This type of spell is common on many coffins of the period. It seems that the spell appeared once on each coffin side, always introduced by another deity (or group of deities in the case of 'all gods'). There are difficulties for understanding the meaning of the spell. H. Willems translates it: 'I am content with it today'.[249] Whatever the real meaning of this phrase, it was of great importance. On the pyramidia the spell appears on the east side, next to the 'opening of the face' formula.[250]

IV. The Nefertem-spell.

First attestation on coffins: Zatip (Da1X)[251], Khakheperreseneb/Aya (Meir)[252], both about Senusret III ?
Appears on coffins from Thebes (T7C, T8NY, T5NY, T6NY, T7NY, T34 T40) and Hu (Hu2, Hu5, Hu6)

---

[248] Version from Nubherredi (T7C).
[249] Willems, *Chests of Life*, 168-169.
[250] Lapp, *Typologie*, 226, 228.
[251] Within a sequence of Pyramid Texts.
[252] Kamal, *ASAE* 14 (1914), 75-78.

Words spoken: NN may appear as Nefertem as lotus at the nose of Ra, may he go forth from the horizont, every day, and at the sight of which the gods purify himself, may appear those who comes, NN at his first place among his brothers, the gods, for all eternity.

The Nefertem-spell is part of the Pyramid Texts (spell 266a-b (249), 267c (250)), but not part of the smaller corpus of the so called pyramidion spells. The Nefertem-spell appears on coffins and other monuments of the late Middle Kingdom and Second Intermediate Period. It is still attested in the Roman period and also became in a slightly different form, part of Book of the Dead chapter 174.[253] The spell appears within the sequence of Pyramid texts on the coffin of Zatip (Da1X) from Dahshur and on the coffin of the 'governor' Khakheperreseneb/Aya from Meir. As main spell, on coffins it was till now only known from Thebes, but seems to have been much more common in Upper Egypt, as the examples from Hu demonstrate. The Theban coffin of Sobekaa (T3Be), most likely dating to the late Twelfth Dynasty, does not yet have the spell, but the opening-of-the-face-formula instead. This might indicate that the use of the spell on coffins was introduced at some point in the Thirteenth Dynasty. Nefertem does not often appear in the Coffin Texts proper.

V. Other 'speeches of gods' on Thirteenth Dynasty coffins:

1. *Words spoken by Ra, I have given a beautiful horizon for NN*

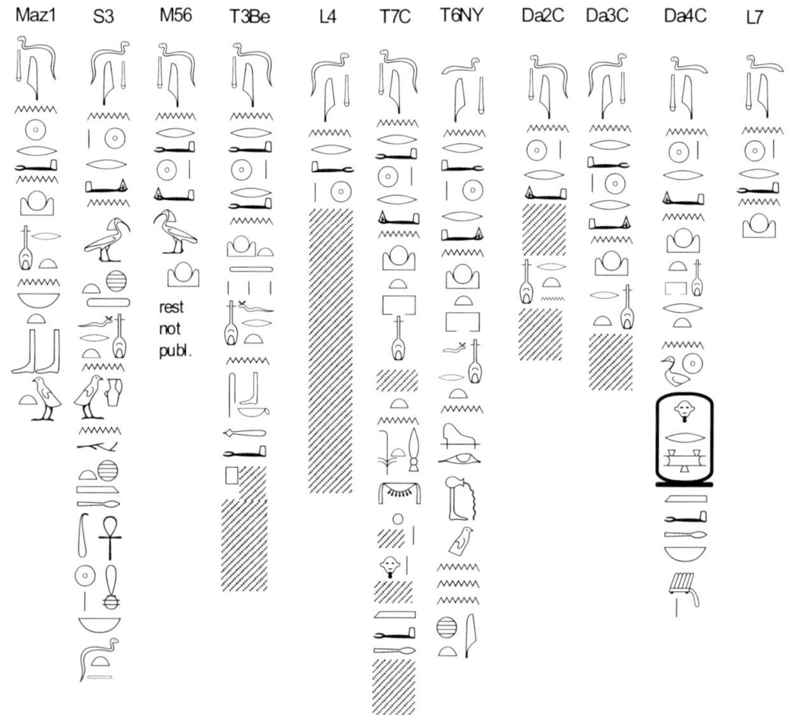

Head end, front side: Bebut (Maz1); Nubheredi (T7C), Nemtyemzaf (T8NY), Senebtisi (?) (L4), Neferet (T5NY); Hapyankhtifi (M56), NN (G2)

Breast, front side: Sobekaa (T3Be)
Front: T40 (slightly different spell)

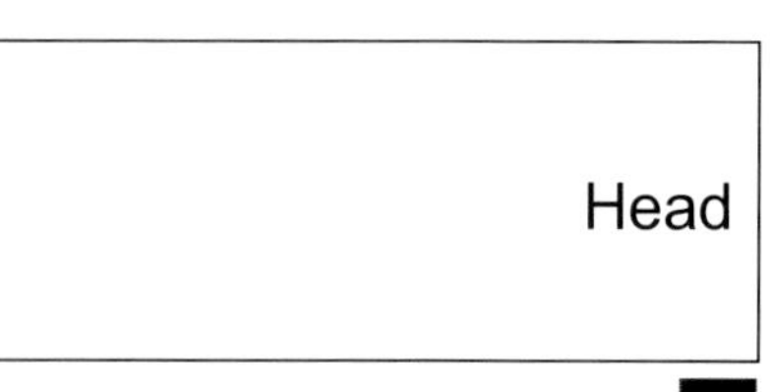

This is one of the most important speeches as it is found on many coffins. It appears already on coffins of the Twelfth Dynasty. On the coffin of Bebut (Maz1) it is the only speech of a god; while the other columns

[253] Lucarelli, in: R. Pirelli (ed.), *Egyptological Studies for Claudio Barocos*, Napoli 1999, 50-52.

just bear 'djed-medu' formulae. In this spell Ra provides the deceased with the 'beautiful horizon'. Perhaps this can be seen in the function of Ra as opening the ways in the Underworld for the deceased.[254] The sun god was traveling the sky on the day and the Underworld in the night. With this function he must have been seen as a good guide for the Underworld too. The horizon was also the dwelling place of Ra.[255]

2. *Words spoken by Ptah-(Sokar): I have given a good reverence for NN*

Foot, right: Nubherredi (T7C), Mi1, Neferet (T5NY), Ikhet (T6NY) ?
Position uncertain: Zatsobek (Da3C),

VI. The Four children of Horus

2. *Words spoken by Amset: I came to attach the left arm of NN*

Breast: front side: Nubherredi (T7C), Ikhet (T6NY), Nemtyemzaf (T8NY), NN (G2), perhaps: Zatsobek (Da3C),

3. *Words spoken by Duamutef: I came to attach the left (i͗3b) arm of NN*

front side: Nemtyemzaf (T8NY), Neferet (T5NY), Ikhet (T6NY) (?), Senebtisi (L4)

4. *Words spoken by Hapy: I have come to attach the right arm of NN*

Breast: back side: Nubherredi (T7C), (perhaps Nubhetepti-khered)

5. *Words spoken by Qebehsenuef: I have come to attach the right leg of NN*

unknown: front side: Zatsobek (Da3C)

6. *Words spoken by Duamutef: I came to attach the left (i͗3b) leg of NN*

unknown position: front side: Zatsobek (Da3C); Duamutef appears also on the front of the coffin of Amenhotep (Da6X), most likely in the region of the leg.

[254] Altenmüller, *Synkretismus in den Sargtexten*, 118.
[255] See the list of attestations in Altenmüller, *Synkretismus in den Sargtexten*, 318.

The relation of the children of Horus to body parts is already found in Coffin Text spell 761[256]:

Your arms are the two sons of Horus, Hapy and Amset
Your legs are Duamutef and Qebehsenuef

This connection is found on almost all coffins with 'speeches of gods'. On the coffin of Sobekaa (T3Be) only Amset (right arm) and Duamutef (right leg) appear on the front side. Hapy and Qebehsenuef appear on the back but in simple *imakhu-kher* formulae. On the coffin of Senebtisi (L4) Duamutef is connected with the left (?) arm. The Amset spell is mostly destroyed. On the coffin of Khnumnakht (S3) the children of Horus are not connected with the limbs but with the body in general. Amset unites the flesh, Duamutef the bones.[257] On the coffin of Senusretankh (Ha1) this connection with body parts is not visible.

In the Thirteenth Dynasty, these spells with the children of Horus became more canonical. Amset is always connected with the left arm and the spell is found on the front (left) side of the coffin. Hapy is connected with the right arm and his spell appears at least once on the right side of the coffin. Duamutef appears so far always in the foot region on the front side of the coffin. On the coffin of Zatsobek (Da3C) he is connected with the left leg. Although the positions of the speeches for Zatsobek's coffin are not recorded, it seems likely that the spell appeared on the left side of the coffin, in the foot region. However, some coffins from Thebes show variations. Here, Duamutef is connected with the right arm, although the spell is placed on the front (left) side of the coffin, in the region of the leg.

7. *Words spoken by Nephthys: I have come to embrace you, NN*

The spell and its variations appears most often on the short end of the coffin, either in the horizontal line or in the columns. In this spell Nephthys takes care of the deceased.

unknown position: Awibre Hor (Da4C)
foot end: NN (T2War), Nubherredi (T7C), Senebhenaf (Aby7)
front (column): Ikhet (T6NY)

8. *Words spoken by Isis: I have come to raise your head, to embrace [your] bones*

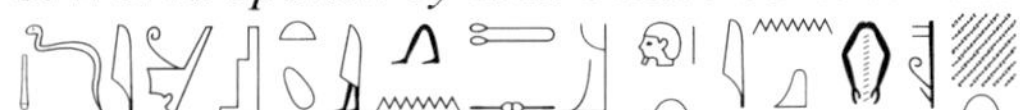

The spell appears on the head end on the coffin of Nubherredi (T7C)[258]

VII. The texts on the lid.

For many coffins with 'speeches of gods', the lid is not preserved, so it is only possible to make some general statements. In the earlier Middle Kingdom an offering formula invoking Anubis was common on the lid.[259] Most lids of the late Middle Kingdom and of the Second Intermediate Period have three lines of texts, although one line is also still attested (Awibre Hor [Da4C] and Nubheteptikhered [Da2C]) for other coffins. For the texts, in general two groups are visible. On several coffins appear spells around the sky goddess Nut, already well known from some coffins of the mid Twelfth Dynasty. This is Pyramid Text spell 368 (638) on Da3-5C, T3Be, Ha1, perhaps also on Hu2. These spell seems to have become standard by the late Twelfth Dynasty.

So far, additionally attested at Thebes (T13C, T34) are the Pyramid Text Spells 252 (272-273a) and 253 (275a-d), appearing on the coffins with 'speeches of gods'. PT 252 seems to confirm that the deceased finally becomes a god (*Lift up your face, you Gods who are in the Duat! NN has come, that you might see*

[256] Altenmüller, *Synkretismus in den Sargtexten*, 151 (a spell found on the early Middle Kingdom coffin of Ima from Thebes); compare Nyord, *Breathing Flesh*, 512-518, especially 515.
[257] Only the front side of the coffin is so far published.
[258] In the orginal the order of the signs is slightly garbled.
[259] Willems, *Chests of Life*, 171-74.

him having become a great god. Lead NN with trembling attire). PT 253 (275a-d) relates to the 'Fields of Yaru', which in the next world is located in the sky: '*He is purified who has purified himself in the Fields of Rushes.*
Re has purified himself in the Fields of Rushes. He is purified, who has purified himself in the Fields of Rushes. This NN has purified himself in the Fields of Rushes'[260] Therefore the placing of the spell on the coffin lid seems logical.[261] The Fields of Rushes appear several times in Pyramid and Coffin Texts. According to Harold Hays, over time there is shift of function visible. In the Old Kingdom they were the place of purification, while in the Middle Kingdom they appear more often as the place of provision of food for the deceased.[262] Interestingly, on the coffins of the Second Intermediate Period there appears the Pyramid Text spell in which the Old Kingdom concept of purification is so important.

Summary

The text decoration on the coffins with 'speeches of gods' shows a combination of different aspects. Several spells clearly relate to the hourly vigil. The children of Horus are coming to fix the arms and the legs of the deceased. The 'opening of the face' formula has a solar aspect. The same is true for the Nefertem-spell, which replaced the 'opening of the face' formula in Upper Egypt at one point in the Thirteenth Dynasty. The Anubis spell on the back of the coffin reflects the wish for the right placement of the deceased's body in the tomb and the western desert. The arms of Anubis express the typical position of that god who is concerned with the mummy.[263] On the head end is found the spell, fixing the deceased between the stars of the sky. All spells found on the lid relate to the sky too. There is mentioned Nut, the sky goddess, and there are the 'Fields of Yaru' and the 'Fields of Rushes'. These are the places where the deceased wished to stay.

[260] Krauss: *Astronomische Konzepte und Jenseitsvorstellungen in den Pyramidentexten*, 275-78.
[261] For sure on T13C, T7NY and T34; also on the model coffin of Khonsu (CG 48404).
[262] Hays, in Bickel, Mathieu, *D'un monde à l'autre, Textes des Pyramides & Texts des Sarcophages*, 175-200
[263] Assmann, *Ägyptische Totenliturgien, I, Totenliturgien in den Sargtexten des Mittleren Reiches*, 146 (6).

Coffin text spell 777

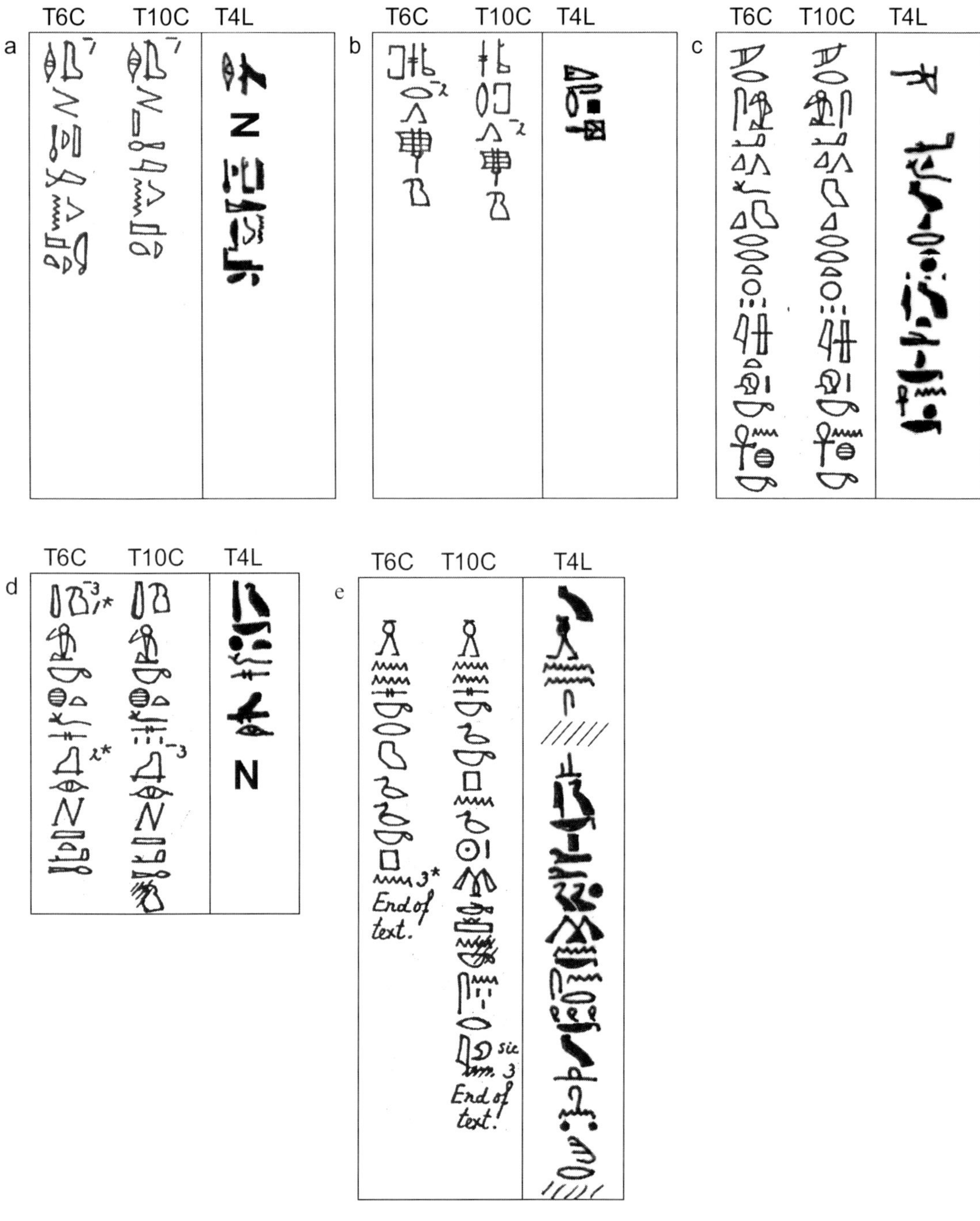

T6C, T10C according to A. de Buck, *The Egyptian coffin texts*, VI, Chicago 1956, 410-414

Coffin Text spell 778

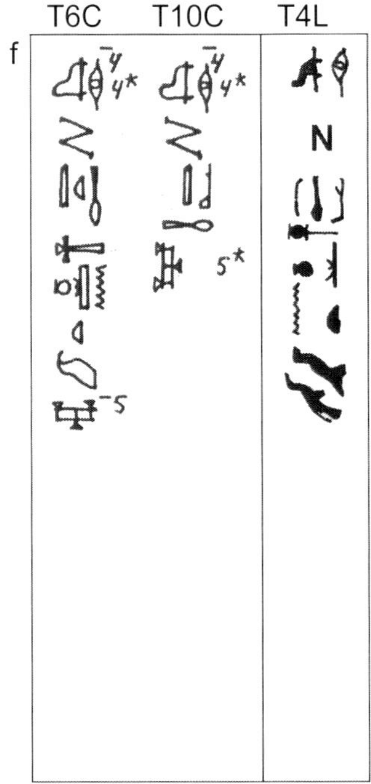

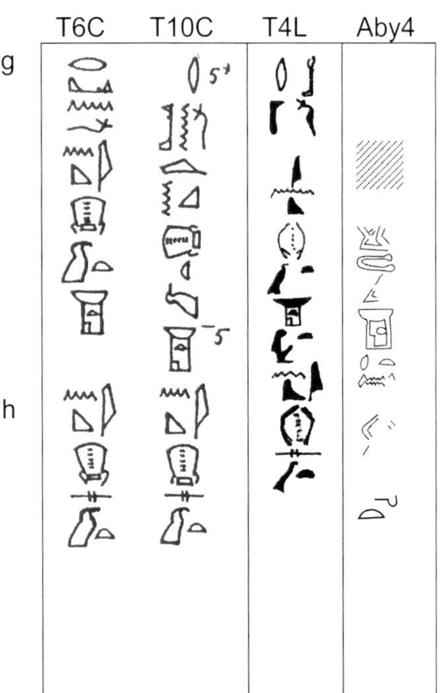

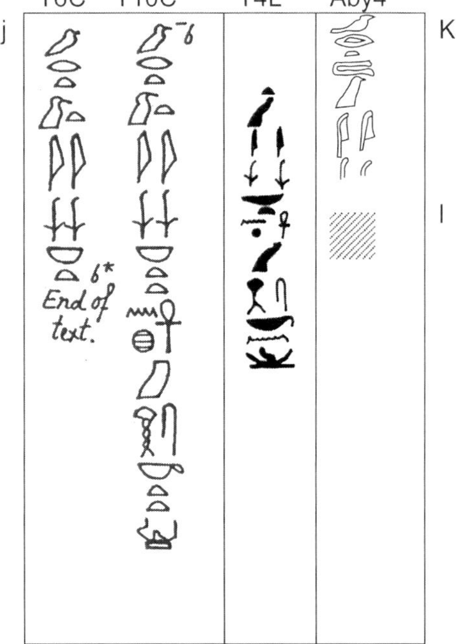

T10C T4L

K

l

6*
End of text.

Coffin Text spell 779

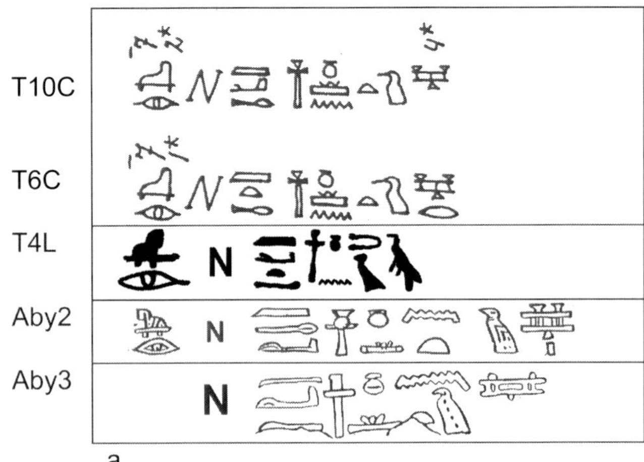

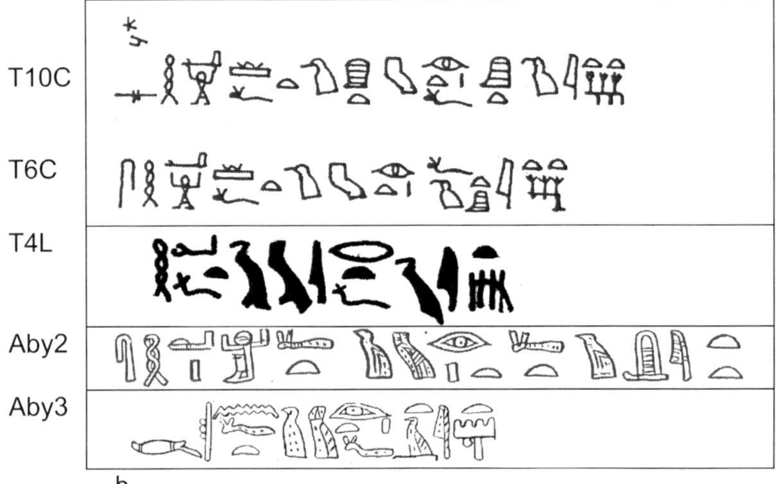

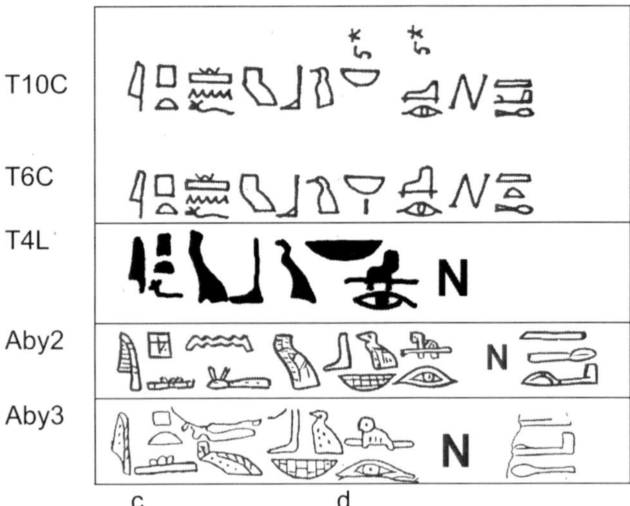

T10C
T6C
T4L
Aby2
Aby3
e

T10C
Sp. 780 follows.
T6C
3* End of text.
T4L
Aby2
Aby3
f

Coffin Text spell 780

	T6C	T10C	T4L	Aby2	Aby3	Aby4	Aby5
g							
h							

	T6C	T10C	T4L	Aby2	Aby4
i					
j					

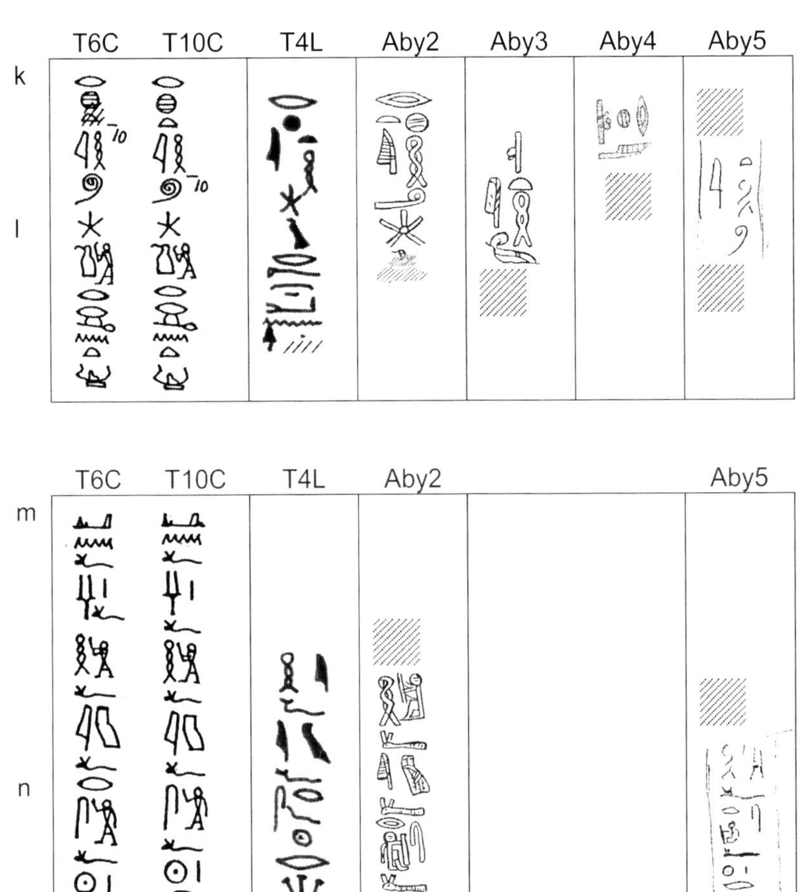

	T6C	T10C	T4L	Aby2		Aby5
m						
n	8* Sp.781 follows.	8* Sp.781 follows.	T4L[1] foll.			

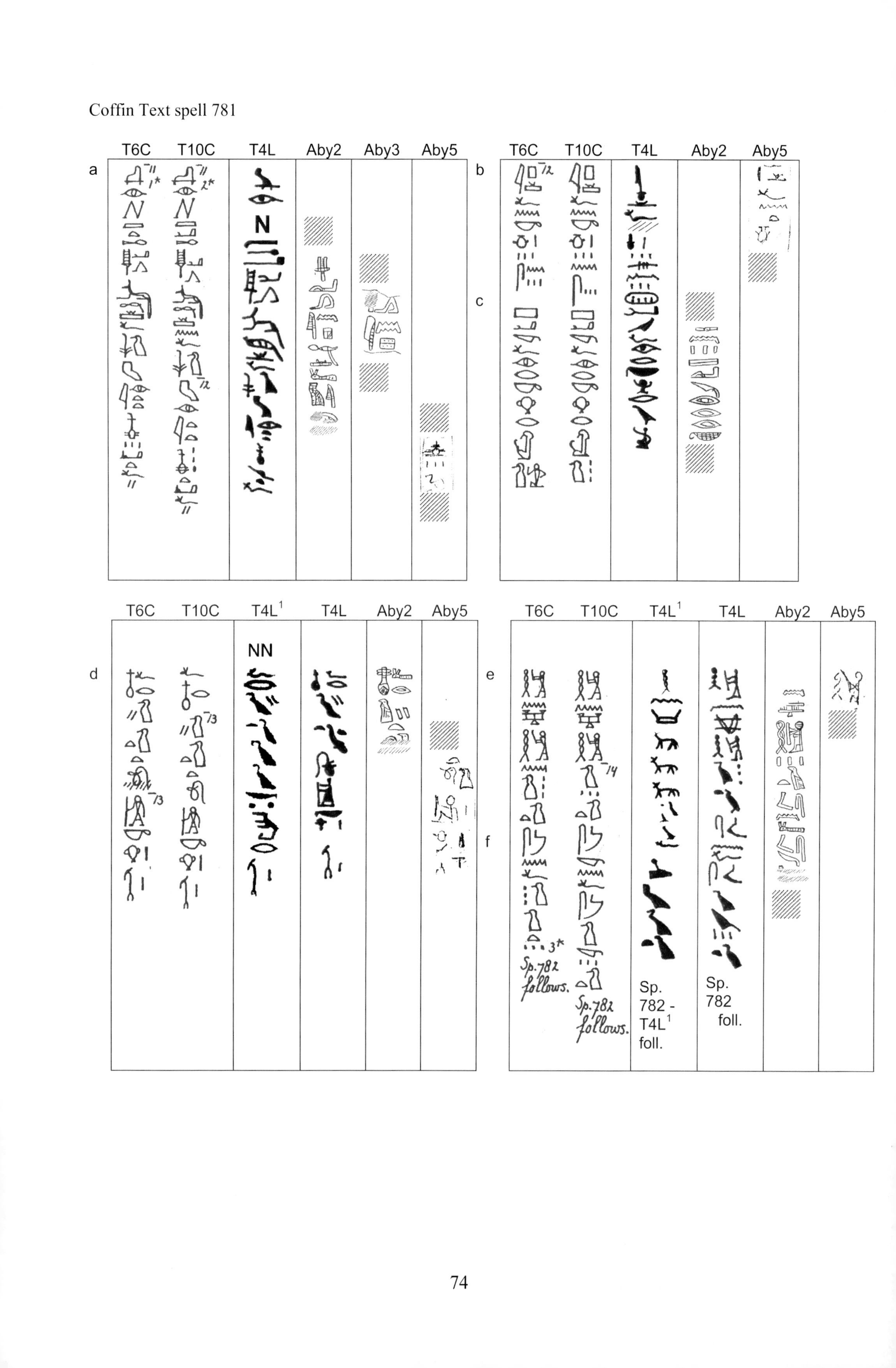

Coffin Text spell 781

	T6C	T10C	T4L	Aby2	Aby3	Aby5
a						

	T6C	T10C	T4L	Aby2	Aby5
b					
c					

	T6C	T10C	T4L[1]	T4L	Aby2	Aby5
d			NN			

	T6C	T10C	T4L[1]	T4L	Aby2	Aby5
e						
f	*Sp. 782 follows.*	*Sp. 782 follows.*	Sp. 782 - T4L[1] foll.	Sp. 782 foll.		

Coffin Text spell 782

g

T6C	T10C	T4L[1]	T4L	Aby2	Aby3	Aby5
14 1* 4*	[14] 2* 15	2				2

h

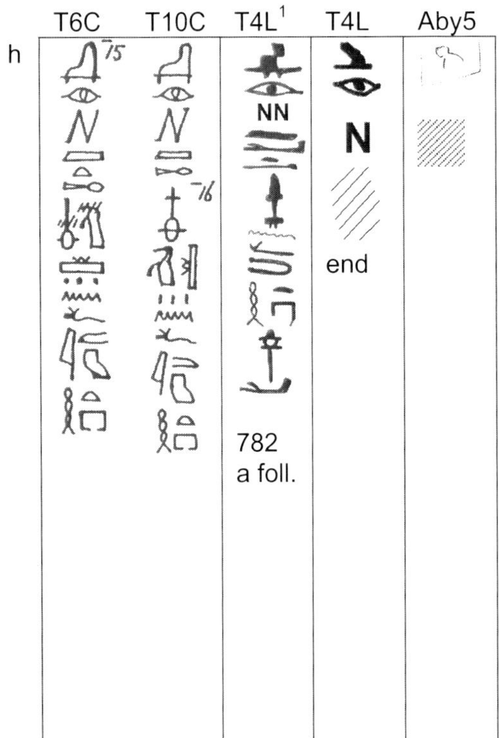

i

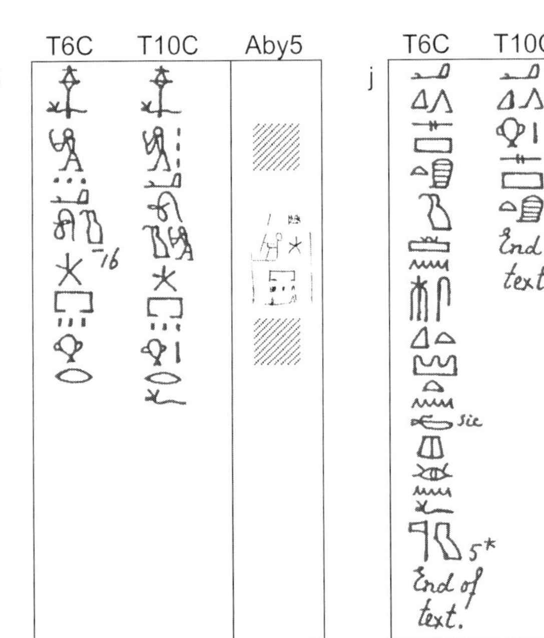

j

T6C	T10C
sic 5* End of text.	5* End of text.

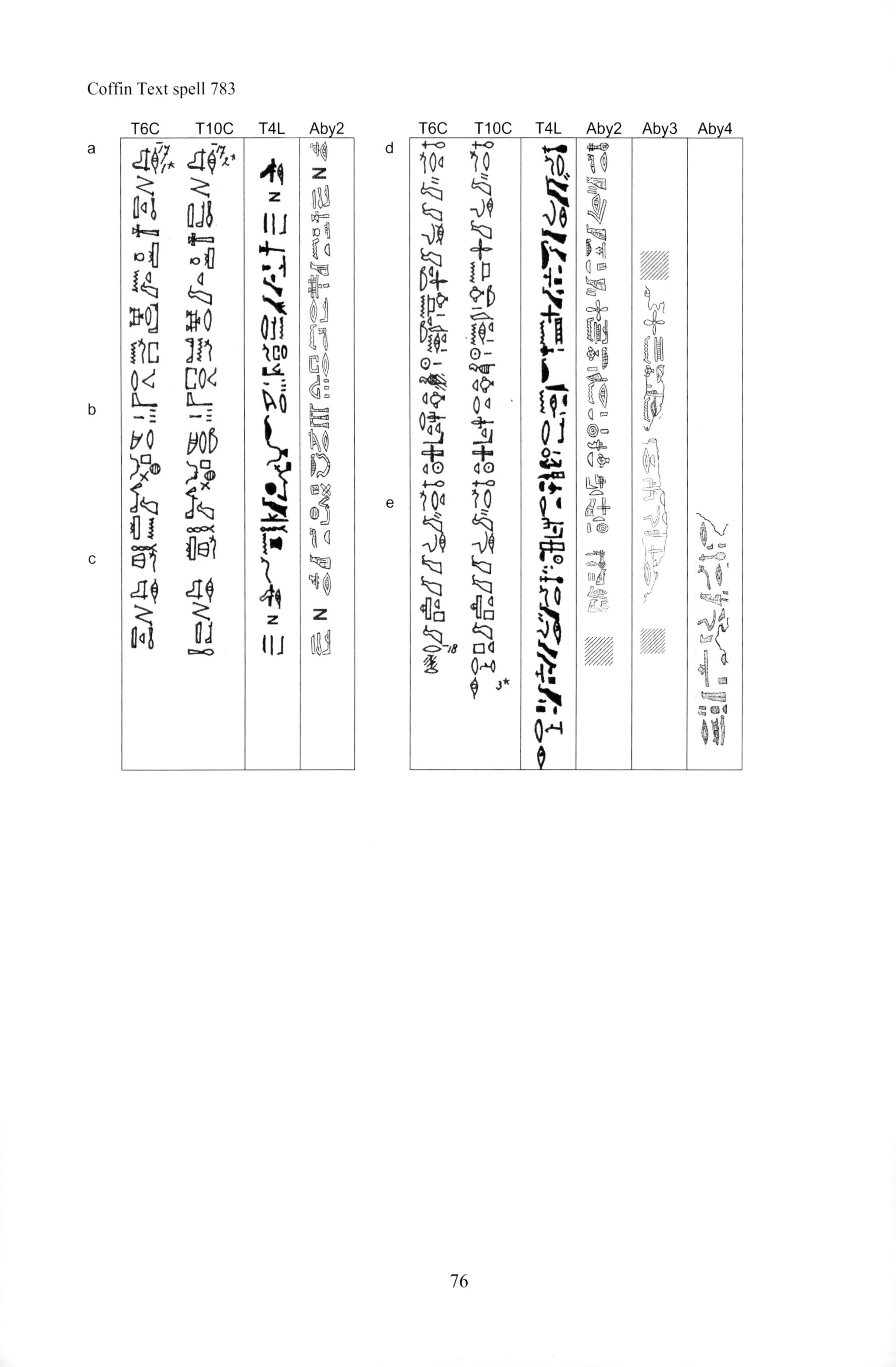

Coffin Text spell 783

	T6C	T10C	T4L	Aby2
a				
b				
c				

	T6C	T10C	T4L	Aby2	Aby3	Aby4
d						
e						

	T6C	T10C	T4L	Aby2	Aby4
f					
g			N	N	
h			N	N	

	T6C	T10C	T4L	Aby2	Aby4
i					
j			N	N	
k					

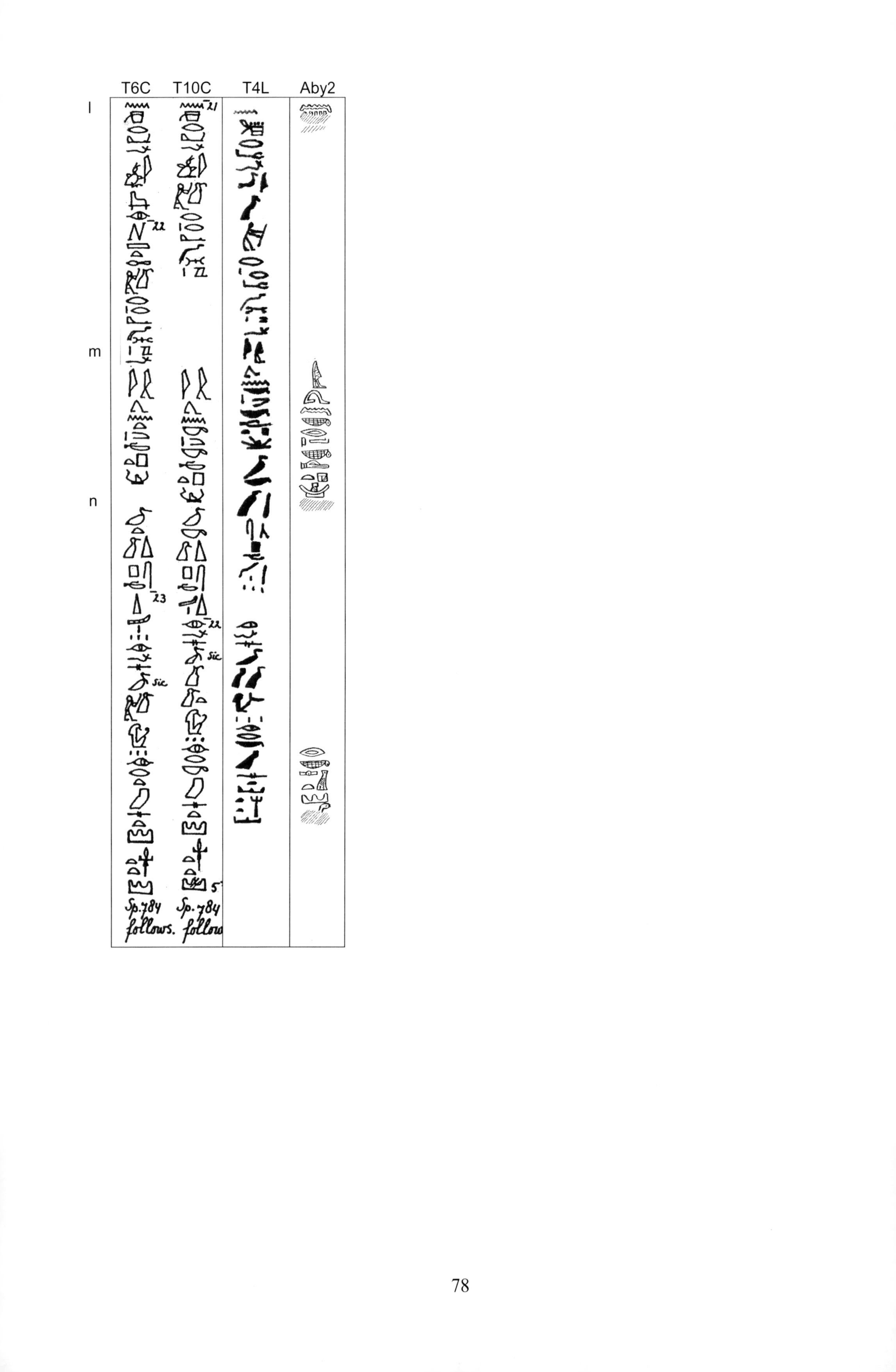

	T6C	T10C	T4L	Aby2
l	22	21		
m	23	22		
n	sic	sic		
	Sp. 784 follows.	5 Sp. 784 follow[s.]		

Coffin Text spell 784

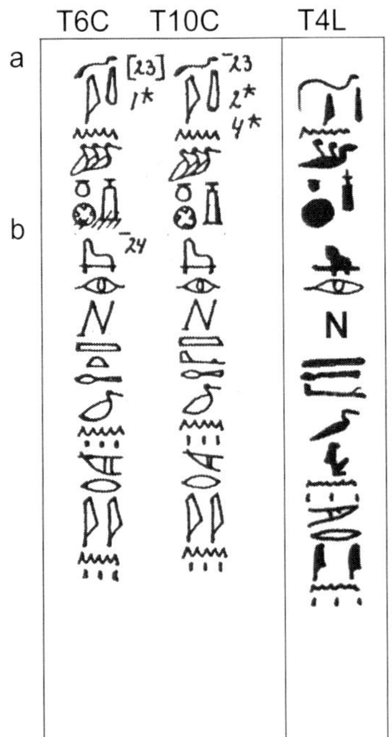

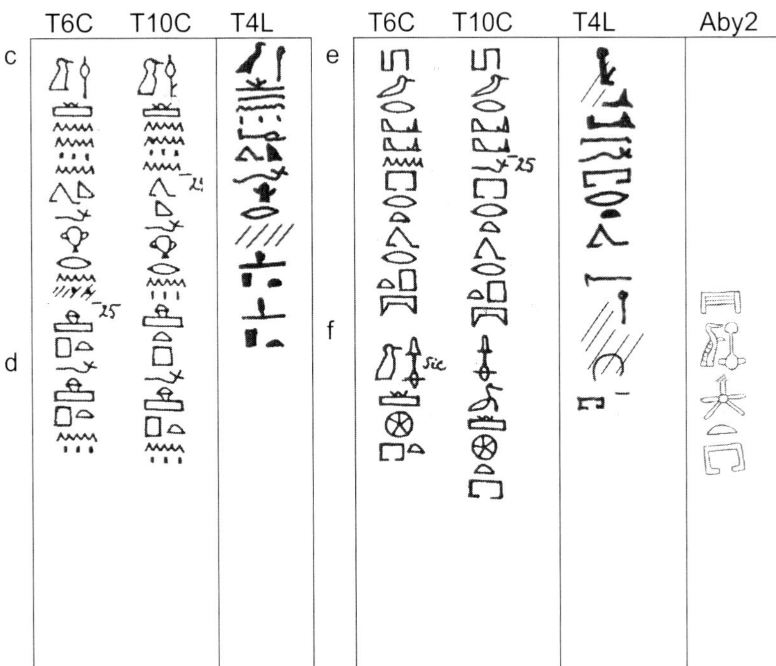

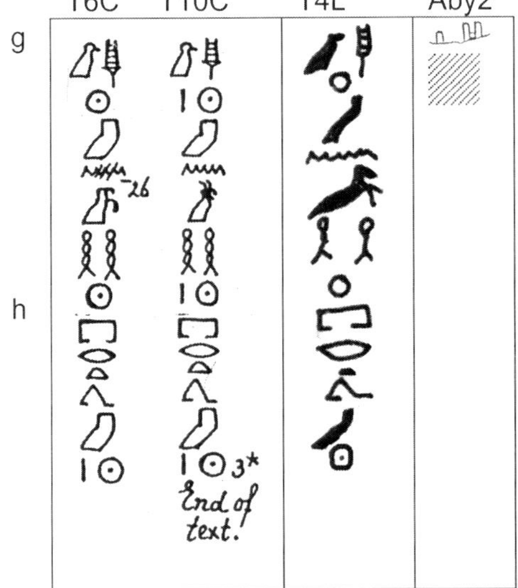

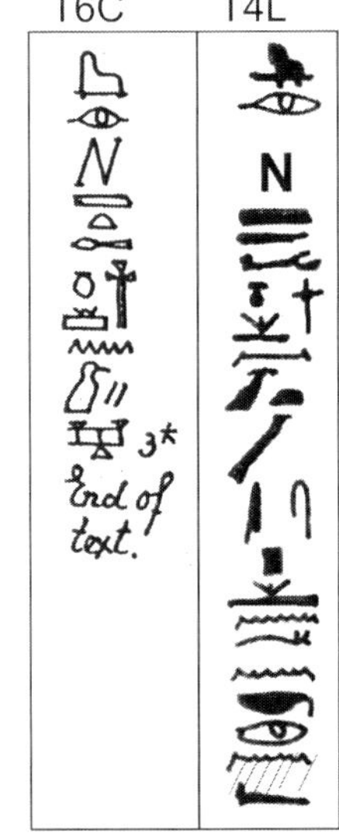

Coffin Text spell 785

	T6C	T10C
j		
k		
l		

	T6C	T10C
m		
n		

	T6C	T10C	Aby3
o			
p			
q			
r			

	T6C	T10C
s	9*	
t	24	
u		

	T6C	T10C	Aby3
v		22	
w	10* 10*		
x			

	T6C	T10C
y	9* 11* End of text. 12*	14*
z		12* End of text.

Translations and comments

CT 777 (on T6C, T10C, T4L, Aby4)

ꜣst-irt NN mꜣꜥ-ḫrw ii n.k ꜣst di.s pri ṯꜣw
mr.s ꜥḳ m ḳrrt imt tp (a).*k*
ꜥnḫ.k mdw.k ḫft.s ꜣst-irt NN mꜣꜥ-ḫrw

the end:

T6C *ini n.s krmwi k pn*
T10C *ini n.s k[rm].k pn rꜥ ḏmd.n.k sn r iwf*
T4L *m ini. n.s* [...] *iw k[rm] p[n] rꜥ ḏmd.n.k sn iwf m ḥtp.sn r* [...]

Comments: (a) On T4L appears here a 'd' (Gardiner D46), perhaps a mistake?

Osiris NN, true of voice, Isis has come to you, she may cause the forthcoming of air,
for she wants that it enters the holes which are in your head ,
so that you might live and speak to her, NN.
T6C : *She has brought these your two kerem (?)-birds.*
T10C: *She has brought the k[erem?]-bird, on the day when you have joined them for flesh.*[264]
T4L*: after she has brought this ... k[erem?]-bird, on the day they unite for you your flesh and are satisfied with you...*

This spell is found on the head end of the coffin. The main figure is Isis[265], here mainly responsible for bringing back the breath to the deceased.[266] The contents of the spell relates to this position on the coffin, at the head end.

CT 778 (on T6C, T10C, T4L, Aby2, Aby3)

ꜣst-irt NN mꜣꜥ-ḫrw nḏ.tw (a) *ḥrw*
rdi.n.f inḳ.tw nbt-ḥwt
inḳ.s tw
ḳd.s tw m rn.s n sšꜣt nbt iḳdw
wrt twii nn nbt

T10C, T4L *ꜥnḫ m sktt*
wṯs.t ḥrw ini.s n.k

T4L *sw ꜥnḫ.k snb*

Comments:
(a) *nḏ.tw* is missing on T10C

Only on T6C, T4L: *Osiris NN*: *Horus has protected you.*
T10C: *NN Horus*
He has caused Nephthys to embrace you and she will embrace you.
She will build you in her name of 'Seshat, mistress of builders'.
The great one it is her, the lady
Only on T10C, T4L: *of life in the night bark, who raises Horus, whom she has brought to you,*
Only on T4L: *that you might live and be healthy.*

---

[264] For the last word as 'flesh', see Nyord, *Breathing Flesh*, 337, n. 3499.
[265] For Isis in the Coffin Texts see in general: Altenmüller, *Synkretismus in den Sargtexten*, 92-94.
[266] Nyord, *Breathing Flesh*, 149.

The spell always appears on the foot end of the coffin. Here, Horus is telling Nephthys[267] to embrace the deceased. After that the goddess builds up the body of the deceased, from which she takes the name 'Seshat, mistress of builders'. Nephthys as 'Seshat', builder of the human body, appears already in the Pyramid Texts (PT 616a-c (364)).[268]

CT 779 (on T6C, T10, T4l, Aby2, Aby3)

ꜣst-irt NN mꜣꜥ-ḫrw nd.tw ḥrw (a)
sḥꜥ.f tw (b) *m irt.f tꜣitt* (Aby3: *mḥ.f m irt.f tꜣit*)
ipt.n.f m bw nb
NN mꜣꜥ-ḫrw mnw.n.k sšrw.k rdit n.k n rnnwtt imit-ḥꜥt ḥrw
ḥḏ-ḥr.k (c) *ḥtp.k*
T10C, T4L, Aby2, Aby3 *m rn.k n ḥḏ-ḥtp*

Osiris NN, Horus has protected you.
He makes you joyful (on Aby3: *he has filled you*) *by means of his woven eye*
which he allotted in every place.
NN, take your linen, that was been given you by Renenutet, who is on the brow[269] *of Horus,*
so that your face may shine and be content
Only on T10C, T4L, Aby2, Aby3: *in your name Hedjhotep.*

(a) On the most coffins Horus is written with the street signs (Gardiner N31), only on T4L with the Horus bird.
(b) on T10C appears here an additional *tꜣ*, most likely a mistake
(c) on Aby3: *sḥḏ-ḥr.k*

The text is always found on the back of the coffin. Its main concern is the linen for the deceased which was essential for the last stage of mummification. The linen was given by Renenutet, who is at the forehead of Horus. The face of the deceased is described as bright in the name of Hedjhotep, who is identified with the deceased.

In the Coffin Texts Renenutet is most often described as being a snake at the forehead and also appears in this spell in this position.[270] Hedjhotep is a god related to garment and weavers. In other sources he supplies the dead with the linen.[271]

CT 780 (on T6C, T10C, T4L, Aby2, Aby3, Aby4, Aby5)

ḏd mdw in bꜣw imntiw
ꜣst-irt NN mꜣꜥ-ḫrw ii ḥr wꜣwt štꜣw
sn.n.f sbꜣw nwn
spr.n.f sbꜣ
prt r pd (T4L, Aby4: *pt*; Aby2: *dpt*)
rḫt iḥ sbꜣ r ḫnt
di n.f ꜥḥꜥ.f ḥw.f im.f sr.f rꜥ r ḥꜣt (T10C, T4L: *wiꜣ*)

Words spoken by the western souls:
NN is the one to come on the hidden paths,
he has opened the gates of the Abyss,
he has reached the gate,

[267] For Nephthys in the Coffin Texts in general: Altenmüller, *Synkretismus in den Sargtexten*, 92-94.
[268] Roeder, *Mit dem Auge sehen*, 288; Budde, *Die Göttin Seschat*, 174-75.
[269] For the 'brow' (*ḥꜣt*) in Coffin Texts: Nyord, *Breathing Flesh*, 170-74.
[270] Altenmüller, *Synkretismus in den Sargtexten*, 124.
[271] Backes, *Rituelle Wirklichkeit*, 93.

*to ascend to the deck (*T4L, Aby4: sky; Aby2: boat),
who knows the rope(s) and who teaches to row.
His sceptre is given to him and he strikes with it when he announces the day in the bow[272]
Only on T10C, T4L: *of the sacred bark.*

The spell appears most often on the back of the coffin. The 'western souls'[273] appear in several Coffin Text spells. In CT 160 (II, 387) they are named as Ra, Sobek and Seth (in some other versions Hathor instead of Ra and Atum instead of Ra appear). They guide the deceased through the underworld. In this context, they appear in this spell too. Here the deceased is walking on the ways of 'western souls' and is passing the 'gates of Nun'.

CT 781 (on T6C, T10C, T4L, Aby2, Aby3, Aby5)
On T4L appears the spell twice in slightly different versions.

ꜣst-irt NN mꜣꜥ-ḫrw ꜥḥꜥ inpw mḥ.n.f sw m irtt mwt.f
ip.f n.k mhrw.sn šꜥ.f iri r.k ḥri mniw
nfr wi twꜣ.k ḥr wꜣs
(for T4L[1] see below)
ḥw.n.hrw ḥw.tw
smꜣ.n.f smꜣw.tw
(for T4L[1]): *hw.n.ḥrw gḥsw … smꜣw*

NN, Anubis is standing there, after he had filled himself with the milk of his mother[274]*;*
he can count to you her (milk) jars and cut the ones who are against you, master of herdsmen,
(for T4L[1] see below) *Horus has beaten those who has beaten you, he has slain those who would slay you who have act against you*

(T4L[1]): *Osiris NN how beautiful you are, when you lean on the was-sceptre,*
Horus has beaten the gazelles and had killed ...

In the Coffin Texts, milk has the main function of nourishment. In this spell Anubis has drunk it to give it to the deceased.[275]

CT 782 (on T6C, T10C, T4L, Aby2, Aby3, Aby5)

ḏd mdw in nfrw kꜣw nbw ḫrt wnniiw ḥḥ
ꜣst-irt NN mꜣꜥ-ḫrw wbꜣw n.f imḥt
ḫsfw ꜥwꜣ dwꜣt ḥr.f
ꜥḳ (ḥr) sšꜣt
(Only on T6C): *n mskt n dgꜣ n.f nṯr im*

Words spoken by those whose kas are fine, the lords of possessions, who will be for ever;
NN, for whom the cave is opened,
driven away for him are the robbers of the underworld.
Enter into the secret place.
Only on T6C: *of the Mesqet (= Milky Way), because see for yourself, the god in it.*[276]

The spell is again concerned with finding the way through the Underworld.

---

[272] The 'bow' of ships appears often in Coffin Texts, Nyord, *Breathing Flesh*, 173, n. 1387.
[273] Leitz, *Lexikon der ägyptischen Götter und Götterbezeichnungen II*, 715-16.
[274] Willems, in W. Clarysse, A. Schoors, H. Willems (editors), *Egyptian Religion, The Last Thousand Years, I, Studies dedicated to the Memory of Jan Quagebeur*, 736-737 translates 'who reckons the hearts of the enemies'
[275] Nyord, *Breathing Flesh*, 330.
[276] compare: Willems, *The Coffin of Heqata*, 265-66.

CT 783 (on T6C, T10C, T4L, Aby2, Aby3)
ꜣst-irt NN nḏ.n.tw ḥrw
rdi.n.f pri nṯrw mr.k wp ḫw
ꜣst-irt Nn mꜣꜥ ḫrw nfrw wi mꜣ.k (T10: *mꜣ*)
wn ḥr.k in irt imntt ḥr iꜣbtt imt rꜥ
nfr wi mꜣꜣ ḥtp w(i) ptr šsp ḥrw nswt.f
ꜣst-irt NN mꜣꜥ-ḫrw ḳd.f sw wn kꜣ.f im
ꜣst-irt NN zꜣ.k ḥrw ḳd.n.f (T10C *ḳd.f*) *tw*
zꜣwti.ky šw tfnwt ḳd.tw
ꜣst-irt NN nḏ.n tw ḥrw
stm.n.f ꜥrty ḫftiw.k
nḏr.f itꜣ (T6C: NN) *r rꜣ ꜥḏt*
ii n.k gs.k-dpt
zꜣ.k spdw spd jbḥ iri.f zꜣwtiw irri.k m zmit-iꜣbt

NN, Horus has protected you
and he has caused the gods to go forth, and you shall desire that the protection will be opened.
NN, how happy are you who see.
Your vision is cleared by the right Eye of Ra which is on the left on the day.
How happy are they who see, how pleased are they who behold, when Horus takes his thrones!
NN forms himself so that his ka may exist thereby;
NN is your son, O Horus, and he has formed you.
O you twins Shu and Tefnut form yourselves.
O NN, Horus has protected you
and he has shut fast the jaws of your foes;
he has seized him who would take (you) to the place of his slaughter. Your protection comes to you
and your son Sopdu the-sharp-toothed acts as protector from whoever would harm the eastern desert.

The spell appears always on the front side of the coffin. The main subject is the protection of the deceased through Horus and the opening of the face of the deceased by the right eye of Ra. Finally the recreating of the deceased is mentioned. The opening of the eye of Ra appears several times in the Coffin Texts.[277] The spell seems to have a strong connection to the 'Opening of the Face'[278] spell often found on late Middle Kingdom coffins and is also placed at the same position on the coffins. The latter spell has a clear solar aspect.

Sopdu, the-sharp-toothed is already attested in the Pyramid Texts and several times in the Coffin Texts. The meaning of the-sharp-toothed is not clear.[279]

CT 784 (T6C, T10C, T4L, Aby2)
ḏd mdw in bꜣw iwnw ꜣst-irt NN mꜣꜥ-ḫrw zꜣ.n mry.n
wḏ.n.n ꜥḳ.f ḥr.n ḥtp.f ḥtp.n
mr-wr dd prt r pt
wbꜣ dwꜣ ꜥḥꜥ m nhh prt m rꜥ
T6C, T4L*: nḏ tw ḥrw*
T4L: *sip n.f n.k*

Words spoken by the souls of Iunu (Heliopolis), Osiris NN, true of voice, our son, our beloved,
we have commanded that that he will enter into us and he might rest in our peace.
Mnevis grants ascent to the sky,
the underworld is open for a lifetime in eternity, for going out on day,
only on T6C, T4L: *O NN, Horus had protected you.*

277 Altenmüller, *Synkretismus in den Sargtexten*, 117.
278 Lohwasser, *Die Formel 'Öffnen des Gesichts'*.
279 Altenmüller, *Synkretismus in den Sargtexten*, 189-90.

only on T4L: *after he forwarded to you…*

The text also always appears on the front of the coffin. The 'souls of Heliopolis' are already known from the Pyramid Texts.[280] They allow the deceased to come to them, while the Mnevis-bull gives access to the way to the sky. The spell has a strong relation to solar aspects. The 'souls of Heliopolis' and the Mnevis-bull are clearly connected to the sun god.[281]

CT 785 (T4C, T10C, Aby3)
ꜣst-irt NN mꜣꜥ-ḫrw tm ḫpr.n.k m rn.k n nṯrw
šm.n.k iw.k sḏr.k rs.k
dr r ḏww ḏbꜣ m iwf.k
mḥ.ti ḫtm.ti m irt-ḥrw
ꜥḥꜥ NN mꜣꜥ-ḫrw nḏ.tw ḥrw
rdi.f n.k Ntrw iṯt (iḫt?).sn m rn.k n ḥwt-sr
mr.n.sn n.k (T6C: m) *ꜥrw*
sḥḏ ḥr.k m ḥḏ
wrt ḥKꜣw.k ꜥꜣ pḥty
šnn n.k nṯrw nbw iḫwt nbwt
isṯ m rn.k n pḫr ḥꜥw-nbw
ꜣst-irt NN mꜣꜥ-ḫrw nb-imꜣḫ
ḳd.k pw ipn wn.k im.f tp tꜣ
ꜥnḫ.ti nhm.k rꜥ nb
wn ḥr.k mꜣ.k rꜥ
ꜣḫ ꜥnꜥ ḏd m rn.k ꜣḫt
fꜣ.f t' n iwtt t'.f wnwt snw.sn n ḫꜣꜣ NN

Oh NN, you have not changed your name of the fathers (T6C: *father*) *of gods.*
You have come and will return whether you have slept or whether you have woken.
Remove the efflux which exuded from your flesh,
you being filled and provided with the Eye of Horus.
Stand up N. Horus has protected you.
He give the gods to you, so take the possession of them in your name of the House-of-the-Noble.
They have loved you and they flee near you;
your face is illumined in the chapel.[282]
O mighty of your magic, greatly strong,
the gods, the lords of all things, circulate about you,
in your name of him who goes about the Isles.
O NN, This is your form, in which you were on earth through him,
you being alive so that you may travel about daily;
your vision is restored so that you may see the sun,
be a spirit, O Baboon, placed in your name of Horizon.
He lifts bread to him who has no bread in the second hour of the night, Oh NN.

This long spell seems to relate to the hourly vigil, where Horus is protecting his father Osiris (=the deceased). The first part is about the efflux from the body of the deceased.[283] The deceased is filled and provided with the eye of Horus after the efflux is removed. In several Coffin Text spells the deceased received the Eye of Horus as nourishment, which seems to be the main meaning of this phrase.[284] Anubis is

[280] Leitz, *Lexikon der ägyptischen Götter und Götterbezeichnungen II*, 713-15.
[281] Willems, *Chests of Life*, 151-54.
[282] Translation: Roeder, *Mit dem Auge sehen,* 321-22; Nyord, *Breathing Flesh*, 160, 1179 reads *ḥḏ-ḥtp.* However, 'Chapel' (*ḥḏ*) seems to fit better.
[283] Nyord, *Breathing Flesh*, 463-464.
[284] Nyord, *Breathing Flesh*, 183; compare also CT 934 (VII, 134a-136i), where offerings to the deceased are labelled as 'Eye of Horus', Willems, H., *The Coffin of Heaqata*, 83-85, 393-403.

forming the deceased. Further aspects are the free movements of the deceased. The spell contains again a reference to the 'opening of the face/vision' to see the sun.[285]

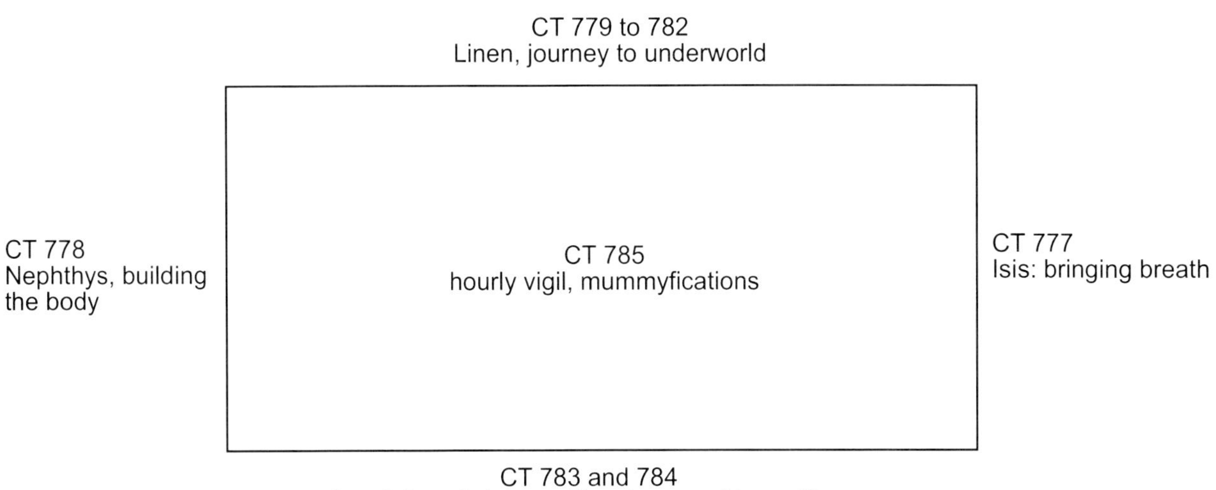

[285] Compare discussion: Nyord, *Breathing Flesh*, 156-57.

Chapter Six: Conclusions

Coffins of the late Twelfth Dynasty

In the late Twelfth Dynasty (after Senusret III) several coffin designs are attested. Most coffins were decorated with one horizontal line at the top and four columns on the long sides and two columns on the short ends. On the short sides often appear images of Isis and Nephthys. Furthermore, several coffins are decorated with a false door under the wedjat eyes on the front or with a palace façade all around. Inner decorations with Coffin Texts are no longer common as in the early Twelfth Dynasty. However, it should be clearly said that there are big problems to date single coffins. Many do not come from proper excavations and other finds from their tomb groups are not published or are basically lost. The prosopographical data of people mentioned on coffins are often limited making it hard to identify the coffin owners with people known from other sources.

In terms of texts there appear in the late Twelfth Dynasty the coffins with pyramidion spells on the long horizontal lines (Ha3, M20, T3Be) and the 'speeches of gods' in the columns (Ha1, L4, Maz1, S3). The 'speeches of gods' show a great variety and it is hard to establish certain rules. However, it is clear that many of them relate to the hourly vigil (*Stundenwache*) and the embalming place of the deceased. A special group of coffins is known for several royal women. Here, the middle coffins are sparsely decorated, with few or no inscriptions on the outside and texts only on the inside (Da1C, Da2X, Da3X, Da4X), or with just one inscription on the lid (L5). These coffins are called 'court type coffins'. At about the same time, an innovation appears on the coffin of a certain Khnumnakht (S3). The main decoration is that of Willems' type IV scheme with a horizontal text line at the top and four columns on the long sides, and two columns on the short sides. However, between the columns on the long sides are added further columns with 'speeches of gods', written in a different style and not fully coloured as the hieroglyphs in the main columns. Altogther, the coffin is decorated on the front with ten columns. The coffin is not inscribed on the inner sides, but there seems to be a wish to add further texts on the coffin.

The 'court type coffins'

In the publication of the Senebtisi burial the term 'court type coffin' was created.[286] It refers to the middle coffin of Senebtisi which was decorated with just one inscribed band of gold at the top. The simplicity of the decoration in connection with the rich use of gold was used as the main element for describing a coffin type. In the publication several further coffins are provided as parallels.[287] These include the coffins of king Awibre Hor (DaC4) and Nubhetepti-khered (Da2C), because they are also decorated with gold foil.[288] However, a clear distinction should be made between the material and the general style of a coffin (wood with gold foil) and the texts of these coffins. Indeed, the text programme on the coffins of king Awibre Hor and Nubhetepti-khered is in many respect identical to other coffins found in different parts of Egypt and they just repeat a common text pattern of the Thirteenth Dynasty found at Dahshur, Abydos, Hu and even as far South as Mirgissa. On all these coffins appear 'speeches of gods', many of them almost identical across the whole country. The coffins of the four royal women buried next to the pyramid of Amenemhat II (Da1C, Da2,3,4X) are totally different and just decorated on the inside. Therefore it seems wise to restrict the label 'court type coffin' to coffins with certain features similar to the middle coffin of Senebtisi.[289] These include gold foil and a very simple outside decoration. Some of these coffins have texts on the inside. These coffins are:

I. The middle coffin of Senebtisi: gold foil, only one text line on the vaulted lid (L5).
II. The four coffins of the royal women buried next to the pyramid of Amenemhat II: gold foil, outside undecorated, vaulted lid, inside is inscribed (Da1C, Da2,3,4X).

---

[286] Mace, Winlock, *The Tomb of Senebtisi at Lisht*, 51, 54-56; compare Williams, *Serapis* 3 (1975-1976), 41-55; Lilyquist, Serapis 5 (1979), 27-28.

[287] Mace, Winlock, *The Tomb of Senebtisi at Lisht*, 32.

[288] In general compare also: Willems, *Chests of Life*, 22, 105; Lapp, in Willems (editor), *The World of the Coffins Texts*, 82.

[289] It might even be asked whether the label 'court type coffin' should be totally dropped.

Other 'court type coffins' are perhaps the inner coffin in tomb no. 10 at Lahun (only gold foil is preserved; it is identical to those on the Dahshur coffins)[290] and those of Hetepet (Sq19X) from Saqqara (no outer decoration, inside decorated with texts). These two coffins are only poorly preserved and so the reconstruction of their original appearance is just a guess.

Coffins of the Thirteenth Dynasty

Most likely, the coffins of the early Thirteenth Dynasty were not different to the examples of the late Twelfth Dynasty. However, few coffins are securely datable to the Thirteenth Dynasty so that any conclusion should be made with great reservation. In the middle of the Thirteenth Dynasty several coffin designs were in use. There were also several text programmes used on these coffin designs. The coffin designs and text programmes are not automatically linked; a certain design can be find with any of the text programmes, although some patterns are visible.

At first, the arrangement of the texts called by Harco Willems *ornamental texts* should be discussed. These are the texts found in the bands on the coffin's outer side. Willems chooses this name to distinguish these ornamental texts from Coffin Texts on the inside.[291] Strictly speaking, the difference between ornamental texts on the outside and the Coffin Texts proper is no longer very useful for the Second Intermediate Period as most coffins were then only decorated on the outside and this decoration includes longer religious texts, some of them, are included in the Coffin Text edition of Adriaan de Buck.

Two trends are visible. Especially, on coffins in Upper Egypt (Thebes, Abydos, Qubbet el-Hawa), the number of columns was increased. On the front up to eight columns could appear, on the back even up to nine. In Lower Egypt and Abydos appear instead of, or as well as coffins with text panels placed between the columns on the outside (Da5X, Da6X, L1Li). Such panels are not yet certainly attested for Twelfth Dynasty coffins, although on some coffins found at Gebelein there are indeed some religious texts on the outside.[292] An offering list on the outside is typical for coffins from Akhmim.[293] These coffins date to the First Intermediate Period and it might be doubted that they had any influence on the coffin development in the Second Intermediate Period. However, in the Twelfth Dynasty is was common to place longer inscriptions on the outside of mastabas.[294] It seems possible that the decoration of panels on coffins was taken directly from there. Texts on the inside of coffins are still known after the Twelfth Dynasty, but are rare. The coffin set of the 'chief lector priest' Sesenebnef (L1-2Li) found at Lisht is in this respect an exception, other examples are the coffins of queen Mentuhotep (T4L) and Herunefer (T6L), (most likely) both found at Thebes. Despite the lack of inside decoration there seems to have been at a certain point a demand for more texts. The inside of the coffins was no longer seen a best place for them and therefore, these longer texts were placed on the coffin outside. There are several types of texts attested on these coffins. They are decorated with Coffin Texts spells 777 to 785 or with pyramidion spells and 'speeches of gods'.[295] These speeches are now more standardised all around the country, if compared with those texts from the late Twelfth Dynasty. There were certainly still many coffins produced with the conventional hetep-di-nisut formula on the long sides and 'revered before' (*im3ḫw ḫr*), followed by the name of a deity, although it is often hard to pinpoint a date for the latter type of coffin. In general, it seems that the coffins at the royal court and those belonging to the highest ruling class were more innovative than those of lower officials and those in the provinces. However, this observation can only be confirmed (or challenged) with the publication of more material.

The longer religious texts, found on the exterior of coffins (in the panels) and on the interior represent a mixture of old and new texts. There are some Coffin Texts, there are some Book of the Dead chapters and there are some texts so far not yet attested anywhere else.

Next to these texts and coffin layouts there are certain details on these coffins typical for the Second Intermediate Period. Several Theban coffins have a black back ground colour (T6C, T10C, T13C, T5-

---

[290] Brunton, *Lahun I*, p. 14.

[291] Willems, *Chests of Life*, 119, 168.

[292] Steindorff, *Grabfunde des Mittleren Reiches in den Königlichen Museen zu Berlin, II. Der Sarg des Sebk-o. – Ein Grabfund aus Gebelein*, 11-19, pl. III-IV; Lapp, *Typologie*, 186

[293] Lapp, *Typologie*, 149

[294] Compare, Allen, *BASOR* 352, November 2008, pl. 1-2, 4-5.

[295] Lapp, in Willems (editor), *The World of the Coffins Texts*, 82-83.

8NY).[296] These coffins are decorated with a high number of columns. They contain 'speeches of gods' or the Coffin Text spells 777-785. Coffins with comparable text programmes (Coffin Text spells 777 – 785) found at Abydos (Aby2-4) have a different back ground decoration; one has painting imitating high quality wood (Aby4) and one other a simple white background (Aby2).

On many of these coffins, but also on several other artifacts placed into the burial chambers of the Second Intermediate Period, the hieroglyphs of animals (birds) are shown without legs or in the case of snakes without tails. These hieroglyphs appear for the first time at the very end of the Twelfth Dynasty on the tomb equipment of the 'king's daughter' Neferuptah[297], daughter of Amenemhat III. These hieroglyphs are common till the end of the Seventeenth Dynasty. It should be noted, that not all coffins of the Second Intermediate Period were decorated with this type of hieroglyphs; there are several examples with 'normal' hieroglyphs. The custom started in the cemeteries of the royal residence, and was later adopted in other parts of the country.[298]

The burial chamber as embalming place/hourly vigil

In this section it will be shown that at the highest court level, coffins and burial equipment often formed a unity. The development seems to have reached its peak under Amenemhat III and in the early Thirteenth Dynasty. The whole burial chamber was arranged like the embalming chamber at the hourly vigil, where the deceased was identified as Osiris and where several deities came to help in the mummification process and in the protection of the deceased. The hourly vigil took place in the night before the dead body was placed into the tomb chamber.[299] The concept of the burial chamber as the embalming chamber at the hourly vigil is still visible at the end of the Thirteenth Dynasty at Thebes and Abydos, although there are noticeable changes in burial equipment and new religious texts appear too. New religious ideas were replacing old ones, while older ones were still alive next to the new ideas.

I. objects from the royal purification tent depicted on coffins

The custom of placing items relating to the royal purification tent into the tomb might go back to the late First Intermediate Period. From Saqqara, there are some early Middle Kingdom coffins where ritual objects relating to royal rituals appear in the 'friezes of objects'. In this context should be mentioned ankh-signs and a sieve, used in ritual at the mummification.[300] Harco Willems has argued that these objects derive indeed from royal rituals connected to the purification tent, and that they appear at Saqqara first, as here were buried the kings of the Old Kingdom and at the end of the First Intermediate these rituals were taken over by high officials and priests, who also used at least some elements of the royal rituals. Outside of the Memphis region these items (but also texts) relating to the purification tent appear first on some coffins found in Upper Egypt (Thebes, Gebelein, Qubbet el-Hawa).[301] These coffins date to the late Eleventh and early Twelfth Dynasty.[302] The next example of a coffin with these objects relating to royal rituals is the sarcophagus of the 'treasurer' Mentuhotep, who was in office in the second part of the reign of Senusret I.[303] After that, the ankh-signs and the sieve are common on many coffins from all parts of Egypt. The decoration of these coffins also include staves and weapons, also found in some of the better preserved tombs of the ruling class. They too might belong to royal rituals.[304]

II. objects from the hourly vigil depicted on coffins and placed into tombs

On coffins and tomb depictions mainly of the Third Intermediate Period a scene occurs showing Osiris lying on a embalming bed. In front of him stands Horus bringing him to life. Around them are arranged several other gods. Evidently, this is a scene from the hourly vigil, where Horus brings his father Osiris to

---

[296] Lapp, *Typologie*, 175
[297] Petrie, *Kahun, Gurob, and Hawara*, 17, pl. V.
[298] Miniaci, *RdE* 61 (2010), 113-134.
[299] Assmann, *Death and Salvation*, 262.
[300] Willems, in van Dijk (editor), *Essays on Ancient Egypt in Honour of Herman te Velde*, 355-57.
[301] Willems, in van Dijk (editor), *Essays on Ancient Egypt in Honour of Herman te Velde*, 353.
[302] Willems, *The Coffin of Heqata*, 25.
[303] Willems, in van Dijk (editor), *Essays on Ancient Egypt in Honour of Herman te Velde*, 356-57.
[304] Willems, *Chests of Life*, 220-21.

life. Under the bed of Osiris are royal insignia. These are crowns, sceptres and weapons. Most of these insignia are identical to those shown in the friezes on the inside of Middle Kingdom coffins and most of these objects are also known as items placed into the burial chambers of the ruling class in the late Middle Kingdom. Because these burials were most often found in cemeteries of the royal court, they were labelled 'court type burials'. From this parallel we can conclude that the 'court type burial' was basically arranged like the embalming chamber at the hourly vigil.

The royal insignia and weapons just described, appear already at the very beginning of the Middle Kingdom in the coffin decorations and even as models in the tomb. One early burial with these elements is that of the local governor Djehutynakht found at Deir el-Bersheh. He dates to the late Eleventh or early Twelfth Dynasty and his burial chamber contained a wooden (model) mace and a was-sceptre.[305] On the coffin of the governor a heqa-sceptre, several staves and a girdle are depicted. There also appears a lion-headed funerary/Osiris bed.[306] We will see that such beds are indeed also known from some high status burials with objects relating to the hourly vigil. It remains uncertain how common this type of burial equipment was in the early Middle Kingdom. Because of the destruction, looting and bad state of publication little is known from these tombs. However, most burials of slightly lower officials as those recorded by J. Garstang for Beni Hasan, do not show these patterns.[307] The main burial goods in these tombs are wooden models of estates and servants, most likely securing the eternal food supply for the deceased.

Fig. 50 Scene from the tomb of king Sheshonq III at Tanis (about 800 BC)[308]

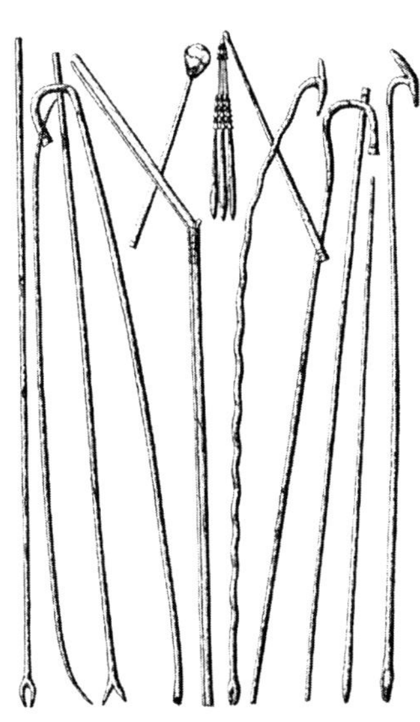

Fig. 51 Weapons and insignia from the tomb of Sesenebnef[309]

However, in the mid Twelfth Dynasty royal insignia became an important element on many coffins all over the country and several royal items were added to the decoration. On the back of the coffin inner side are shown royal crowns, cobras and vultures, but also, not automatically on the same coffins, sticks, royal sceptres and weapons.[310] In the 'court type burials' these royal insignia suddenly became the main items placed into the burial chamber around the deceased. There were no longer wooden models of estates and servants nor even statues of the deceased.

305 Doxey, in: Freed, Berman, Doxey, Picardo, *The Secrets of Tomb 10A, Egypt 2000 BC*, 141, fig. 98, 99.
306 Berman, in: Freed, Berman, Doxey, Picardo, *The Secrets of Tomb 10A, Egypt 2000 BC*, fig. 74, 75.
307 Garstang, *The Burial Customs of Ancient Egypt.*
308 Montet, *Les constructions et le tombeau de Chéchanq III à Tanis*, pl. XXX.
309 Gautier/Jéquier, *Mémoire sur les Fouilles de Licht*, 74-79, fig. 97.
310 Willems, *Chests of Life*, 220-21.

III. From the First Intermediate Period on it is also visible that the deceased was directly identified as Osiris, king of the underworld. This did not so much happen in the 'ornamental texts' but more often in the Coffin Texts.[311] In the 'ornamental texts' this happens rarely. One important example is the anthropoid coffin of Userhet, found at Beni Hassan.[312] It has been noted that in the New Kingdom Book of the Dead papyrus of Nu, the deceased is most often called 'Osiris' in the *s3ḫw* ('glorification') chapters.[313] Indeed the mummified body of the deceased was called *s3ḥ* and early mummiform figures, including anthropoid coffins, seem to represent the deceased in the form of *s3ḥ*.[314] Thus, the deceased was transformed into a divine-like status.[315]

The royal insignia placed into the 'court type burials' almost automatically imply that the deceased using the ritual was identified as Osiris. From the sources it is hard to decide whether the deceased was indeed really identified with the god or whether there was the belief that the deceased should receive the same treatment as that god of the Underworld. However, the royal ritual does not appear on all coffins and only a small number of deceased were called Osiris on their coffin (or on other monuments). Certainly a wider range of rituals and beliefs circulated in the Middle Kingdom. In the late Middle Kingdom, there are now basically two types of burials. At the royal court, the highest elite was buried in 'court type burials'. On the other hand there are many burials of people of lower status where there is often no sign that the deceased was identified as Osiris. Other aspects were seen as more important in these burials.[316]

In the early Middle Kingdom, the focus of the inscriptions on the coffin is a good burial in the West and the eternal food supply. In the Underworld, the deceased most likely kept his status as a human being. At the beginning of the Twelfth Dynasty a shift is visible. The outer decoration of many coffins received additional columns in which several gods appear. These gods are those also appearing in the hourly vigil, the place and ritual where Osiris was mummified and brought back to life.[317] The burial equipment of the early Middle Kingdom often had a different focus. The well known wooden models most likely had the task of securing the eternal food supply. Only certain objects, not regularly found in burials had different functions. Here a set of staves from the tomb of Gemniemhat (Saqqara) should be mentioned.[318]

In the late Middle Kingdom the hourly vigil becomes most important.[319] The outer decoration of many late Twelfth and almost all decorated Thirteenth Dynasty coffins relate to a great part to the hourly vigil. Offering formulae almost totally disappear. This is no longer just visible on the coffin inscriptions. In the burial equipment of the late Twelfth and early Thirteenth Dynasty, belonging to the highest level of the ruling class, objects were found also relating to the hourly vigil. This development seems to have reached its peak in the early Thirteenth Dynasty, when the text on the coffin exterior and the whole tomb decoration seem to have formed one unit, representing the hourly vigil. The 'speeches of gods' relate in particular to the ritual. There are the children of Horus taking care of the legs and arms of the deceased; Isis and Nephthys are taking further care of the body, while other gods are responsible for taking the deceased to the best places in the next world, Geb in the desert, Ra at the beautiful horizon and Nut between the imperishable stars.

The 'court type burials'

The 'court type burials' are mainly known from the undisturbed burials of several royal women found at Dahshur, Lisht and Hawara. These burials all have certain patterns in common.

---

[311] Altenmüller, *Synkretismus in den Sargtexten*, 42.

[312] Bourriau, *Pharaohs and Mortals, Egyptian art in the Middle Kingdom*, 91-92, no. 72, pl. III.3.

[313] Lapp, *The Papyrus of Nu*, 34.

[314] Taylor, *Death and Afterlife in Ancient Egypt*, 16-17, 222-223; compare also the vignette in the papyrus of Muthetepti, where the mummy is called 'sah'; Faulkner, *The Ancient Egyptian Book of the Dead*, fig. on p. 178-179

[315] Whelan, *Mere Scraps of Rough Wood?, 17th – 18th Dynasty Stick Shabtis in the Petrie Museum and other Collections*, 46.

[316] Grajetzki, *EVO* 30 (2007), 51; for these burials in general see: Bourriau, 'Patterns of change in burial customs', 3-20; Miniaci, Quirke, *BIFAO* 109 (2009), passim, especially table on p. 369.

[317] Willems, *Chests of Life*, 141-147.

[318] Jørgensen, *Catalogue, Egypt I*, 148.

[319] According to Assmann, *Altägyptische Totenliturgien III, Osirisliturgien in den Papyri der Spätzeit*, 230 the concept of the hourly vigil only developed in the early Middle Kingdom.

1. The deceased was placed in a set of several coffins. The outer one is often a sarcophagus, rarely decorated. The middle coffin is a rectangular coffin, often decorated with inscribed gold foil. The inner coffin is in many cases anthropoid, but there are also examples where there was just a mummy mask.
2. Next to the deceased, often within the middle coffin were placed royal insignia. They include:
    a. two types of was-sceptres (one with a plain staff, one with a curved staff)
    b. a heqa-sceptre
    c. a mace
    d. a flail
    e. a dagger
    f. bows and arrows

Some 'court type burials' have additional objects:

3. a girdle, decorated with beads in the shape of the plants of Upper and Lower Egypt[320]
4. a vessel for 'pure water'

This type of vessel is mainly found in 'court type burials' belonging to the king and the king's family. In tombs of private individuals it is so far not attested for certain. Some of them are inscribed, but not all of them. Some of these vessels bear a text known from Ptolemaic times as accompanying the second libation in the second night hour of the hourly vigil. Furthermore, the Book of the Dead papyri of Gautseshen and Pennesuttawy, two of the four sources for Book of the Dead chapter 178, contain a copy of this libation passage.[321]

  a. Sithathoriunet (alabaster; with longer text)[322]
  b. Khenmetneferhedjet (alabaster, with longer text)[323]
  c. Amenemhat III (alabaster, fragment)[324]
  d. Neferuptah (in pyramid of Amenemhat III; alabaster, fragments of inscription)[325]
  e. Neferuptah (own burial; silver; with offering formula)[326]
  f. King Hor, two examples (alabaster, with human head and text)[327]

The texts on the vessels of Sithathoriunet and Amenemhat III seem to be quite similar, although the text of the latter is partly lost and some fragments might indicate some different phrasings. The text of king Awibre Hor is a very much shortened version. That of Khenmetneferhedjet is not yet fully published.

The whole burial equipment, at least of the core group of these 'court type burials' relates certainly to the hourly vigil. This is especially clear from later depictions, where Osiris is shown on the Osiris-bed and Horus in front of him, bringing him to life (fig. 50). Under the bed of Osiris are shown royal insignia, sceptres, weapons and crowns; most of these items were also found in 'court type burials'. The presenting of the ankh sign and was-sceptere was an important part of the hourly vigil in the second hour.[328] It seems clear that the texts on the coffins and the burial equipment formed one unity. One wonders whether these

---

[320] Patch, in Eldamaty, Trad (editors), *Egyptian Museum Collections around the World, volumne II*, 905-916.

[321] Quirke, in: Grallert/Grajetzki (editors), *Life and Afterlife in the Middle Kingdom and Second Intermediate Period*, London 2007, 104-105.

[322] Petrie, Flinders/Brunton/Murray, *Lahun II*, XXV, 7, XXVI; Forman, Quirke, *Hieroglyphs and the Afterlife in Ancient Egypt*, fig. on p. 71 (with translation of text: NN, receive this, your cool water which is from the land that begets everything that lives, all those things that this land gives; indeed it is the land that begets everything that lives, in truth from everything comes forth. May you live on them, may you revive upon them. May you live and revive upon this breath that is within it. It begest you, and you come forth. You live on all that is desired and perfect that is therein.).

[323] Arnold, *MDAIK* 36 (1980), 20, pl. 15a.

[324] Petrie, *Kahun, Gurob, and Hawara*, 17, pl. V (translation: NN, receive this, your cool water, which is in that land that begets everything that live, all those things that ths land gives…that begets everything that lives…. comes forth).

[325] Petrie, *Kahun, Gurob, and Hawara*, 17, pl. V.

[326] Farag/Iskander, *The Discovery of Neferwptah*, 15, fig. 10, pl. XIVc, XVc.

[327] de Morgan, *Fouilles à Dahchour Mars-Juin 1894*, 90, fig. 210 (translation: NN, receive this, your cool water, which was created in the land, in Heliopolis. May you live on them in the House of the Benben in Heliopolis, may you receive it, may you live of it for eternity.).

[328] Assmann, *Altägyptische Totenliturgien III, Osirisliturgien in den Papyri der Spätzeit*, 59-60

insignia were used in embalming rituals in the purification tent. Indeed it had been noted that some of the staves were found broken[329] and one wonders whether this happened during a ritual.

The last securely datable 'court type burials' belong to king Awibre Hor and the 'king's daughter' Nubhetepti-khered (see pp. 98-99), both from the early Thirteenth Dynasty. Coffins with 'speeches of gods' are still attested later, indeed they form the main bulk of coffins so far, firmly datable to the Thirteenth Dynasty. Little has survived from their burial equipment, so that is remains uncertain whether there were still 'court type burials'.

Altogether there is visible a development in which more and more royal symbols were taken over in the burials of the ruling class. This process started with objects relating to rituals of the (royal) purification tent; from the beginning of the Middle Kingdom a selection of these objects began to be placed into the tomb chamber. At the same time, the same items appear on the friezes of objects on the coffins and related rituals appear in the Coffin Texts. At the end of the Twelfth Dynasty the whole burial chamber at the highest social level was arranged like the embalming place/purification tent of Osiris, king of the dead. Texts on the coffins and the objects placed next to the deceased are connected to the hourly vigil, which took place at the very end of the embalming and rapping in the purification tent.[330] The deceased was not only treated but even named as 'Osiris' in many funerary texts.

Coffins of the late Thirteenth and Sixteenth Dynasty and the hourly vigil

As mentioned above, in about the middle of the Thirteenth Dynasty, a new text programme on coffins appears. These are the so-called Coffin Texts spells 777-785. So far these coffins have only been found at Abydos and Thebes; indeed from about seven coffins found at Abydos, and datable to the Second Intermediate Period, four coffins (Aby2, Aby3, Aby4, Aby5) bear this text programme. The coffin of Zemathor (Aby5) indicates that this text programme was already known in the period around the reigns of Sobekhotep II to Sobekhotep IV. One wonders whether Abydos was the place where this corpus was composed. Altogether, these spells also refer to the hourly vigil and there are many connections to the 'speeches of gods'. On the short ends appear Isis and Nephthys taking care of the deceased's body. On the front is the opening of the sight an important point which relates to the 'opening of the face' formula found on many coffins with 'speeches of gods'/pyramidion spells. The right placement of the deceased in the Underworld is another important aspect of these spells. These spells seems to be fuller and longer versions perhaps indeed spoken at rituals, while the short 'speeches of gods' might have been specifically composed for placement on coffins. Both text types for coffins coexisted at the same time, being two different variations for a coffin decoration, although the 'speeches of gods' are not only restricted to certain places in Egypt and were introduced at the end of the Twelfth Dynasty.

Some coffins have additional texts. In the Thirteenth Dynasty, there were sometimes added text panels on the exterior or the inside of the coffin decoration. Here, often new spells appear, some of them will later enter the corpus of the Book of the Dead. These texts often carry other rituals or liturgies.[331]

End of Middle Kingdom coffin tradition

A group of coffins is datable to the very end of the Second Intermediate Period and to the early Eighteenth Dynasty. These coffins differ greatly in detail but still have certain patterns in common. The decoration is quite eclectic and borrows elements from early Middle Kingdom coffins, such as objects on the outside decoration, the palace façade and even perhaps the hetep-di-nisut formula.[332]

Typical features are:

1. inscriptions are rarer
2. checkerboard pattern and/or imitation of mats
3. wedjat eyes are placed on both long sides. On some coffins there are two wedjat eyes on each side, on other coffins there is one single eye on each side. Perhaps the latter examples are later in date. The

[329] de Morgan, *Fouilles à Dahchour Mars-Juin 1894*, 95; de Morgan, *Dahchour II*, 60; Gautier/Jéquier, *Mémoire sur les Fouilles de Licht*, 79.

[330] Assmann, *Ägyptische Totenliturgien, I, Totenliturgien in den Sargtexten des Mittleren Reiches*, 272-273.

[331] For the coffin of queen Mentuhotep: Quirke, *Journal of Ancient Near Eastern Religions* 5 (2005), 228-237

[332] This observation should be made with great caution. All these elements might have been there in the Second Intermediate Period, while just the evidence is missing. Still too few coffins are published from Thebes.

placement of the eyes on either side of the coffin relates perhaps to the new position of the body in the coffin. In the Old and Middle Kingdom the body was always placed on the left side with the head to the North, thus looking to the East. In the Second Intermediate Period the body was placed on its back.[333] The coffin decoration responded to that. There are some fragments where the eyes were placed at the head end (p. 56, 59-60), but on other coffins we find two eyes on each long side. Later, one eye was placed on each long side.

4. in the panels between the text lines appear figures and objects. The lying Anubis jackal is common, but there are also other motifs often only attested once for one coffin.

Some of these coffins provide a clue for a date. In the coffin of Aabed (Sq18) from Saqqara was found a dagger with the name of king Apophis and with a coffin (T38) found at Thebes were found several inscribed royal cartouches, the last one being that of king Ahmose.

Distribution

Most decorated rectangular coffins of the Second Intermediate Period come from just a few sites. These are Thebes, Abydos and the area from Hawara up to Saqqara, the region of the power centre in the Middle Kingdom. A few other examples were found at places such as Elephantine, Hu or Beni Hasan. In general this reflects the research on Second Intermediate Period sites but also a shifting pattern of wealth. Thebes and Abydos are major centres of the Second Intermediate Period. However, the case of Hu might indicate that coffins at provincial sites are also to be expected, but these cemeteries are yet not excavated or the preservation conditions for wood are not good. This is the case for the Qau-Badari region with several burial grounds of the period and Edfu where there is also a partly excavated Second Intermediate Period cemetery but with few coffin fragments. Indeed, the only recorded decorated coffin at Edfu, belongs to the Twelfth Dynasty.[334] So, in general there is the impression that decorated and inscribed rectangular coffins were still common throughout the Second Intermediate Period, but through the increasing poverty of the country they became less common than in the classical Middle Kingdom.

In contrast, the coffins with longer religious texts seem to be restricted to the Memphite region, Thebes and Abydos. In discussing the development of the Book of the Dead, it has been argued that in the beginning it was restricted to the king and members of the royal family.[335] However, the evidence indicates that the coffins with longer religious texts (and the first attestations of the Book of the Dead) were restricted to people connected to the royal court. This includes the king's family, but also high officials, such as the 'treasurer' Amenhotep (Da6X). Indeed, the cemeteries mentioned are those, where we can expect royal burials and those of the courtiers at the king's court.[336] Therefore, longer religious texts on coffins were in the Second Intermediate Period restricted to a small circle of people at the royal court. Is that a reflection of an impoverished country in this period?

[333] Bourriau, in H. Willems (editor), *Social Aspects of Funerary Culture in the Egyptian Old and Middle Kingdoms Proceedings of the international symposium held at Leiden University 6-7 June, 1996*, 1-20

[334] Michałowski, Deschores, de Lineage, Manteuffel, Żejmo-Żejmis, *Tell Edfou 1939*, pl. XLVII, no. 16.

[335] Gestermann, in: B/ Backes, I. Munro, S. Stöhr, *Totenbuch-Forschungen, Gesammelte Beiträge des 2. Internationalen Totenbuch-Symposiums 2005*, Wiesbaden 2006, 103 (Gestermann discusses mainly the Book of the Dead versions of the early New Kingdom, the picture of the late Thirteenth Dynasty and Second Intermediate Period might be slightly different).

[336] For royal burials at Abydos see: Landua-McCormack, *Dynasty XIII Kingship in Ancient Egypt: A study of political power and administration through an investigation of the Royal Tombs of the Late Middle Kingdom.*

Appendix I: List of 'court type burials'

Deir el-Bersheh

Djehutynakht
Perhaps the earliest burial which can be called a 'court type burial' or which has at least elements of it, is that of Djehutynakht, governor of Hermopolis who was buried at Deir el-Bersheh. The deceased governor was placed in two decorated coffins. Within the second coffin were several further items, some of them typical for 'court type burials'. There was a sceptre with a jackal head, a long bow, and a staff. In the burial was also found a girdle (pl. XV), similar to the one in the tomb of Senebtisi and Neferuptah. Most typical are a mace and a flail.[337] The body of the deceased was placed on a bed with lion heads. The governor is not exactly datable, but a date around Amenemhat II seems to be most likely.[338]

Dahshur

1. Ita[339]
The tomb of Ita at Dahshur was excavated by de Morgan and his team. It was found next to the pyramid of Amenemhat II in a gallery tomb consisting of two burials. The 'king's daughter' Ita was buried in a set of three coffins. There was an outer undecorated sarcophagus, a middle wooden rectangular coffin and an inner anthropoid coffin. The middle box coffin was inscribed on the inside, mostly with Pyramid Texts. The mummy was richly adorned with jewellery. The tomb dates perhaps under Amenemhat III.[340]

Other finds next to the mummy (not including jewellery):

flagellum
dagger[341]
a mace
different sceptres (on the drawing of the burial are visible: a heqa-sceptre, a was-sceptre and a simple (?) plain stave; all on the left side of the mummy; on the right, slightly under the mummy a long 'double' staff)
on the ground of the burial chamber were found several bronze tools
a canopic box with four canopic jars
an incense burner
under the head was found a clay disc
From this tomb comes perhaps a scarab with the throne name Nimaatre (Amenemhat III)[342]

2. Khnumet[343]
The tomb of the 'king's daughter' Khnumet was found next to the pyramid of Amenemhat II at Dahshur. The burial was undisturbed. The funeral equipment was similar to those of Ita. The tomb dates perhaps under Amenemhat III too.[344]

undecorated sarcophagus
inscribed wooden middle coffin
remains of an anthropoid inner coffin
under the head was a clay disc
jewellery
two maces
sceptres (was and heqa), gilded and broken
bow

---

[337] Kamal, *ASAE* 2 (1901), 221.
[338] Willems, *Chests of Life*, 74-75.
[339] de Morgan, *Dahchour II*, 45-55.
[340] Fay, *The Louvre Sphinx and Royal Sculpture from the Reign of Amenemhat III*, 44; compare Arnold, in E. Czerny, I. Hein, H. Hunger, D. Melman, A. Schwab (editors), *Timelines, Studies in Honour of Manfred Bietak I*, Leuven, 47, n. 2.
[341] de Morgan, *Dahchour II*, pl. VI.
[342] Suggested by Allen, *The Art of Medicine*, 24-25, no. 13.
[343] de Morgan, *Dahchour II*, 55-68.
[344] Fay, *The Louvre Sphinx and Royal Sculpture from the Reign of Amenemhat III*, 44, 46.

a jewellery box in the tomb chamber with the jewellery
pottery
inscribed wooden canopic box[345]

3. Itaweret[346]
The 'king's daughter' Itaweret was found in another gallery tomb next to the pyramid of Amenemhat II at Dahshur. The tomb was found undisturbed. The tomb dates perhaps under Amenemhat III.[347]

The tomb contained:
an uninscribed sarcophagus
inscribed wooden coffin
inner anthropoid coffin
to the left of the mummy were found
staves, sceptres, one mace, a bow, a flagellum, an axe ('une houe') and several other wooden objects, gilded

in the second chamber:
an inscribed canopic box[348]
pottery with food
a wooden figure of a swan
a rectangular table
a round table
a wooden box with the alabaster vessels for oil; it contained the inscriptions (?), that it once contained a pair of gilded sandals and a board on which there was a mirror, a diadem

4. Zathathormeryt[349]
The tomb of Sithathormerit was found by de Morgan next to the pyramid of Amenemhat II at Dahshur. Sithathormerit does not bear the title 'king's daughter' as the three other women buried next to her and with almost an identical tomb equipment.[350] The tomb dates perhaps under Amenemhat III.[351]

Following the short description of de Morgan the tomb contained the following objects:

an outer sarcophagus
the inscribed wooden coffin (Coffin CG 28101)
an inner anthropoid coffin
sceptres and weapons on the left side of the body

the second room contained:
vases
a round table
box for alabaster containing eight vessels with oil
inscribed canopic box

bones of cattle
box with nine oil vases
inscribed canopic box with four canopic vases[352]

5. Zathathor ('king's daughter', buried next to the pyramid of Senusret III at Dahshur)
several beads of a flail[353]

---

[345] Lüscher, *Kanopenkästen*, 75-76.
[346] de Morgan, *Dahchour II*, 73-74.
[347] Fay, *The Louvre Sphinx and Royal Sculpture from the Reign of Amenemhat III*, 44-45.
[348] Lüscher, *Kanopenkästen*, 75-76.
[349] de Morgan, *Dahchour II*, 74-76.
[350] de Morgan, *Dahchour II*, 74-76.
[351] Fay, *The Louvre Sphinx and Royal Sculpture from the Reign of Amenemhat III*, 44, 46-47.
[352] Lüscher, *Kanopenkästen*, 75-76.

6. Neferthenut ('king's wife', buried next to the pyramid of Senusret III at Dahshur)
two mace heads[354]

7. Zatwerut (undisturbed, but not yet published)
girdle [355]
'sticks, staves'[356]

8. Khenmetneferhedjet ('king's wife')[357]
mace heads made of granite and alabaster
a vase for 'pure water'

9. Aat ('king's wife')[358]
mace heads made of crystal and limestone

10. king Awibre Hor[359]

shrine with a statue of the king
stela with religious texts (Pyramid Texts)
stela with offering formula
round offering table with offering formula
two water jars in the shape of canopic jars
statue of the king (found in shaft)
long box with sceptres
staff with a Horus head
staff with big middle part
several broken was-sceptres
two broken arrows
mace
basket
a small box
wooden vessels
long beads
two big jars
three big plates
six bottles

sarcophagus
wooden coffin
mummy mask
in coffin:
different sceptres
two alabaster vessels
flaggelum
bracelets and armlets
falcon collars
wooden dagged, gilded

rough funerary statue
gold disc
rosette

---

353 Arnold, *Senwosret III*, 124.
354 de Morgan, *Dahchour I*, 73; Arnold, *Senwosret III*, 63.
355 Patch, D.C., in Eldamaty, Trad (editors), *Egyptian Museum Collections around the World, volume II*, 905-916.
356 Arnold, *Egyptian Archaeology* 9 (1996), 24.
357 Arnold, *MDAIK* 36 (1980), 20, pl. 15a.
358 Arnold, *MDAIK* 36 (1980), 20.
359 Aufrere, *BIFAO* 101 (2001), 1-41.

pendant
a wooden band, gilded
vulture head
gold leaf from the mummy mask and the mummy covering
two beads with the king's name
schist object, unknown function
mallet

11. Nubhetepti-khered
The burial contained:
a long box with staves
a mace
nine arrows
one heqa-sceptre
two was-sceptres, both broken (in antiquity?)
two sceptres with big middle part
a wooden mirror
a za-symbol

a second box contained eight alabaster vessels with the names of oils written on them

coffin decorated with gold leaf[360] placed into a rock cut sarcophagus
inner anthropoid coffin
the mummy was adorned:
a diadem, with uraeus and vulture (belonging to diadem or coffin?)
a falcon collar
a golden dagger
two bracekets and two armlets
one flaggelum
two alabaster vases
two (?) was-sceptres

there was gilded canopic box with four canopic jars
several pottery vessels ('queen's ware')

Hawara

1. Neferuptah[361]

The tomb contained:
outer sarcophagus with a short inscription
middle wooden coffin adorned with gold leaf
inner anthropoid coffin
a set of ten alabaster vessels for sacred oils
a large alabaster jar
flail
mace (only the mace head is preserved)
was-sceptre (only the eyes are preserved)
another sceptre
girdle

two silver hes-vases
a silver jar
a set of pottery vessels including three beer jars, 14 bowls and 59 model vessels
an offering table in alabaster

---

[360] A reconstruction of the coffin: Grajetzki, *Bulletin of the Egyptian Museum*, 73-74, fig. 3.
[361] Farag/Iskander, *The Discovery of Neferwptah.*

2. Iunefer (tomb 51), datable under Amenemhat III[362]
beads of a flail
mace head

Harageh

1. Tomb 608[363]
beads of a flail

2. Tomb 280[364], belonging to Iamyt ('lady of the house'). This burial is the clearest example of a 'court type burial' at Harageh. There are the beads of a flail as well as a wooden (model) dagger, similar to the one found in the tomb of the king Awibre Hor. The 'wooden implement' might be seen in the same context.
beads of a flail
wooden dagger
'wooden implement'

3. Tomb 105[365]
beads of a flail

4. Tomb 110[366]
beads of a flail

5. Tomb 108[367]
beads of a flail

6. Tomb 49[368]
beads of a flail

7. Tomb 162[369]
beads of a flail

8. Tomb 17[370]
beads of a flail

9. Tomb 171[371]
beads of a flail

[362] Petrie/Wainwright/Mackay, *The Labyrinth, Gerzeh and Mazghuneh*, 36; The name Iunefer was found on two canopic jars and on a shabti; the tomb also contained the fragments of a coffin with the name 'Akhet-hotep'. For the date of Iunefer see, Grajetzki, Whelan, *SAK* 37 (2008), 125-26; Akhet-hotep might be contemporary or an intrusive burial. It remains uncertain who of these was buried in the 'court type' style.
[363] Engelbach, *Harageh*, pl. LXII, the tomb chamber was lined with limestone slabs and is therefore one of the most elaborate ones at Harageh. Two limestone eyes found might indicate an anthropoid coffin; gold foil was discovered.
[364] Engelbach, *Harageh*, pl. LX (the tomb belongs again to the richer ones at Harageh, with gold foil, an inscribed canopic chest and canopics).
[365] Engelbach, *Harageh*, pl. LIX.
[366] Engelbach, *Harageh*, pl. LIX.
[367] Engelbach, *Harageh*, pl. LIX.
[368] Engelbach, *Harageh*, pl. LVIII.
[369] Engelbach, *Harageh*, pl. LIX.
[370] Engelbach, *Harageh*, pl. LVIII.
[371] Engelbach, *Harageh*, pl. LIX.

Lahun

1. Tomb no. 7[372]
   Beads of flail
   Beads of girdle?

2. Tomb 650
   beads of a flail[373]

3. tomb of a certain Senusret... (905)
This is a disturbed tomb consisting of the remains of mastaba with little fragments of relief decoration. The sarcophagus in the tomb chamber was made of different slabs of stone. There were found canopic jars with human heads and beads from a flail; other beads belong to jewellery. A copper tool was found and the head of a wooden staff (pottery types: 32M, 37j).[374]

4. Tomb 906
   beads of a flail[375]

Lisht

1. The tomb of Senebtisi[376]

Next to the mummy of Senebtisi were found on the left side several staves and other objects:
   a double staff (*pḏ-ꜥḥꜥ*)
   heqa-scepter
   straight staff with forked bottom
   dam – sceptre with curly staff
   was-sceptre
   straight staff
   two bows
   flagellum
   mace
   dagger
   girdle

other objects found in the tomb:
   a wig box with the remains of a wig
   a stave box, containing a mace, a piece of a crook staff, and other wooden pieces not identified
   two shrine-shaped boxes
   canopic box with four canopic jars

The outer coffin was decorated with spells of gods. Only parts of them are preserved. The middle coffin was only decorated with one inscription on the lid.

2. The tomb of Sesenebnef

The objects found[377]:

   mace
   flagellum

---

[372] Brunton, *Lahun I, The Treasure*, 15.
[373] Petrie/Brunton/Murray, *Lahun II*, pl. XLVIIIA (tomb register).
[374] Petrie/Brunton/Murray, *Lahun II*, pl. XLVIIIA (tomb register).
[375] Petrie/Brunton/Murray, *Lahun II*, pl. XLVIIIA (tomb register).
[376] Mace, Winlock, *The Tomb of Senebtisi at Lisht.*
[377] Gautier/Jéquier, *Mémoire sur les Fouilles de Licht*, 74-79, fig. 97.

bow
was-sceptre, curley
was-sceptre, plain
two heqa-sceptree
plain staff with forced end, closed
plain staff with forked end, open
plain staff with thicker bottom end
plain staff
double staff

3. 'French Tomb'

bead from a flail.

The tomb dates under Senusret III or later.[378]

4. There were several other 'court type burials' at Lisht, none of these are so far published. In at least 13 burials were found remains of a beaded garment, also known from the burials of Senebtisi, Neferuptah and Sitwerut.[379] For tomb 5102 it is reported that several staves were found.[380]

Meir

The burial of the 'overseer of sealers' Uhkhotep[381]
sceptres
flail

The burial of the 'steward' Hapyankhtifi[382]
staves
was-sceptres
flail
mace

Riqqeh

Tomb 166 of Zawadjet[383]
Two rectangular coffins, an inner anthropoid coffin and a mummy mask. The inside of one coffin is decorated with friezes of objects including a number of objects also known from 'court type burials'.
beads of a flail
was-sceptre
heqa-sceptre

Thebes

Tomb K03.5 (Dra Abu el-Naga)[384]
was-sceptre
aba-sceptre

---

378 Arnold, *Middle Kingdom Tomb Architecture at Lisht*, 32.
379 Bourriau, in Quirke (editor), *Discovering Egypt from the Neva, The Egyptological Legacy of Oleg D Berlev*, 57.
380 Mace, Winlock, *The Tomb of Senebtisi at Lisht*, 85.
381 Kamal, *ASAE* 12 (1912), 113
382 Mace, Winlock, *The Tomb of Senebtisi at Lisht*, 85, 92, 101, 103.
383 Engelbach, *Riqqeh and Memphis VI*, 23-25; pl. V.2, XXII, 8, XXIII.
384 Polz, *Für die Ewigkeit geschaffen, Die Särge des Imeni und Geheset*, 8, figs. 120, 121.

Appendix II: Coffin Texts and Book of the Dead chapters on coffins of the Thirteenth to Seventeenth Dynasty

In the Middle Kingdom funerary texts were mainly written on the inside of the coffin and are therefore called Coffin Texts. In the New Kingdom many funerary texts were placed on papyrus rolls and these texts are therefore called 'Book of the Dead', although the Ancient Egyptian name – 'Going forth on the Day' – of this composition is known. Most of the funerary texts of the Second Intermediate Period were still written on the coffin and at first glance it seems logical to call these Coffin Texts too. However, there seems to be a shift in the function of texts and many spells known from the later Book of the Dead appear already on coffins of the Second Intermediate Period. The most famous example is the coffin of queen Mentuhotep (T4L), on which the texts are often regarded as the first example of the 'true' Book of the Dead. Therefore it might be wise to make clear the difference, between Coffin Texts and the Book of the Dead. If it is indeed only the writing medium, all funerary texts on coffins of the Second Intermediate Period should still be called Coffin Texts.

Indeed, there was also a shift in function and contents between these two corpora. Assmann describes the world of Coffin Texts as belonging to the world of the embalming chamber and hourly virgil. Many of the Coffin Texts are liturgies and he argues that many were read in the cult for the dead in the embalming chamber.[385] Therefore they appear always on the coffin inside or in the coffin chamber so as to be close to the deceased. In contrast some Books of the Dead chapters describe in their entity the journey of the deceased in the underworld. They open with the arrival of the deceased in the underworld and close with the journey in the solar barque where the deceased wished to join in.[386]

The Book of the Dead is often illustrated with vignettes, while these are rare in the Coffin Texts. Further differences are 'discovery notes'. These are short paragraphs added to some Book of the Dead chapters and describe how and where these chapters were found. Most of them are given an old age and often kings of the First and Second Dynasty are mentioned under whom it is said that these chapters are written.[387] Another difference is the number of spells or chapters. There are about 200 chapters for the Book of the Dead, while more than 1000 are known for the Coffin Texts. Altogether, there is certainly a difference between these two text corpora.

Evidently there was in the Second Intermediate Period an ongoing production of new funerary texts. Some were only used for a short period of time (such as Coffin Text spells 777-785), but others were still used in the New Kingdom and became part of the Book of the Dead. In the end, each Book of the Dead spell might have had its own history. Therefore, it might be wise to look at each single spell, while the merging of some of these texts might have taken place at a later time. It is sometimes stated that the Book of the Dead was at one point in the Second Intermediate Period 'edited' in Thebes.[388] However, looking at the evidence in general, it seems more likely that each spell was created or edited at a different time. For example, the spell for the mummy mask is in its New Kingdom version already attested in the Thirteenth Dynasty (on the coffin of queen Keminub, Da5X).[389] As part of Book of the Dead spell 151 it is only attested in the New Kingdom.[390]

The same can be assumed for the place of the compositions. Whether Thebes was the main centre of this text production – as proposed – might be doubted.[391] Some of the earliest versions of Book of the Dead chapters come indeed from the Memphite-Fayum region, such as the texts on the coffin of queen Keminub (Da5X) or those on the coffins of Sesenebnef (L1-2Li). Furthermore, Abydos must be mentioned. It is the cult centre of Osiris. A high percentage of the coffins with Coffin Text spells 777 to 785 come from Abydos. One wonders whether these spells were composed there. At least for the 'Abydos formula' on the

[385] Assmann, *Ägyptische Totenliturgien, I, Totenliturgien in den Sargtexten des Mittleren Reiches*, 17; H. Willems announced a detailed study of these texts: Willems, *Les Textes des sarcophages et la démocratie*, 228.
[386] Lapp, *The Papyrus of Nu*, 49.
[387] Quirke, *Journal of Ancient Near Eastern Religions* 5 (2005), 235-36.
[388] Gestermann, in Backes, Munro, Stöhr, *Totenbuch-Forschungen*, 113, n. 40.
[389] Lüscher, *Untersuchungen zu Totenbuch Spruch 151*, 52-53.
[390] Munro, *Untersuchungen zu den Totenbuch-Papyri der 18. Dynastie*, 349.
[391] Parkinson, Quirke, in *Studies in Pharaonic Religion and Society in Honour of J. Gwyn Griffths*, 48; Gestermann, in: Backes, Munro, Stöhr, *Totenbuch-Forschungen, Gesammelte Beiträge des 2. Internationalen Totenbuch-Symposiums 2005*, Wiesbaden 2006, 113.

coffin of Zemathor this seems certain. There is almost no other place where the spell might be composed. The spell appears on a coffin with the spells CT 777 to 785. The placing on these two texts on one coffin is not a proof at all that the latter composition was composed in Abydos, but might be an indication.

Table: occurrence of certain features on coffins

Key:
IV - Willems coffin type IV
I/d Imax/dd mdw – simple *imꜣḫw ḫr* or *ḏd mdw* formula on the outside in the columms
SOG1 - 'speeches of gods', not standardised
SOG2 - 'speeches of gods', standardised
7-9 Coffins with seven to nine columns on the long sides
CT – Coffin Text spells 777 to 785
panels - text panels between the column, on the exterior
Inc. Hier – incomplete hieroglyphs
black – coffin outside is black
eyes – 1 = just one eye on each longe side; 2 = two eyes on each long side
mats – mat pattern/checkerboard pattern

Bold: coffin is connected with a king's name:

Da4C (Awibre Hor), T4L (Djehuty), T10C, T6C (Sewahenre), Sq18 (Nebkhepeshre Apophis), 37/59 (Thutmosis I, Thutmosis II), Saqqara II (Amenhotep I), NN T37 (Ahmose)

	IV	I/d	SOG1	SOG2	Inc. Hier	7-9	CT	panels	black	eyes	mats
Da1	x	x									
S3	x	x	x			x					
L4	x		x								
Haw2	x ?		x		x						
Da4C	x			x	x						
Da2C	x			x	x						
T34			x		x	x					
L1Li	x	x			x			x			
Da6X	x			x	x			x			
Aby5					x	x	x	x			
Aby7	x?			x	x			x	?		
T7C				x	x	x			x		
T5-8NY				x	x	x			x		
T10C					x	x	x		x		
T6C					x	x	x		x		
T4L					x	x	x				
Aby2-4					x	x	x				
T38						x					x
37/63											x
T33	x	x									x
T36	x	x								2	x
T37		x								2	
Sq18	x	x								1	x
37/7										1	
37/59										1	x
Saqqara II										1	x

Bibliography

Allen, G. T., *Occurrences of Pyramid Texts with Cross Indexes of These and Other Egyptian Mortuary Texts*, Chicago 1950

Allen, J. P., *The Art of Medicine in Ancient Egypt*, New York 2005

Allen, J. P., Coffin Texts from Lisht, In: *The World of the Coffin Texts, Proceedings of the Symposium, held on the occasion of the 100th birthday of Adriaan de Buck*, Leiden, December 17-19, 1992, Leiden 1996, 1-15

Allen, J. P., *The Egyptian Coffin Texts, Volume 8*, Middle Kingdom Copies of Pyramid Texts, Chicago 2006

Allen, J. P., 'The Historical Inscription of Khnumhotep at Dahshur: Preliminary Report', *BASOR* 352, November 2008, 29-39

Altenmüller, B. *Synkretismus in den Sargtexten*, Göttinger Orientforschungen IV, 7

Arnold, D., 'Dahschur, Dritter Grabungsbericht', *MDAIK* 36 (1980), 15-21

Arnold, D., *The Pyramid of Senwosret I, The South Cemeteries of Lisht I*, New York 1988

Arnold, D., 'Two Mastabas of the Twelfth Dynasty at Dahshur', in *Egyptian Archaeology* 9 (1996), 23-25

Arnold, D., *The Pyramid Complex of Senwosret III at Dahshur, Architectural Studies*, New York 2002

Arnold, D., *Middle Kingdom Tomb Architecture at Lisht*, New York 2008

Arnold, Do., 'The Fragmented Head of a Queen Wearing the Vulture Headdress', in E. Czerny, I. Hein, H. Hunger, D. Melman, A. Schwab (editors), *Timelines, Studies in Honour of Manfred Bietak* I, Leuven, Paris, Dudley, MA 2006, 47-54

Assmann, J., *Ägyptische Totenliturgien, I, Totenliturgien in den Sargtexten des Mittleren Reiches*, Heidelberg 2002

Assmann, J., *Altägyptische Totenliturgien II, Totenliturgien und Totensprüche in Grabinschriften des Neuen Reiche*s, Heidelberg 2005

Assmann, J., *Death and Salvation in Ancient Egypt* (translated by D. Lorton), New York 2005

Assmann, J., *Altägyptische Totenliturgien III, Osirisliturgien in den Papyri der Spätzeit*, Heidelberg 2008

Aston, D.A., *Tell el-Dab'a XII, A Corpus of Late Middle Kingdom and Second Intermediate Period Pottery*, Vienna 2004

Aufrere, S., 'Le roi Aouibrê Hor: Essai d'interprétation du matériel découvert par Jacques de Morgan à Dahchour (1894)' *BIFAO* 101 (2001), 1-41

D'Auria, S.; P. Lacovara; C. R. Roehrig (editors), *Mummies and Magic, The Funerary Arts of Ancient Egypt*, Boston 1988

Backes, B., *Rituelle Wirklichkeit: Über Erscheinung und Wirkungsbereich des Webergottes Hedjhotep und den gedanklichen Umgang mit einer Gottes-Konzeption im alten Ägypten*, Rites Egyptiens, Brepols 2001

von Beckerath, J., *Untersuchungen zur politischen Geschichte der zweiten Zwischenzeit in Ägypten*, Glückstadt/New York 1965

Ben-Tor, D., with contributions by A. J. Allen, J. P. Allen, 'Seals and Kings', *BASOR* 315 (1999), 47-74

Berlev, O., 'Стела Вюрцбургского университетского музея (XIII Династия)', палестинский сборник, 25 (1974), 26-31

Berlev, O., A contemporary of King Sewah-en-re, *JEA* 60 (1974), 106-113

Berman, L., M., 'The Coffins and Canopic Chests of Tomb 10', in: R. Freed, L. M. Berman, D. M. Doxey, N. S. Picardo, *The Secrets of Tomb 10A, Egypt 2000 BC*, Boston 2009, 105-135

Bienkowski, P., A. M. J Tooley, *Gifts of the Nile*, Liverpool 1995

Bourriau, J., *Pharaohs and Mortals, Egyptian art in the Middle Kingdom*, Cambridge 1988

Bourriau, J., 'Patterns of change in burial customs', in S. Quirke (editor) *Middle Kingdom Studies*, Whistable 1991, 3-20

Bourriau, J., 'The Dolphin Vase from Lisht', in P. Der Manuelian (editor*), Studies in Honor of William Kelly Simpson, Vol.I*, Boston 1996, 101-116

Bourriau, J., 'Beyond Avaris : The Second Intermediate Period in Egypt Outside the Eastern Delta', in: E. D. Oren (editor), *The Hyksos : new historical and archaeological perspectives proceedings of the International Seminar on Cultural Interconnections in the Ancient Near East ; held for 16 consecutive weeks at the Univ. of Pennsylvania Museum of Archaeology and Anthropology during the spring term, January - April 1992*, University Museum monographs 96, Philadelphia 1997, 159-182

Bourriau, J., 'Change of Body Position in Egyptian Burials from the Mid XIIth Dynasty until the early XVIIIth Dynasty', in H. Willems (editor), *Social Aspects of Funerary Culture in the Egyptian Old and Middle Kingdoms Proceedings of the international symposium held at Leiden University 6-7 June, 1996*, Leuven 2001, 1-20

Bourriau, J., 'The contribution of the excavation of Lisht North Cemetery to Middle Kingdom Studies', in S. Quirke (editor), *Discovering Egypt from the Neva, The Egyptological Legacy of Olge D Berlev*, Berlin 2003, 51-59

Bourriau, J., 'Mace's Cemetery Y at Diospolis Parva', in D. Magee, J. Bourriau, S. Quirke (editors), *Sitting beside Lepsius, Studies in Honour of Jaromir Malek at the Griffith Institut*e, Leuven, Paris, Walpole, MA 2009, 39-98

Brunton, G., Lahun I, *The Treasure*, London 1920

Brunton, G., R. Engelbach, *Gurob*, London BSAE 41, 1927

Bruyère, A. B., *Rapport sur les fouilles de Deir el Médineh (1929)*, le Caire 1930
Budde, D. *Die Göttin Seschat*, Leipzig 2000
Carrier, C. *Textes des Pyramides de l'Égypte Ancienne, Tome VI, Annexes*, Paris 2009
Carter, H., Earl of Carnavon, *Five years' explorations at Thebes; a record of work done 1907-1911*, London, New York 1912
Daressy, G., 'Un poignard du temps des rois pasteurs', *ASAE, 7* (1906), 115-120
Dodson, A., *The Canopic Equipment of the Kings of Egypt*, London/New York 1994
Dolzani, C., *La Collezione Egiziana del museo dell academia dei concordi in Rovigo*, Rome 1969
Doxey, D. M., 'The Djehutynakht's burial goods', in Berman, in: R. Freed, L. M. Berman, D. M. Doxey, N. S. Picardo, *The Secrets of Tomb 10A, Egypt 2000 BC*, Boston 2009, 137-149
Downes, D., *The Excavations at Esna*, 1905-1906, Warminster 1974
Dreyer, G. 'Saqqara', in *Deutsches Archäologisches Institut, Abteilung Kairo, Rundbrief, September 2007*, 19-21
Edel, E., *Die Felsgräbernekropole der Qubbet el-Hawa bei Assuan, I. Abbteilung Band 1*, Paderborn, München, Wien, Zürich 2008, 436
Engelbach, R., *Riqqeh and Memphis VI*, 1915
Engelbach, R., *Harageh*, London 1923
von Falck, M., 'Text- und Bildprogramm ägyptischer Särge und Sarkophage der 18. Dynastie: Genese und Weiterleben', *SAK* 34 (2006), 125 - 140
Farag, N./Iskander, Z., *The Discovery of Neferwptah*, Cairo 1971
Faulkner, R. O., (edited by C. Andrews*), The Ancient Egyptian Book of the Dead*, London 1985 (revised edition)
Fay, B., *The Louvre Sphinx and Royal Sculpture from the Reign of Amenemhat III*, Mainz am Rhein 1996
Firth C.M.,/B. Gunn, *Excavations at Saqqara: Teti pyramid cemeteries*, Cairo 1926
Forman, W/S. Quirke, *Hieroglyphs and the Afterlife in Ancient Egypt*, London 1996
Franke, Doss., see Franke, D., *Personendaten*
Franke, D., *Personendaten aus dem Mittleren Reich (20.-16. Jahrhundert v. Chr.), Dossiers 1-796*, Wiesbaden 1984
Franke, D., 'The Middle Kingdom offering formulas: a challenge', *JEA* 89 (2003), 39-57
Gautier MM.J.-E. /G. Jéquier, *Mémoire sur les Fouilles de Licht*. Cairo 1902
Garstang, J., *El Arabah: A Cemetery of the Middle Kingdom*, London, 1901
Garstang, J., *The Burial Customs of Ancient Egypt*, London, 1907
Geisen, C., *Die Totentexte des verschollenen Sarges der Königin Mentuhotep aus der 13. Dynastie: ein Textzeuge aus der Übergangszeit von den Sargtexten zum Totenbuch*, Wiesbaden 2004
Gestermann, L., 'Aufgelesen: Die Anfänge des altägyptischen Totenbuchs', in: B. Backes, I. Munro, S. Stöhr, *Totenbuch-Forschungen, Gesammelte Beiträge des 2. Internationalen Totenbuch-Symposiums 2005*, Wiesbaden 2006, 101-113
Graefe, E., *Das Grab des Padihorresnet, Obervermögensverwalter der Gottesgemahlin des Amun (Thebanisches Grab Nr. 196)*, Tunrnhout 2003
Graefe, E., *Die Doppelgrabanlage "M" aus dem Mittleren Reich unter TT 119 im Tal el-Asasif in Theben West*, Aegypticaca Monasteriensia 5, Aachen 2007
Grajetzki, W., 'Der Schatzmeister Amenhotep und eine weitere Datierungshilfe für Denkmäler des Mittleren Reiches', *Bulletin de la Société d'égyptologie*, 19 (1995), 5-11
Grajetzki, W., *Die höchsten Beamten der ägyptischen Zentralverwaltung zur Zeit des Mittleren Reiches*, Berlin 2000
Grajetzki, W., *Two Treasurers of the Late Middle Kingdom*, Oxford 2001
Grajetzki, W., *Harageh, an Egyptian burial ground for the rich around 1800 BC*, London 2004
Grajetzki, W., 'Reconstructing the coffins of king Hor, the 'king's daughter' Nubhetep-khered and the 'lady of the house' Satsobek', *Bulletin of the Egyptian Museum* 2 (2005), 71-78
Grajetzki, W., 'The Coffin of the "King's Daughter" Neferuptah and the Sarcophagus of the "Great King's Wife" Hatshepsut', *GM*, 205 (2005), 55-66
Grajetzki, W., 'Another early source for the Book of the Dead: The Second Intermediate Period Burial D 25 at Abydos', *SAK* 34 (2006), 205-216
Grajetzki, W., 'The Second Intermediate Period model coffin of Teti in the British Museum (EA 35016)', *BMSAES* 5 (2006), 1-12
Grajetzki, W./P. Whelan, 'The mummiform figure of Senankh from Abydos', *SAK* 37 (2008), 125-30
Habachi, L., *Elephantine IV, The Sanctuary of Heqaib*, Mainz am Rhein 1985
Hayes, W. C., *Royal Sarcophagi of the XVIII Dynasty*, Princeton 1935
Hayes, W. C., *The Scepter of Egypt I, From the Earliest Times to the End of the Middle Kingdom*, New York 1953
Hays, H. M., 'Transformation of Context: The Field of Rushes in Old and Middle Kingdom Mortuary Literature', in S. Bickel, B. Mathieu, *D'un monde à l'autre, Textes des Pyramides & Texts des Sarcophages*, Cairo 2004, 175-200
Hoffmeier, J. K., 'The Coffins of the Middle Kingdom: The Residence and the Regions', in *Middle Kingdom Studies*, edited by Stephen Quirke, Whistable 1991, 69-85
Ikram S./A. Dodson, *The Mummy in Ancient Egypt*, London 1998

James, T. G. H., *The Mastaba of Khentika called Ikheki*, London 1953
Janosi, P., 'Keminub - eine Gemahlin Amenemhets II.?', In, *Zwischen den beiden Ewigkeiten, Festschrift Gertrud Thausing*, M. Bietak [Hrsg.], 94 – 101
Jéquier, G., *Le Monument funéraire de Pepi II*, Tome III, Cairo 1940
Jørgensen, M., *Catalogue, Egypt I (3000 – 1550 B.C.), Ny Carlsberg Glyptotek*, Copenhagen 1996
Kamal, A. B., 'Rapport sur les Fouilles executes à Deîr-el-Bershé', *ASAE* 2 (1901), 206-222
Kamal, A. B.,, 'Rapport sur les fouilles exécutées dans la zone comprise entre Déîrout au nord et Déîr-el-Ganadlah, au sud (suite)', *ASAE* 12 (1912), 97-127
Kamal, A. B., 'Rapport sur les fouilles executes dans la zone comprise entire Déîr rout au Nord et Déîr-el-Ganadlah au Sud', *ASAE* 14 (1914), 45-87
Kees, H., *Totenglaube und Jenseitsvorstellungen der alten Ägypter* (2nd edition), Berlin 1956
Kemp, B.J./R.S Merrillees, *Minoan Pottery in Second Millennium Egypt*, Mainz 1980
Krauss, R., *Astronomische Konzepte und Jenseitsvorstellungen in den Pyramidentexten*, Wiesbaden 1997
Landua-McCormack, D., *Dynasty XIII Kingship in Ancient Egypt: A study of Political Power and Administration through an Investigation of the Royal Tombs of the Late Middle Kingdom*, Ann Arbor 2008
Lapp, G., 'Der Sarg des Jmnj mit einem Spruchgut am Übergang von Sargtexten zum Totenbuch', *SAK* 13 (1986), 135-147
Lapp, G., *Typologie der Särge und Sargkammern von der 6. bis 13. Dynastie*, Heidelberg 1993
Lapp, G., 'Die Entwicklung der Särge von der 6. bis zur 13. Dynastie', in H. Willems (editor), *The World of the Coffins Texts*, Leiden 1996
Lapp, G., *The Papyrus of Nu*, London 1997
Leitz, C. (editor), *Lexikon der ägyptischen Götter und Götterbezeichnungen I-VII*, Leuven, Paris, Dudley, MA, 2002
Lilyquist, C., *Ancient Egyptian Mirrors from the Earliest Times through the Middle Kingdom*, Berlin 1979
Lilyquist, C., 'A note on the Date of Senebtisi and other Middle Kingdom Groups', *Serapis* 5 (1979), S. 27-28
Lohwasser, A., *Die Formel "Öffnen des Gesichts"*, Beiträge zur Ägyptologie 11, Veröffentlichungen der Institute für Afrikanistik und Ägyptologie der Universität Wien 58, Vienna 1991
Lüscher, B., *Untersuchungen zu den ägyptischen Kanopenkästen*, Hildesheimer ägyptologische Beiträge 31, Hildesheim 1990, 75-76
Lüscher, B., *Untersuchungen zu Totenbuch Spruch 151*, Wiesbaden 1998
Martin, G., *Egyptian administrative and private-name seals, principally of the Middle Kingdom and Second Intermediate Period*, Oxford 1971
Michałowski, K., Deschores, Ch., de Lineage, J., Manteuffel, J., Żejmo-Żejmis, M., *Tell Edfou 1939, Fouilles Franco-Polonaises, Rapports*, Cairo 1950
Miniaci, G., 'The incomplete hieroglyphs system at the end of the Middle Kingdom', *RdE* 61 (2010), 113-134
Miniaci, G., 'Il potere nella 17a dinastia: il titolo "figlio del re" e il ripensamento delle strutture amministrative nel Secondo Periodo Intermedio', In Pernigotti, Sergio ; Marco Zacchi (eds), *Il tempio e il suo personale nell'Egitto antico : Atti del quarto Colloquio, Bologna - 24/25 settembre 2008*, Bologna 2010, 99-131
Miniaci, G.; S. Quirke, 'Reconceiving the Tomb in the Late Middle Kingdom, The Burial of the Accountant of the Main Enclosure Neferhotep at Dra Abu al-Naga', *BIFAO* 109 (2009), 349-383
Montet, P., *Les constructions et le tombeau d'Osorkon II a Tanis*, Paris 1947
Montet, P., *Les constructions et le tombeau de Chéchanq III à Tanis*, Paris 1960
Moreno Garcia, J. C., 'Administration territoriale et organisation de l'espace en Égypte au troisième millénaire avant J.-C./5: ges-per', *ZÄS* 126 (1999), 116 - 131
Morgan, J. de, *Fouilles à Dahchour Mars-Juin 1894*, Vienna 1895
Morgan, J. de, *Fouilles à Dahchour 1894-1895*, Vienna 1903
Munro, I. *Untersuchungen zu den Totenbuch-Papyri der 18. Dynastie*, London, New York 1987
Naville, E./T. E. Peet/H. R. Hall, *Cemeteries of Abydos II*, London 1914
Nyord, R., *Breathing Flesh, Conceptions of the Body in the Ancient Coffin Texts*, Copenhagen 2009
O'Connor, D., 'The 'Cenotaphs' of the Middle Kingdom at Abydos', in *Mélanges Gamal eddin Mokhtar*, Cairo 1985, 161-177
Parkinson, R./S. Quirke, 'The Coffin of Prince Herunefer and the Early History of the Book of the Dead', in *Studies in Pharaonic Religion and Society in Honour of J. Gwyn Griffths*, London 1992, 37-51
Patch, D.C., 'The Beaded Garment of Sit-werut', in M. Eldamaty, M. Trad (editors), *Egyptian Museum Collections around the World, volume II*, Cairo 2002, 905-916
Peet, T. E., *Cemeteries of Abydos II*, London 1914
Peet, T. E., W. L. S. Loat, *Cemeteries of Abydos I*II, London 1913
Petrie, W.M.F., *A Season in Egypt*, London 1888
Petrie, W.M.F., *Kahun, Gurob, and Hawara*, London 1890
Petrie, W.M.F., *Diospolis Parva: the cemeteries of Abadiyeh and Hu*, 1898-9, London 1901
Petrie, W.M.F., *Scarabs and Cylinder with Names*, London 1917

Petrie, W.M.F./Wainwright, G. A./Mackay, E., *The Labyrinth, Gerzeh and Mazghuneh*. BSAE XXI, London 1912
Petrie, W.M.F.,/Brunton, G./Murray, M., *Lahun II*, London 1923
von Pilgrim, C., Elephantine XVIII, *Untersuchungen in der Stadt des Mittleren Reiches und der Zweiten Zwischenzeit*, AV 91, Mainz am Rhein 1996
Polz, D.(editor), *Für die Ewigkeit geschaffen, Die Särge des Imeni und Geheset*, Mainz 2007
Polz, D., *Der Beginn des Neuen Reiches, Zur Vorgeschichte einer Zeitenwende*, Berlin, New York 2007
Postel, L., '<<Rame>> ou <<course>>? : Enquête lexicographique sur le terme hpt', *BIFAO* 103 (2003), 377-420
Quirke, S., review of Geisen, Mentuhotep, *Journal of Ancient Near Eastern Religions* 5 (2005), 228-237
Quirke, S., '<<Book of the Dead Chapter 178>>: A Late Middle Kingdom Compilation or Excerpts?', in: S. Grallert, W. Grajetzki (editors), *Life and Afterlife in the Middle Kingdom and Second Intermediate Period*, London 2007, 105-127
Quirke, S., 'Four Titles: What is the Difference?', In: D. P. Silverman, W. K. Simpson, J. Wegner, in, *Archaism and Innovation: Studies in the Culture of Middle Kingdom Egypt*, New Haven, Philadelphia, 2009, 305-316
Ranke, H., *Die ägyptischen Personennamen*, Bd. I-III. Glückstadt, 1935, 1949, 1977
Richards, J., *Society and Death in Ancient Egypt, Mortuary Landscapes of the Middle Kingdom*, Cambridge 2005
Roeder, H., *Mit dem Auge sehen, Studien zur Semantik der Herrschaft in den Toten- und Kulttexten*, SAGA 16, Heidelberg 1996
Ryholt. K.S.B., *The Political Situaton in Egypt during the Second Intermediate Period*, Kopenhagen 1997
Seidlmayer, S. J., *Gräberfelder aus dem Übergang vom Alten zum Mittleren Reich*, SAGA 1, Heidelberg 1990
Seiler, A., Tradition & Wandel, *Die Keramik als Spiegel der Kulturentwicklung Thebens in der Zweiten Zwischenzei*t, Mainz am Rhein 2005
Seipel, W. (editor), *Götter Menschen Pharaonen*, Speyer 1993
Simpson, W. K., *The Terrace of the Great God at Abydos: The Offering Chapels of Dynasties 12 and 13*, New Haven and Philadelphia 1974
Snape, S., *Mortuary Assemblages from Abydos*, Liverpool 1986 (unpublished PhD)
Stefanović, D., *The non-royal regular feminine titles of the Middle Kingdom and Second Intermediate Period: Dossiers*, London 2009
Steindorff, G., *Grabfunde des Mittleren Reiches in den Königlichen Museen zu Berlin, I. Der Sarg des Mentuhotep*, Berlin 1901
Steindorff, G., *Grabfunde des Mittleren Reiches in den Königlichen Museen zu Berlin, II. Der Sarg des Sebk-o. – Ein Grabfund aus Gebelei*n, Berlin 1901
Stewart, H.M., *Mummy Cases & Inscribed Funerary Cones in the Petrie Collection*, London 1986
Taylor, J., *Death and Afterlife in Ancient Egypt*, London 2001
Tiradritti, F., *L'Egittologo Luigi Vassalli, 1812-1887, disegni e documenti nei Civici Istituti Culturali Milanesi*, Milano 1994
Tiradritti, F., 'Luigi Vassalli and the archaeological season at Western Thebes (1862-3)', In M. Marée (editor), *The Second Intermediate Period (Thirteenth-Seventeenth Dynasties), Current Research, Future Prospects*, Leuven, Paris, Walpole, MA, 2010
Vercoutter, J., *Mirgissa II, Les nécropoles*, Paris 1975
Vercoutter, J., *Mirgissa II, Les necropolis, Part 2, Études anthropologiques.Études archéologiques*, Paris 1975
Vernus, P., 'Deux Inscriptions de la XIIe Dynastie provenant de Saqqara', *RdE* 28 (1976), 119-138
Whelan, P., *Mere Scraps of Rough Wood?, 17th – 18th Dynasty Stick Shabtis in the Petrie Museum and other Collections*, London 2007
Willems, H., *Chests of Life*, Leiden 1988
Willems, H., *The Coffin of Heqata (Cairo JdE 36418)*, Leuven 1996
Willems, H., 'Anubis as a judge', W. Clarysse, A. Schoors, H. Willems (editors), *Egyptian Religion, The Last Thousand Years, I, Studies dedicated to the Memory of Jan Quagebeur*, Leuven 1998, 719-743
Willems, H., 'The Embalmer Embalmed, Remarks on the Meaning of the Decoration of Some Middle Kingdom Coffins', in: Jacobus van Dijk (editor), *Essays on Ancient Egypt in Honour of Herman te Velde*, Gronningen 1997, 343-72
Willems, H., *Les Textes des sarcophages et la démocratie*, Paris 2008
Williams, B., 'The Date of Senebtisi at Lisht and the Chronology of Major Groups and Deposits of the Middle Kingdom', *Serapis* 3 (1975-76), S. 41-55
Winlock, H. E., 'The Tombs of the Kings of the Seventeenth Dynasty at Thebes', *JEA* 10 (1924), 217-77
Yoshimura, S. (edit.), *Excavating in Egypt for 40 years, Waseda University Expedition 1966-2006*, Tokyo 2006
Yoshimura, S. (edit.), *Excavating in Egypt for 40 years, Waseda University Expedition 1966-2006*, Tokyo 2008

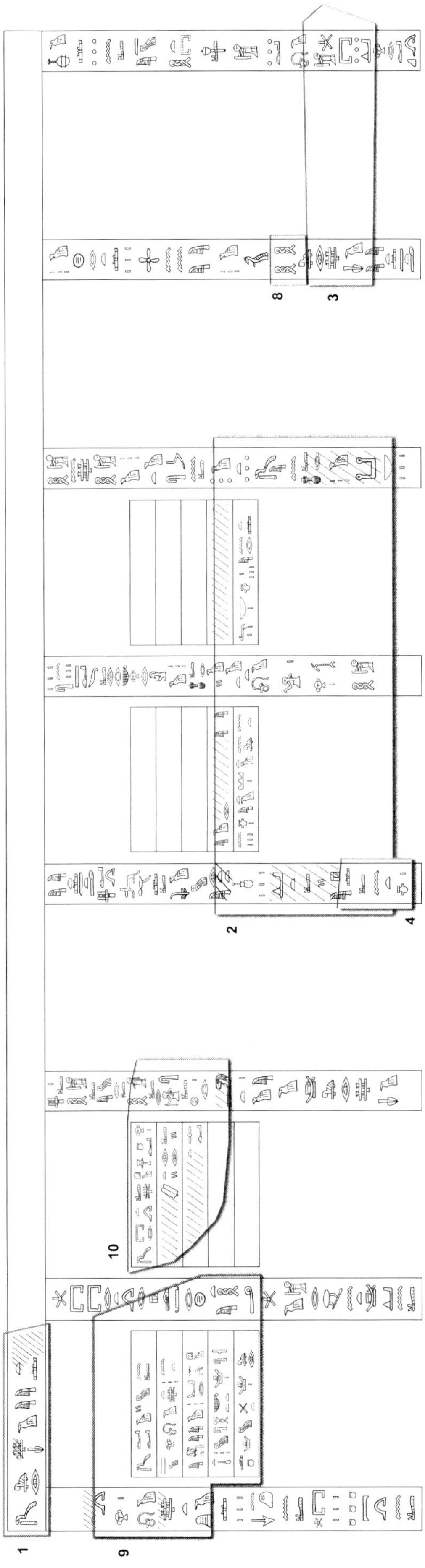

Plate I. Reconstruction of the back side of Zemathor's coffin (drawing: Paul Whelan). The numbers refer to those of Garstang's notebook copies.

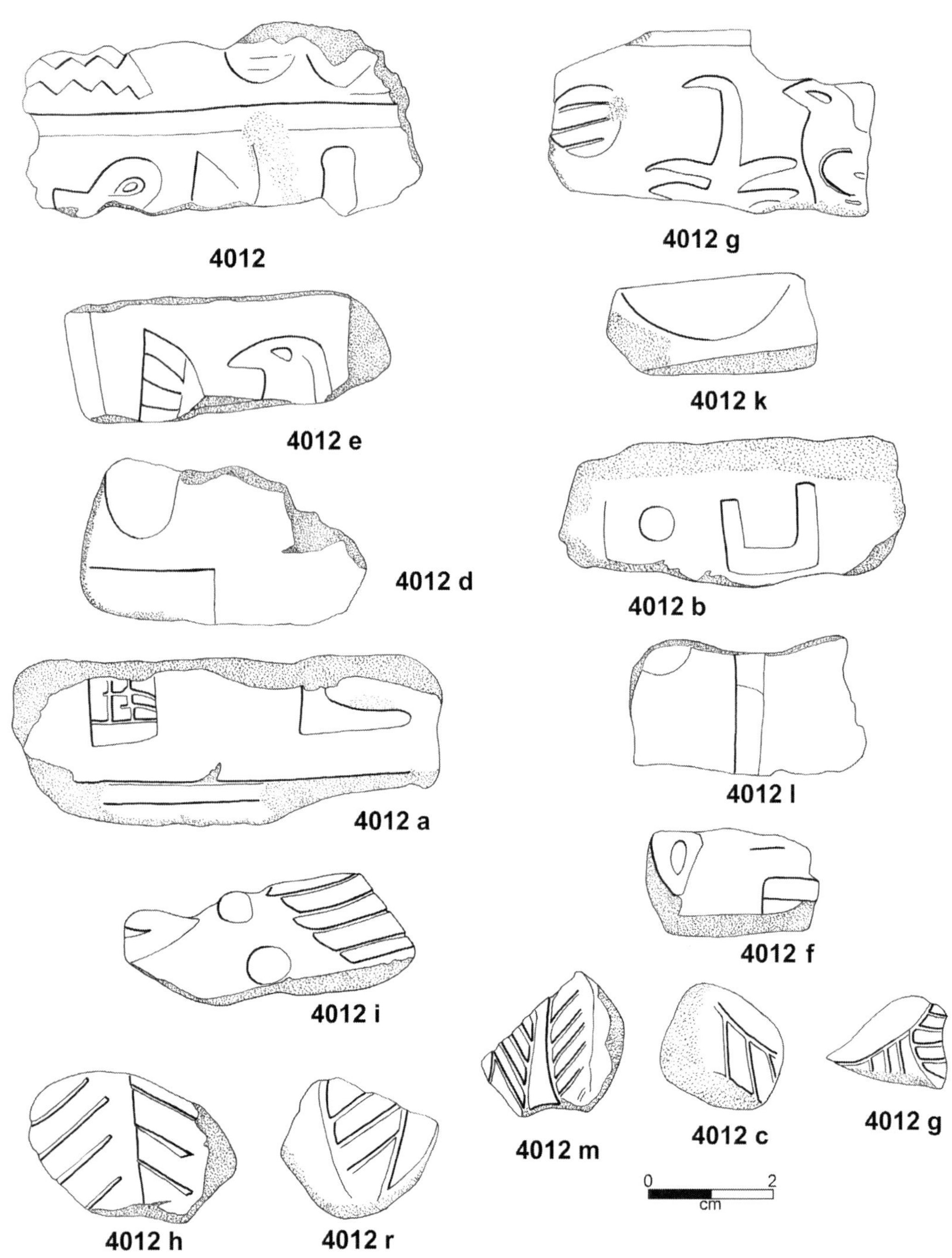

Plate II. Plaster fragments found in tomb 6 at Abydos (drawing: Paul Whelan)

Plate III. The stela of Khonsu, drawn from the photographic picture on plate X

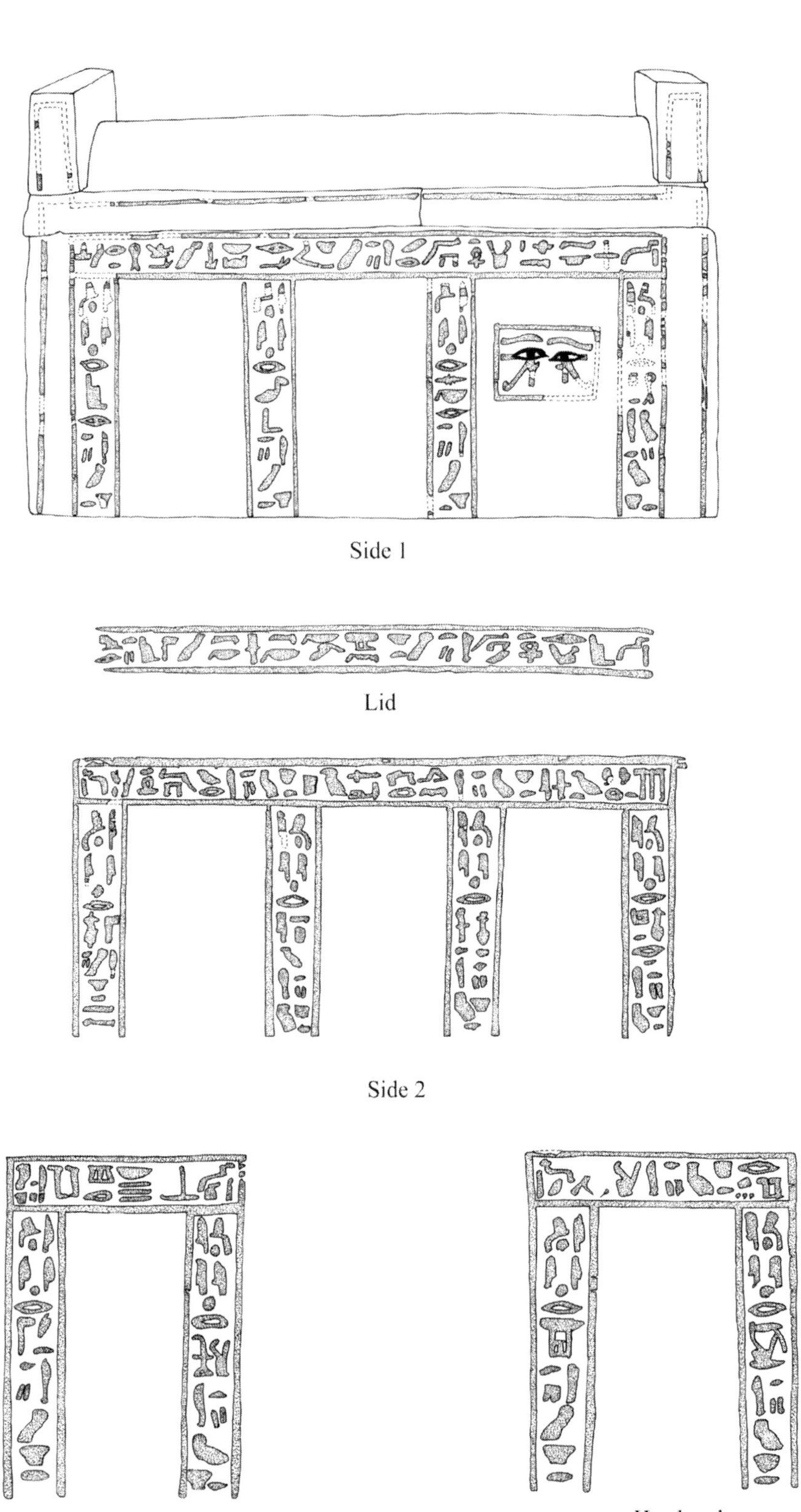

Plate IV. The model coffin of Nemtyemweskhet (drawing: Paul Whelan)

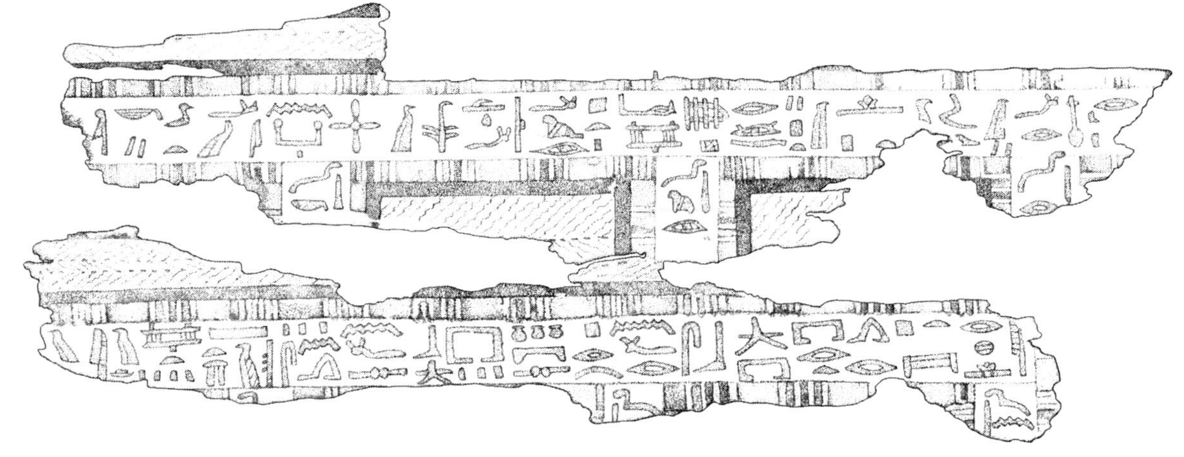

Plate V. The long sides on the coffin of Dedmut – Aby4 (drawing: Paul Whelan)

Plate VI. The fragments of the canopic box of Dedmut (drawing: Paul Whelan)

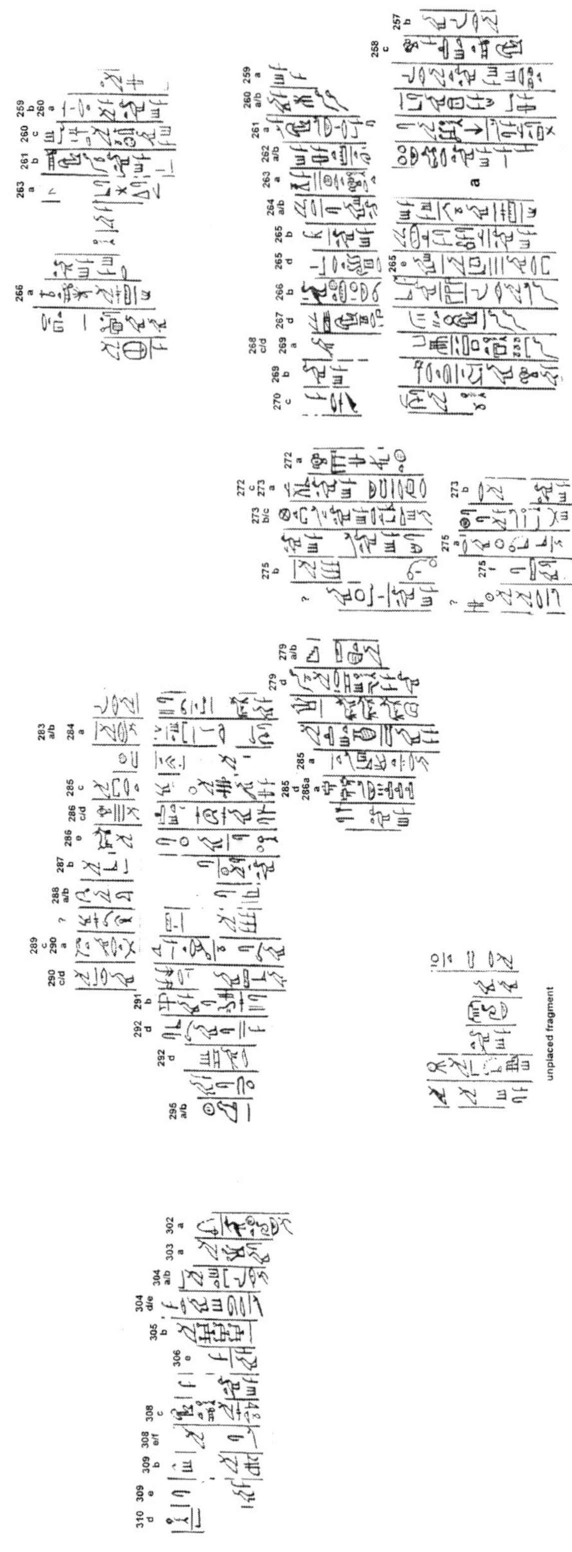

Plate VII. The texts on the coffin of Zatip, rearrangend

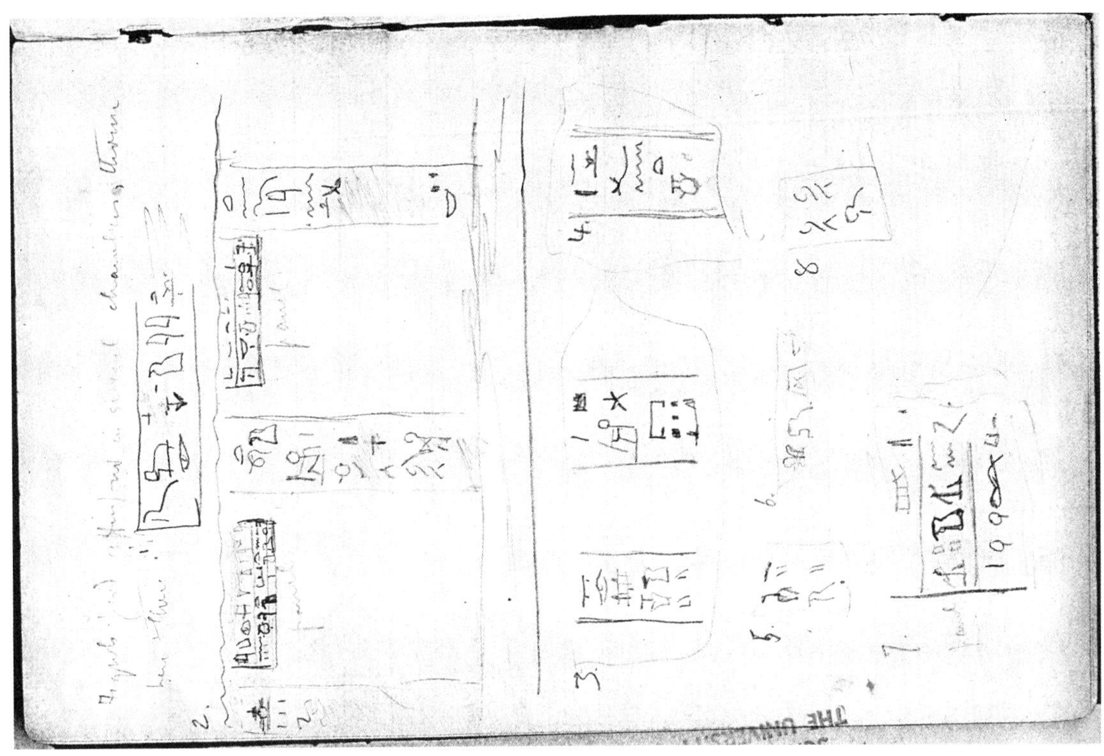

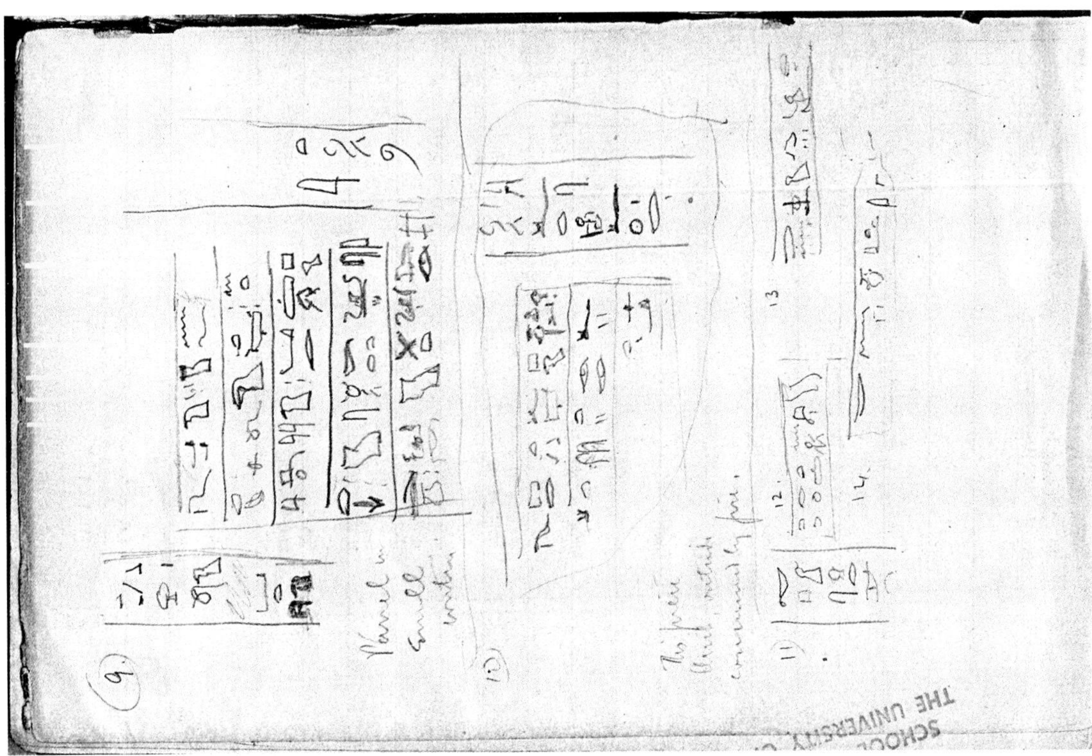

Plate VIII. Notebook drawings of Zemathor's coffin © Liverpool University; Garstang's notebook

Plate IXa. Stela of Khons, excavation photograph © Liverpool University

Plate IXb. Head of a canopic jar, Manchester Museum (photo: author).

Plate X. Stela of Khonsu, excavation photograph © Liverpool University

Plate XIa The long sides on the coffin of Dedmut – Aby4; picture: © Egyptian Exploration Society

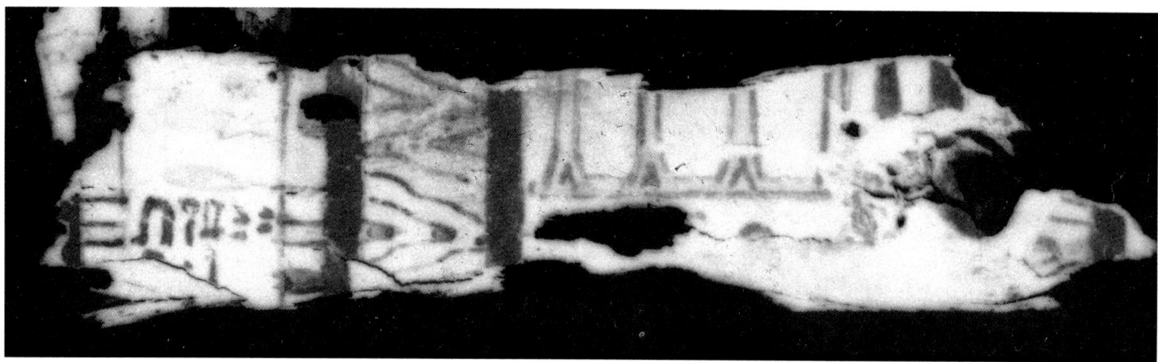

Plate XIb. Fragments of the canopic box from tomb C66; Abydos; pictures: © Egyptian Exploration Society

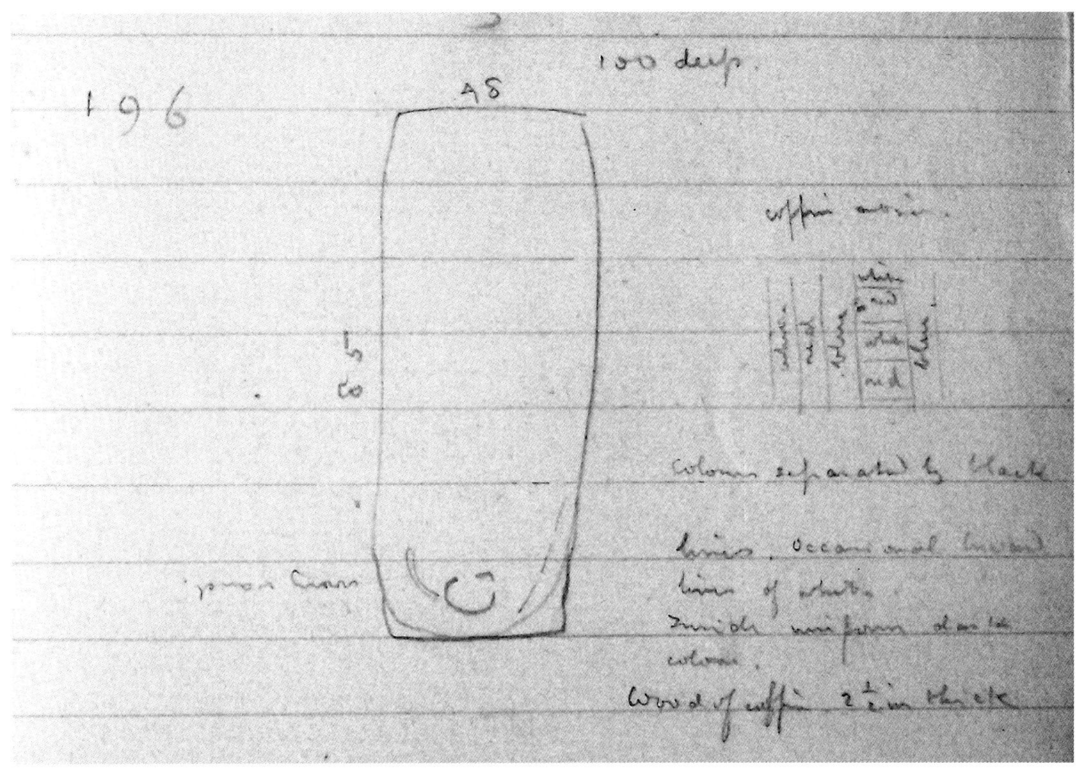

Plate XIIa. notebook entry: Tomb Hu Y 196 (Hu1) © Petrie Museum of Egyptian Archaeology

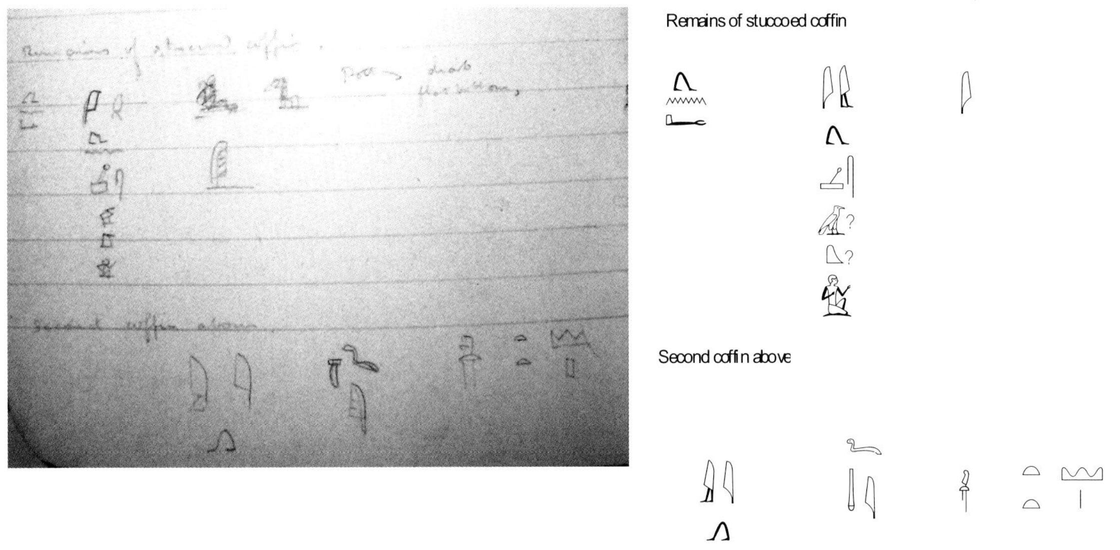

Plate XIIb. notebook entry Tomb Hu Y 219 (Hu2) © Petrie Museum of Egyptian Archaeology

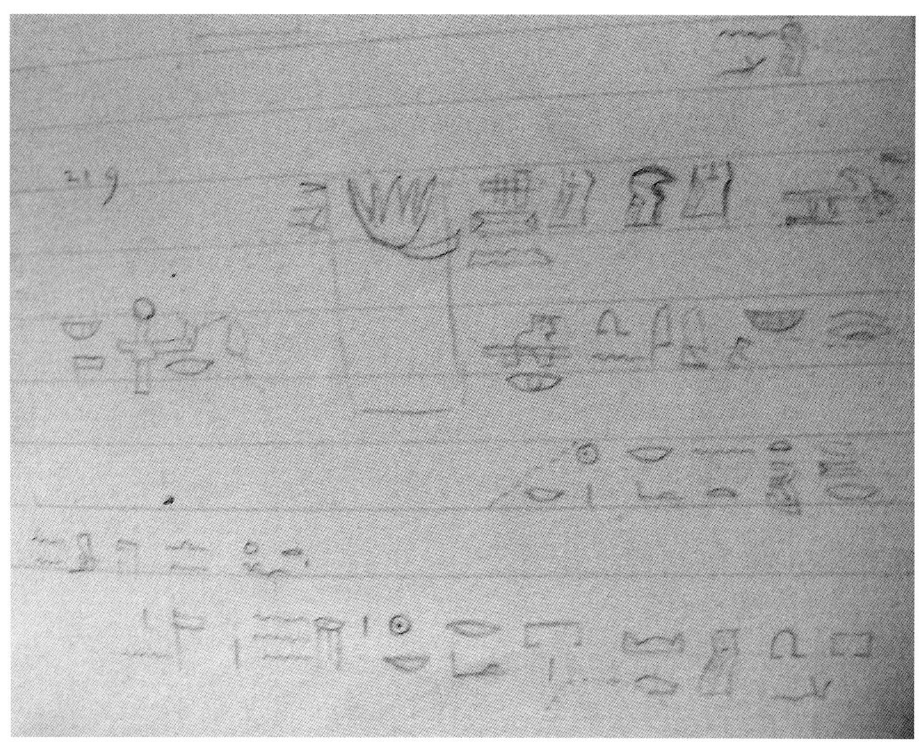

Plate XIIIa. Tomb Hu Y 219 (Hu2) © Petrie Museum of Egyptian Archaeology

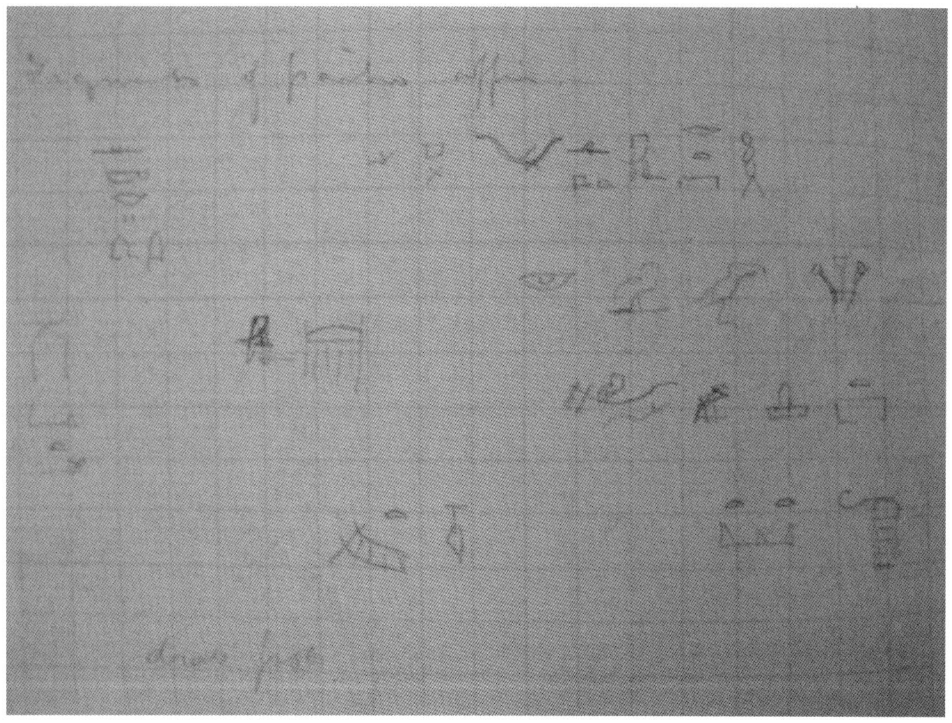

Plate XIIIb. Tomb Hu Y 467 (Hu4) © Petrie Museum of Egyptian Archaeology

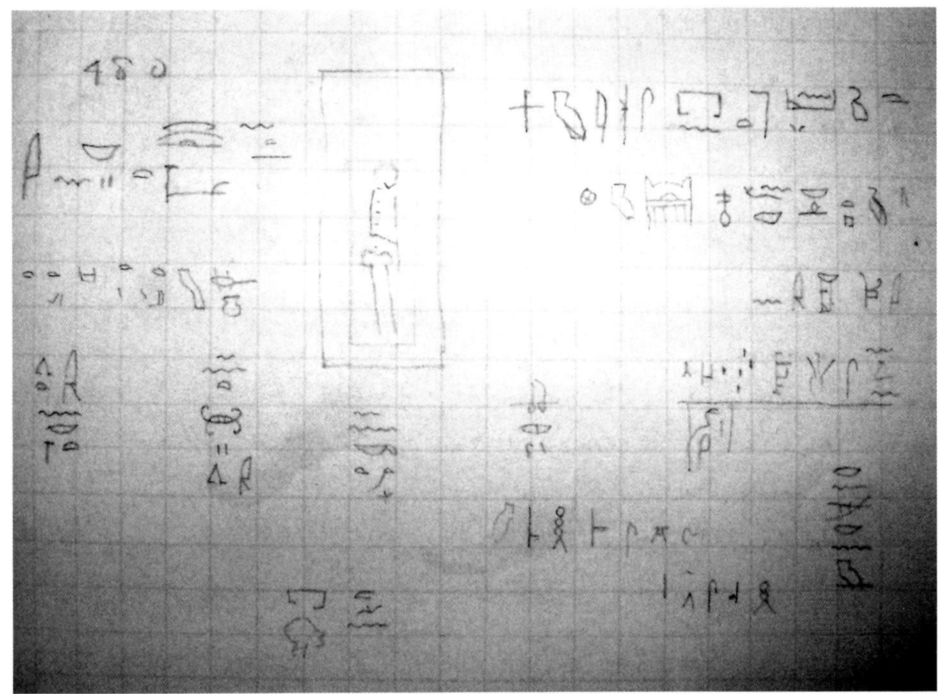

Plate XIVa. Tomb Hu Y 480 (Hu5) © Petrie Museum of Egyptian Archaeology

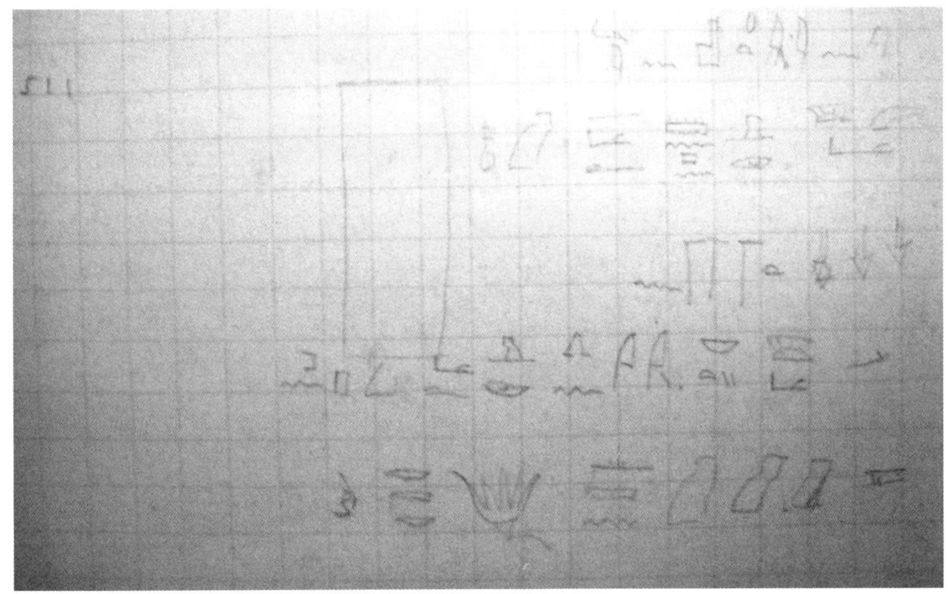

Plate XIVb. Tomb Hu Y 511 (Hu6) © Petrie Museum of Egyptian Archaeology

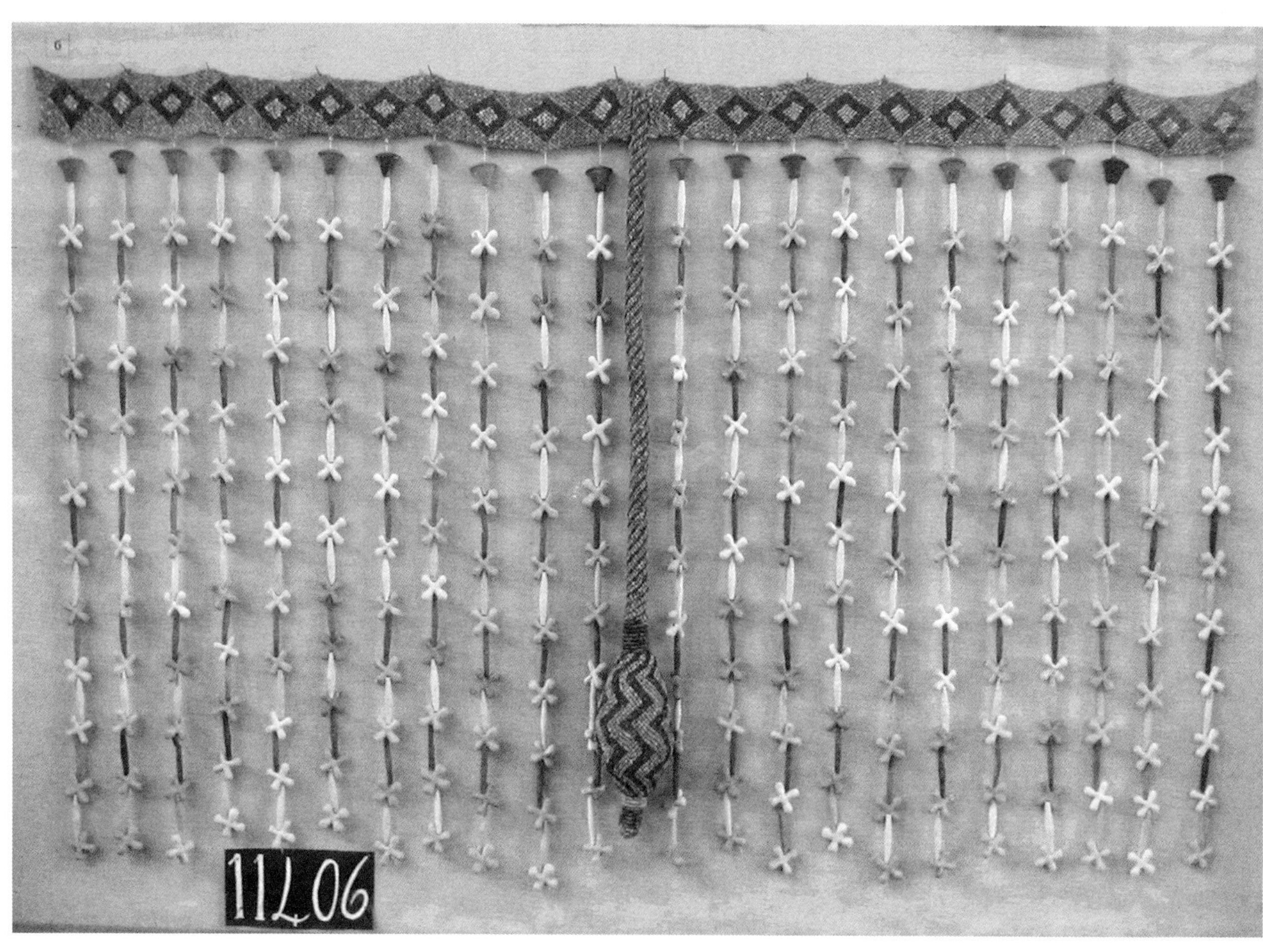

Plate XV. Belt from the tomb of Djehutynakht at Deir el-Bersheh; Cairo, Egyptian Museum; photo © Gianluca Minaci